SECOND EDITION

Learning Unix for OS X

Dave Taylor

Beijing · Boston · Farnham · Sebastopol · Tokyo

Learning Unix for OS X

by Dave Taylor

Copyright © 2016 Dave Taylor. All rights reserved.

Printed in the United States of America.

Published by O'Reilly Media, Inc., 1005 Gravenstein Highway North, Sebastopol, CA 95472.

O'Reilly books may be purchased for educational, business, or sales promotional use. Online editions are also available for most titles (*http://safaribooksonline.com*). For more information, contact our corporate/institutional sales department: 800-998-9938 or *corporate@oreilly.com*.

Editor: Rachel Roumeliotis	**Indexer:** Judy McConville
Production Editor: Nicole Shelby	**Interior Designer:** David Futato
Copyeditor: Sonia Saruba	**Cover Designer:** Randy Comer
Proofreader: Rachel Head	**Illustrator:** Rebecca Demarest

January 2016:   Second Edition
September 2012:   First Edition

Revision History for the Second Edition
2016-01-19:   First Release

See *http://oreilly.com/catalog/errata.csp?isbn=9781491939987* for release details.

The O'Reilly logo is a registered trademark of O'Reilly Media, Inc. *Learning Unix for OS X*, the cover image, and related trade dress are trademarks of O'Reilly Media, Inc.

While the publisher and the author have used good faith efforts to ensure that the information and instructions contained in this work are accurate, the publisher and the author disclaim all responsibility for errors or omissions, including without limitation responsibility for damages resulting from the use of or reliance on this work. Use of the information and instructions contained in this work is at your own risk. If any code samples or other technology this work contains or describes is subject to open source licenses or the intellectual property rights of others, it is your responsibility to ensure that your use thereof complies with such licenses and/or rights.

978-1-491-93998-7

[LSI]

Table of Contents

Interfaces to Unix

Unix can be used as it was originally designed: on typewriter-like terminals, from a prompt on a command line. Most versions of Unix also work with window systems, or graphical user interfaces (GUIs). These allow each user to have a single screen with multiple windows—including "terminal" windows that act like the original Unix interface.

OS X includes a simple terminal application for accessing the command-line level of the system. That application is called the Terminal and is closely examined in Chapter 2.

While you can use your Mac quite efficiently without issuing commands in the Terminal, that's where we'll spend all of our time in this book. Why?

- Every Macintosh has a command-line interface. If you know how to use the command line, you'll always be a power user.

- As you become a more advanced Unix user, you'll find that the command line is actually much more flexible than the graphical Mac interface. Unix programs are designed to be used together from the command line—as "building blocks"—in an almost infinite number of combinations, to do an infinite number of tasks. No window system I've seen has this tremendous power.

- You can launch and close any Mac program from the command line.

- Once you learn to use the command line, you can use those same techniques to write *scripts*. These little (or big!) programs automate jobs you'd have to do manually and repetitively with a window system (unless you understand how to program a window system, which is usually a much harder job). See Chapter 10 for a brief introduction to scripting.

- In general, text-based interfaces are much easier than graphical computing environments for visually impaired users.

I'm not saying that the command-line interface is right for every situation. For instance, using the Web—with its graphics and links—is usually easier with a GUI web browser within OS X. But the command line is the fundamental way to use Unix. Understanding it will let you work on any Unix system, with or without windows. A great resource for general OS X information (the GUI you're probably used to) is *OS X El Capitan: The Missing Manual*, by David Pogue (Pogue Press/O'Reilly).

How This Book Is Organized

This book will help you learn Unix on your Mac fast. It is organized in a way that gets you started quickly and then expands your Unix horizons, chapter by chapter, until you're comfortable with the command line and with X11-based open source applications and able to push further into the world of Unix. Specific commands, for example, may be previewed in earlier chapters and then explained in detail in later chapters (with cross-references so you don't get lost). Here's how it's all laid out:

Chapter 1, Why Use Unix?

> Graphical interfaces are useful, but when it's time to become a power user—really forcing your Mac to do exactly what you want, when you want it—nothing beats the power and capability of the Unix command line. You'll see exactly why that's the case in this first chapter.

Chapter 2, Using the Terminal

> It's not the sexiest application included with OS X, but the Terminal, found in the */Applications/Utilities* folder, opens up the world of Unix on your Mac and lets you peek inside the inner workings. This chapter explains how to best use it and customize it for your own requirements.

Chapter 3, Exploring the Filesystem

> Once you start using Unix, you'll be amazed at how many more files and directories are on your Mac—information that's hidden from the graphical interface user. This chapter takes you on a journey through your Mac's filesystem, showing you how to list files, change directories, and explore the hidden nooks and crannies of El Capitan.

Chapter 4, File Management

> Now that you can move around in your filesystem, it's time to learn how to look into individual files; copy or move files around; and even create, delete, and rename directories. This is your first introduction to some of the most powerful Unix commands, too, including the text-based *vi* editor.

Chapter 5, Finding Files and Information

> If you've ever looked for a file with the Finder or Spotlight, you know that some types of searches are almost impossible. Looking for a file that you created exactly 30 days ago? Searching for that file with the Finder will prove to be an exercise in futility. But that's exactly the kind of search you can do with Unix's *find*, *locate*, and *grep* commands, as well as Spotlight's command-line utilities.

Chapter 6, Redirecting I/O

> One of the most powerful elements of the Unix command line is that you can easily combine multiple commands to create new and unique "super-commands" that perform exactly the task you seek. You'll learn exactly how you can save a command's output to a file, use the content of files as the input to Unix commands, and even hook multiple commands together so that the output of one is the input of the next. You'll see that Unix is phenomenally powerful, and easy, too!

Chapter 7, Multitasking

As mentioned earlier, Unix is a *multitasking* operating system that allows you to have lots of applications running at the same time. In this chapter, you'll see how you can manage these multiple tasks, stop programs, restart them, and modify how they work, all from the Unix command line.

Chapter 8, Taking Unix Online

Much of the foundation of the Internet was created on Unix systems, and it's no surprise that you can access remote servers, surf the Web, and interact with remote filesystems, all directly from the command line. If you've always wanted more power when interacting with remote sites, this chapter dramatically expands your horizons.

Chapter 9, Of Windows and X11

The graphical interface in OS X is the best in the industry. Elegant and intuitive, it's a pleasure to use. But it turns out that there's another Unix-based graphical interface lurking in your Mac system, called the X Window System, or X11 for short. This chapter shows you how to install X11 and gives you a quick tour of a couple of the very best X11 applications available for free on the Internet.

Chapter 10, Where to Go from Here

With all its commands and command-line combinations, and the addition of thousands of open source utilities free for the downloading, you can spend years learning how to best take advantage of the Unix environment. In this final chapter, I offer you some directions for your further travels, including recommendations for books, websites, and similar resources to investigate.

Conventions Used in This Book

The following typographical conventions are used in this book:

Plain text

Indicates menu titles, menu options, menu buttons, and keyboard accelerators (such as Alt and Control).

Italic

Indicates new terms, URLs, email addresses, pathnames, filenames, and file extensions.

`Constant width`

Used for program listings, as well as within paragraphs to refer to program elements such as variable or function names, databases, data types, environment variables, statements, and keywords.

`Constant width bold`

Shows commands or other text that should be typed literally by the user.

`Constant width italic`

Shows text that should be replaced with user-supplied values or by values determined by context.

Menus/navigation

Menus and their options are referred to in the text as File→Open, Edit→Copy, etc. Arrows are also used to signify a navigation path when using window options; for example, System Preferences→Screen Effects→Activation means you would launch System Preferences, click on the icon for the Screen Effects preferences panel, and select the Activation pane within that panel.

Pathnames

Pathnames are used to show the location of a file or application in the filesystem. Directories (or folders for Mac and Windows users) are separated by forward slashes. For example, if you see something like "launch the Terminal application (*/Applications/Utilities*)" in the text, that means the Terminal application can be found in the *Utilities* subfolder of the *Applications* folder.

↵

A carriage return (↵) at the end of a line of code is used to denote an unnatural line break; that is, you should not enter these as two lines of code, but as one continuous line. Multiple lines are used in these cases due to printing constraints.

Menu symbols

When looking at the menus for any application, you will see some symbols associated with keyboard shortcuts for a particular command. For example, to open a document in Microsoft Word, you could go to the File menu and select Open (File→Open), or you could issue the keyboard shortcut ⌘-O.

Figure P-1 shows the symbols used in the various menus to denote a keyboard shortcut.

Rarely will you see the Control symbol used as a menu command option; it's more often used in association with mouse clicks to emulate a right-click on a two-button mouse or for working with the *bash* shell.

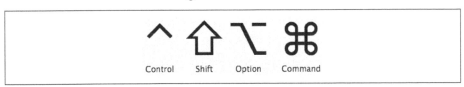

Figure P-1. Keyboard accelerators for issuing commands

$, #

The dollar sign ($) is used in some examples to show the user prompt for the *bash* shell; the hash mark (#) is the prompt for the *root* user.

This icon signifies a tip, suggestion, or general note.

This icon indicates a warning or caution.

Using Code Examples

This book is here to help you get your job done. In general, you may use the code in this book in your programs and documentation. You do not need to contact us for permission unless you're reproducing a significant portion of the code. For example, writing a program that uses several chunks of code from this book does not require permission. Selling or distributing a CD-ROM of examples from O'Reilly books does require permission. Answering a question by citing this book and quoting example code does not require permission. Incorporating a significant amount of example code from this book into your product's documentation does require permission.

We appreciate, but do not require, attribution. An attribution usually includes the title, author, publisher, and ISBN. For example: "*Learning Unix for OS X*, by Dave Taylor. Copyright 2016 Dave Taylor, 978-1-4919-3998-7."

If you feel your use of code examples falls outside fair use or the permission given above, feel free to contact us at *permissions@oreilly.com*.

Safari® Books Online

Safari Books Online (*www.safaribooksonline.com*) is an on-demand digital library that delivers expert content in both book and video form from the world's leading authors in technology and business.

Technology professionals, software developers, web designers, and business and creative professionals use Safari Books Online as their primary resource for research, problem solving, learning, and certification training.

Safari Books Online offers a range of product mixes and pricing programs for organizations, government agencies, and individuals. Subscribers have access to thousands of books, training videos, and prepublication manuscripts in one fully searchable database from publishers like O'Reilly Media, Prentice Hall Professional, Addison-Wesley Professional, Microsoft Press, Sams, Que, Peachpit Press, Focal Press, Cisco Press, John Wiley & Sons, Syngress, Morgan Kaufmann, IBM Redbooks, Packt, Adobe Press, FT Press, Apress, Manning, New Riders, McGraw-Hill, Jones & Bartlett, Course Technology, and dozens more. For more information about Safari Books Online, please visit us online.

How to Contact Us

Please address comments and questions concerning this book to the publisher:

O'Reilly Media, Inc.
1005 Gravenstein Highway North
Sebastopol, CA 95472
800-998-9938 (in the United States or Canada)
707-829-0515 (international or local)
707-829-0104 (fax)

We have a web page for this book, where we list errata, examples, and any additional information. You can access this page at *http://bit.ly/learn-unix-osx-2*.

To comment or ask technical questions about this book, send email to *bookquestions@oreilly.com*.

For more information about our books, courses, conferences, and news, see our website at *http://www.oreilly.com*.

Find us on Facebook: *http://facebook.com/oreilly*

Follow us on Twitter: *http://twitter.com/oreillymedia*

Watch us on YouTube: *http://www.youtube.com/oreillymedia*

The Evolution of This Book

This book is loosely based on the original O'Reilly title *Learning the Unix Operating System*, by Jerry Peek, Grace Todino, and John Strang. There are lots of differences in this book to meet the needs of OS X users, but the fundamental layout and explanations are the same. The El Capitan edition is the sixth OS X custom edition of this title. As OS X keeps getting better, so does this little book!

- There are thousands of open source and otherwise freely downloadable Unix-based applications. Can't afford Adobe Photoshop but still want a powerful graphics editor? The GNU Image Manipulation Program (GIMP) offers a viable alternative (see Chapter 9).

- Want to search for files by when they were created, or by whom? Difficult in the Finder or Spotlight, but it's a breeze with Unix (see Chapter 5).

- How about managing your files and file archives in an automated fashion? Tricky to set up with the GUI tools, but in Unix, you can set up a *cron* job to handle this at night while you sleep.

Fundamentally, Unix is all about power and control. As an example, consider the difference between using Force Quit from the Apple menu and the Unix programs *ps* and *kill*. While Force Quit is more attractive, as shown in Figure 1-1, notice that it lists only graphical applications.

Figure 1-1. Force Quit doesn't show all running applications

By contrast, the *ps* (process status—say "pea-ess" to sound like a Unix guru) command used from within the Terminal application (*/Applications/Utilities/Terminal*) shows a complete and full list of every application, utility, and system process running on your Mac, as shown here:

```
$ ps -acx
    PID TTY          TIME CMD
```

```
   1 ??          0:10.28 launchd
  11 ??          0:01.41 UserEventAgent
  12 ??          0:01.86 kextd
  14 ??          0:01.15 notifyd
  15 ??          0:02.83 securityd
  16 ??          0:00.24 diskarbitrationd
...
1526 ??          0:51.39 iTunes
1573 ??          0:00.07 taskgated
1583 ??          0:24.08 Google Chrome Helper
1539 ttys000     0:00.04 login
1540 ttys000     0:00.04 -bash
1568 ttys000     0:00.21 vi
1586 ttys001     0:00.03 login
1587 ttys001     0:00.02 -bash
```

That's more than the few applications Force Quit shows you. Of course, the next thing that's probably running through your head is, "Sure, but what does all that output in the Terminal mean to me, and what do I do with it?" This is the key reason to learn and work with the Unix side of OS X: to really know what your Mac's doing and be able to make it match what you want and need your Mac to do.

Okay, now let's go back and look at the output from running the *ps -acx* command. First off, you'll see that we added some *options* (or *flags* or *switches*) to the *ps* command; the options are the *-acx* bit. Flags are spoken by letter, so this would be pronounced as "pea-ess minus aye-sea-ex." These options tell *ps* to display all of the programs and processes being run by all of the users (including you and the system itself) on the system. When the Terminal displays the results of the *ps -acx* command, you'll see that it adds a line of "headers" or column titles to the output:

```
$ ps -acx
  PID TTY           TIME CMD
   16 ??         0:00.24 diskarbitrationd
```

Think of the headers the same way you would when looking at a Numbers spreadsheet with a bunch of columns. Each column in that spreadsheet should have a column head to help define what you see underneath. The same applies here. In the very first line of the information returned, you'll see the following headers:

PID

Lists the command's process identification number (or PID, for short).

TTY

Tells you the terminal the process is running in. If you see two question marks (??), that means the process isn't associated with a specific Terminal window or display: typically it's a system-level command or utility, as is the disk arbitration program listed above (*diskarbitrationd*—the final "d" stands for *daemon*, an always-running system-level task).

TIME

Tells you the amount of time it took to run that particular process, or how long that process has been running, in minutes and seconds. For example, the 0:00.24 you see in the preceding output means that it took, roughly, a quarter of a second for the *diskarbitrationd* process to start and run.

CMD

Gives you the specific command that's being run. You can also ask for the entire pathname to the process that's running, including any starting flags or options that might have been invoked. For example, */sbin/diskarbitrationd* tells you that the process that's running is *diskarbitrationd*, located in the */sbin* directory.

Great! So now you know what all that means, but you still don't know how this relates to Force Quit, right? Be patient, we're getting there!

Once you know the PID number of a process, you can then issue the Unix *kill* command to, well, kill that process. For example, let's say that Microsoft Word decides to lock up on you and you're stuck with the Spinning Beach Ball of Death (SBBoD). After you finish tearing out your hair in frustration, you need to *kill* Microsoft Word, but in order to do so, you first need its process number. For this, we'll use the *grep* command, which is basically a Unix search tool that you use to search for words or, as numbers in files, or in this case, the output of a command:

```
$ ps -ax | grep Word
  1634 ??          0:02.50 /Applications/Microsoft Office 2011/Microsoft
                   Word.app/Contents/MacOS/Microsoft Word -psn_0_766139
  1645 ttys002     0:00.00 grep Word
```

This tells us that Microsoft Word's PID is 1634, as noted by the first number in the command output. Now all you need to do to *kill* Word is issue the following command:

```
$ kill 1634
```

After typing that and hitting the Return key (an activity known as "entering a command"), Microsoft Word promptly quits, closing all its windows. It won't save anything you've done since your last save, but since Word was locked in a deep freeze you wouldn't have been able to save your changes anyway, right? And if you had used the Force Quit window, you wouldn't have been able to save changes there, either.

Batch Renames and Extracting File Lists

Here's another example. Suppose you just received a thumb drive from a client with hundreds of files in a single folder. Now let's say that you only need those files that have the sequence *-nt-* or *-dt-* as part of their filenames, and that you want to copy them from the thumb drive to your home directory. Within the Finder, you'd be doomed to going through the list manually, a tedious and error-prone process. But on the Unix command line, this becomes a breeze:

```
$ cd /Volumes/Thumb
$ cp *-dt-* *-nt-* ~
```

The first command, *cd /Volumes/Thumb*, takes you to the *Volumes* directory, which is where the thumb drive (named *Thumb*) is actually mounted on your Mac's filesystem. The second command, *cp *-dt-* *-nt-* ~*, breaks down as follows:

cp

This is Unix's copy command.

-dt- *-nt-*

This tells the *cp* command to look for any items on the thumb drive that contain either *-dt-* or *-nt-* in their filenames. Unix recognizes the asterisks (*) as wildcards in the command string. By placing an asterisk before and after each item (**-dt-** and **-nt-**), you're telling Unix to find any file that has either *-dt-* or *-nt-* anywhere in its filename.

~

The tilde character (or squiggle, in Unix-speak) simply refers to the current user's home folder (or directory).

By placing the tilde (~) at the end of the command line, you're telling *cp* to copy each file it finds that has *-dt-* or *-nt-* in its filename to your home directory.

Fast, easy, and doable by any and all OS X users.

There are a million reasons why it's helpful to know Unix as an OS X power user, and you'll see them demonstrated time and again throughout this book.

Finding Hidden Files

You might not realize it if you only work in the Finder, but your system has thousands of additional files and directories that are hidden from view, but easily found from the command line. Most of these hidden files are known in the Unix world as *dot files*, because each file or directory has a period (.) as the first character of its name. For example, in your home directory you probably have a file called *.profile* that contains specific instructions on how you want your command shell set up when it's launched. But when you view your home folder in the Finder, this file is hidden, as shown in Figure 1-2. Instead, all you see are the default set of folders (*Desktop, Documents, Movies, Music, Pictures, Public*) along with any additional files and folders you've created.

To view the dot files in the Terminal, type the file listing command (*ls*), along with its *-a* option (for *list all*, which shows the hidden dot files). Suddenly you'll see that there are lots more files in that directory:

```
$ ls -aF
./                  .dropbox/      .vuescanrc      Music/
../                 .dvdcss/       Applications/   Pictures/
.CFUserTextEncoding .lesshst       Desktop/        Presentations/
.DS_Store           .nchsoftware/  Documents/      Public/
.Trash/             .profile       Downloads/      VirtualBox VMs/
.android/           .ssh/          Dropbox/        bin/
.bash_history       .subversion/   Library/
.cups/              .viminfo       Movies/
```

Figure 1-2. The Finder doesn't show hidden files and folders that you can see in the Terminal with standard Unix commands

Personally, though I don't always need the power, I like knowing that I can get to, view, and even edit every file on my computer if I need to. All I need to do is launch the Terminal application (which I actually have permanently available in my Dock, so it's always just one click away), type in a few simple commands, and I'm on my way.

Folders or Directories?

If you're new to the whole Unix thing, you're going to need to learn Unix-speak. In the graphical world, such as with OS X or Windows, you're used to working with a graphical user interface (GUI) that lets you see everything visually. When you create a new file, it gets stored in a folder of some sort, even if you save the file to your Desktop (which is, in its own right, a folder).

But in Unix, folders are referred to as *directories*. That's right, folders and directories are one and the same. It's an odd sort of translation, but when Unix was first developed, there was no GUI; all you had was a text-based terminal to type into, and you were darned happy to have that, especially as you were walking 10 miles uphill in the snow to and from school each day. But I digress!

Directories were set up as part of the hard drive's *filesystem*, or the structure in which directories and files are stored on the system. And the way you get to a folder (er, directory) in Unix is to enter its *file path*, using forward slashes between the directory names. For example, the file path to your home directory (again, think folder) is actually:

```
/Users/your_name
```

where *your_name* would be replaced by your short username. Or use the power user shortcut ~, as shown earlier!

At the very top of your Mac's filesystem, you have the root directory, denoted with a single forward slash (/). As noted in the previous example, to specify a particular directory or file, all you need to do is place the path after this leading slash.

This takes a little getting used to, but once you get the hang of entering Unix file paths, you'll find that it's actually a faster way to get around (particularly if you can type faster than it takes you to move the cursor around in the graphical world).

Just remember: folders are directories, and when working on the Unix side of your Mac, we'll refer to folders as directories throughout the book.

Thousands of Free Applications

This should appeal to anyone who is a part of the Macintosh community: by warming up to Unix and its command line, you are joining the much-lauded free software movement, since OS X is based on a free, open source Unix operating system called *Darwin*. What's excellent is that there are thousands of different applications available for open source operating systems, including design, development, scientific, and business applications that compare quite favorably to expensive commercial alternatives. And don't make the mistake of assuming that all open source applications are command-line tools and utilities! Some of the very best applications, like the GIMP graphics editor (*http://www.gimp.org*) and the NeoOffice suite (*http://www.neooffice.org*), are designed to work either within the X Window System (also known as X11), a standard Unix graphical interface that Apple includes with your OS X system, or directly in OS X El Capitan's graphical environment.

Power Internet Connections

If you're someone who uses the Internet daily, you already know that there are a bunch of useful Mac OS X applications available to help you be more efficient. Unfortunately, lots of them seem to have a price tag attached—even a simple FTP program like Fetch (*http://www.fetchsoftworks.com*). But why spend $29 on an application when you can use OS X's built-in *ftp* command-line utility for free?

cp original_file copied_file
Copies the *original_file* (or files) from one location to another.

mv original_file new_file
Moves a file or files; the original is deleted once the operation is complete.

rm filename
Removes a file, set of files, or folder(s) full of files.

 Use the *rm* command with caution; there's no "Trash" to which things are moved. Once you've used *rm* to delete something, it's gone forever.

pwd
Displays your present working directory; this is where you currently are in the filesystem.

cd directory_name
Changes to the specified directory in the filesystem. Without any arguments, it's a shortcut for changing back to your home directory.

man command_name
Accesses OS X's built-in documentation for the Unix commands. To read the manpage for the *ls* command, for example, type **man ls**.

less filename
Displays a long text file, one screen at a time. Pressing the space bar gets the next page when you're ready, and pressing q at any time quits the program and returns you to the command prompt.

grep pattern filename(s)
Searches for the specified pattern across as many files as you desire—a fast way to find that email message you sent to Uncle Linder, for example.

top
Shows you which applications and processes are running on your system, including those that the Finder's Force Quit window ordinarily hides.

A Simple Guided (Unix) Tour

Enough talking about what Unix can do; it's time to flex your fingers, open up your Mac, and try a few commands so you can get a sense of how it all works!

The first step is to launch the Terminal application through which you'll interact with the command shell. Terminal is tucked into the *Utilities* folder within your *Applications* folder.

Since you'll be using the Terminal application throughout this book (and hopefully in the future, as you grow more comfortable with Unix), you should drag the Terminal's icon to the Dock so it's always at the ready. Or, if the Terminal's already running, you can Control-click on its icon in the Dock (or just click and hold down the button for a few seconds) and select Options→Keep in Dock, as shown in Figure 1-3.

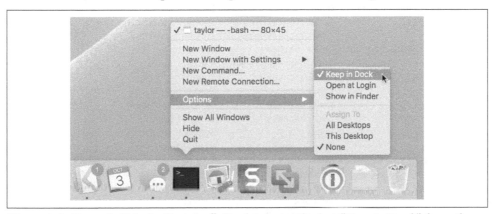

Figure 1-3. Control-click the Terminal's Dock icon, and select "Keep in Dock" from the Options menu so it will always be there when you need it

Throughout the following examples, type in the commands you see in **bold**, pressing the Return key after each one (again, this is known as "entering a command" in Unix-speak). Preceding each command, I've included some comments to let you know what you're about to do.

Without any arguments, the *cd* command moves you to your home directory:

```
$ cd
```

The *pwd* (present working directory) command shows you the path for the directory you're currently in:

```
$ pwd
/Users/taylor
```

Use the *ls* command to list the files in your home directory; compare this listing with the picture of the Finder window shown in Figure 1-2. If you omit the *-a* option, all the hidden dot files stay hidden in this directory:

```
$ ls
Applications    Downloads    Movies      Presentations    bin
Desktop         Dropbox      Music       Public
Documents       Library      Pictures    VirtualBox VMs
```

Now let's change directories to your *Library* folder:

```
$ cd Library
```

Use the *ls* command again to see what's inside (there's very little here you'll need to mess with):

```
$ ls
Accounts                Fonts               Preferences
Address Book Plug-Ins   Fonts Disabled      Printers
Application Scripts      GameKit             PubSub
Application Support      Google              Safari
Assistants              Group Containers    Saved Application State
Audio                   IdentityServices    Screen Savers
Autosave Information     Input Methods       Services
Caches                  Internet Plug-Ins   Social
Calendars               Keyboard Layouts    Sounds
ColorPickers            Keychains           Spelling
Colors                  LanguageModeling    StickiesDatabase
Compositions            LaunchAgents        Suggestions
Containers              Logs                SyncedPreferences
Cookies                 Mail                VirtualBox
CoreData                Messages            Voices
Dictionaries            Metadata            WebKit
Favorites               Mobile Documents    com.apple.nsurlsessiond
Filters                 Network             iMovie
FontCollections         PreferencePanes     iTunes
```

Now let's go back a directory. For this, use the .. shortcut for moving up one directory in the filesystem. In this case, since you were in your *Library* folder (e.g., */Users/taylor/Library*, or just *~/Library*), the following command moves you back to your home directory (as noted by the *pwd* command that follows):

```
$ cd ..
$ pwd
/Users/taylor
```

Finally, when it's time to quit the Terminal, use the *exit* command rather than just quitting the application with ⌘-Q:

```
$ exit
```

Don't worry if you aren't sure exactly what each of those commands does; we'll explore each one in great detail as the book proceeds.

There's a whole world of Unix inside your OS X system, and it's time for you to jump in and learn how to be more productive and more efficient, and gain remarkable power as a Mac user. Ready? Let's go!

## CHAPTER 2

Using the Terminal

With a typical Unix system, a staff person has to set up an account for you before you can use it. With OS X, however, the operating system installation process automatically creates a default user account. The account is identified by your *username*, which is usually a single word or an abbreviation. Think of this account as your office —it's your personal place in the Unix environment.

When you log in to your OS X system, you're automatically logged into your Unix account as well. In fact, your Desktop and other customized features of your OS X environment have corresponding underpinnings in the Unix environment. Your files and programs can be accessed either through the Finder or through a variety of Unix command-line utilities that you can use in OS X's Terminal application.

In this chapter, you'll not only learn about the Terminal and how to customize it for your own needs, but you'll also gain an understanding of the command-line nature of OS X when accessed through the Terminal. If you're used to moving your cursor around and clicking on buttons, this might seem wonderfully—or awkwardly—retro, but as is so often the case, the differences between the Finder and the Terminal are part of what makes the Terminal, and Unix, so remarkably powerful.

Launching the Terminal

The way you use Unix on OS X is through an application known as the Terminal, or, to Mac geeks, *Terminal.app* (pronounced "Terminal dot app"). Open a Finder window, head to *Applications*, then look in *Utilities*, as shown in Figure 2-1. Double-click on "Terminal" and it will start up, presenting you with a dull, uninspiring white window with black text that says "Last login:" and a shell prompt.

Figure 2-1. Finding Terminal in the Utilities folder

 By default, the Terminal uses *bash* as its shell. If you'd like to configure it to use a different shell, you can do so by selecting Terminal→Preferences and specifying the shell to use. I talk about that in "What Is a Shell?" on page 19, later in this chapter.

Most OS X applications you've run to this point probably have a pretty graphical interface and allow you to move the cursor around with your mouse or trackpad. Move it over something you want to do, and you can simply click for the action to take place. The Terminal is different, though: your mouse gets a rest for a while as you type in the commands on your keyboard, ending each line with a Return.

Syntax of a Unix Command

Unix command lines can be simple, one-word entries, such as the *date* command. They can also be more complex; you may need to type more than the command or program name. The command can be the name of a Unix program (such as *date*), or it can be a command that's built into the shell (such as *exit*). You probably don't need to worry about this!

A Unix command can have *arguments*. An argument can be an option or a filename. The general format for a Unix command line is:

```
command option(s) filename(s)
```

There isn't a single set of rules for writing Unix commands and arguments, but these general rules work in most cases:

- Enter commands in lowercase. Unix is case-sensitive, so *echo* and *ECHO* are not synonymous.

- *Options* modify the way in which a command works. Options are often single letters, prefixed with a dash (-, also called a "hyphen" or "minus") and set off by any number of spaces or tabs. Multiple options in one command line can be set off individually (such as *-a -b*). In most cases, you can combine them after a single dash (such as *-ab*), but most command documentation won't tell you whether this will work; you'll have to try it.

  Some commands also have options made from complete words or phrases and starting with two dashes, such as *--delete* or *--confirm-delete*. When you enter a command line, you can use this option style, the single-letter options (which each start with a single dash), or both.

- The argument `filename` is the name of a file you want to use. Most Unix programs also accept multiple filenames, separated by spaces or specified with wildcards (see Chapter 4). If you don't enter a filename correctly, you may get a response such as "`filename`: no such file or directory" or "`filename`: cannot open."

  Some commands, such as *who*, have arguments that aren't filenames.

- You must type spaces between commands, options, and filenames. You'll need to "quote" filenames that contain spaces. For more information, see Chapter 4.

- Options come before filenames.

- In a few cases, an option has another argument associated with it; type this special argument just after its option. Most options don't work this way, but you should know about them. The *sort* command is an example of this feature: you can tell *sort* to write the sorted text to a filename given after its *-o* option. In the following example, *sort* reads the file *sortme* (given as an argument), and writes to the file *sorted* (given after the *-o* option):

  ```
  $ sort -o sorted -n sortme
  ```

  I also used the *-n* option in that example, but *-n* is a more standard option specifying a numeric rather than alphabetic sort; it has nothing to do with the final argument (*sortme*) on that command line. So, I also could have written the command line this way:

  ```
  $ sort -n -o sorted sortme
  ```

  Don't be too concerned about these special cases, though. If a command needs an option like this, its documentation will say so.

- Command lines can have other special characters, some of which you'll see later in this book. They can also include several separate commands. For instance, you can write two or more commands on the same command line, each separated by a semicolon (;). Commands entered this way are executed one after another by the shell.

OS X has a lot of commands! Don't try to memorize all of them. In fact, you'll probably need to know just a few commands and their options. As time goes on, you'll learn these commands and the best way to use them for the work you need to do.

Let's look at a sample command. The *ls* program displays a list of files. You can use it with or without options and arguments. If you enter:

```
$ ls
```

you'll see a list of filenames. But if you enter:

```
$ ls -l
```

there will be an entire line of information for each file. The *-l* option (a dash and a lowercase letter "L") changes the normal *ls* output to a long format. You can also get information about a particular file by using its name as the second argument. For example, to find out about a file called *chap1*, enter:

```
$ ls -l chap1
```

Many Unix commands have more than one option. For instance, *ls* has the *-a* (all) option for listing hidden files. You can use multiple options in either of these ways:

```
$ ls -a -l
$ ls -al
```

You must type at least one space between the command name and the dash that introduces the options. If you enter `ls-al`, the shell reports back with:

```
ls-al: command not found
```

Exercise: Entering a Few Commands

The best way to get used to the Terminal is to enter some commands. To run a command, type the command and then press the Return key. Remember that almost all Unix commands are typed in lowercase. Try issuing the commands shown in Table 2-1 to see what results are produced in the Terminal.

Table 2-1. Sample Unix commands to test out

Task	Command
Get today's date and time.	*date*
List logged-in users.	*who*
Obtain more information about users.	*who -u, finger,* or *w*

Task	Command
Find out who is at your terminal.	*who am i*
Enter two commands in the same line.	*who am i;date*
Mistype a command.	*woh*

In this session, you've tried several simple commands and seen the results on the screen.

Types of Commands

When you use a program, you'll want to know how to control it. How can you tell it what job you want done? Do you give instructions before the program starts, or after it's started? There are several general ways to run programs on an OS X system, and it's good to be aware of them:

Graphical programs

Some programs work only within the graphical window environment. On OS X, you can run these programs using the *open* command. For instance, when you type **open -a Chess** at a command prompt, the Chess application (*/Applications*) launches and opens one or more windows on your screen. The program has its own way to receive your input—through menus and buttons on its windows, for instance. Although you can't interact with these graphical programs using traditional Unix utilities, OS X includes the *osascript* utility, which lets you run Apple-Script commands from the Unix shell.

Noninteractive Unix programs

You can run many Unix programs (though we generally call them "commands" when they're being typed in) directly at a shell prompt. These programs work within a specific command window and you control them from the Unix command line—that is, by typing options and arguments at a shell prompt before you start the program. After you start the program, wait for it to finish; you generally don't interact with it.

Interactive Unix programs

Some Unix programs that work in the Terminal window have commands of their own. (For examples, see Chapters 3 and 4.) These programs may accept options and arguments on their command lines, but once you start a program, it prints its own prompt and/or menus, and it understands its own commands. It also takes instructions from your keyboard that weren't given on its command line.

For instance, if you enter **ftp** at a shell prompt (refer back to the example in "Power Internet Connections" on page 7), you'll see a new prompt from the *ftp* program. At this prompt, you can enter certain FTP commands for transferring files to and from remote systems. When you enter the special command **quit** to quit the *ftp* program (or you can use **bye**), *ftp* stops prompting you for more input. Once you quit FTP, you're returned to the standard Unix shell prompt, where you can enter other Unix commands.

Changing the Terminal's Preferences

To change the Terminal's preferences, go to Terminal→Preferences. This opens the complicated Preferences window, as shown in Figure 2-2.

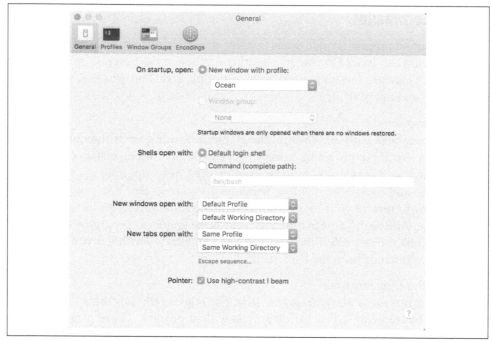

Figure 2-2. The Terminal Preferences window lets you configure the settings for your Terminal windows

At the top of the window is a row of buttons that let you select which options to configure: General, Profiles, Window Groups, and Encodings. The names suggest what each does, but let's have a closer look anyway, particularly since some of these settings definitely *should* be changed (in my view).

General

When you first open the Terminal Preferences, the General settings are displayed, as shown in Figure 2-2. This lets you manage the overall behavior of a window, including its color scheme (my default is "Ocean"), what shell you'd like to use, and even what happens when you open a specific tab.

What Is a Shell?

A *shell*, at least in the Unix world, is the environment in which you work on the Unix side of things. To put this into context, when you're using the graphical user interface for OS X, you're using OS X's native "environment." With Unix, however, everything is text-based, and the shell offers you an interface in which to issue commands, and to configure how your shell environment works and behaves.

Shells also offer their own scripting languages, which allow you to write mini-programs for mundane things, such as displaying a message to tell you to clean the litter box, or much larger tasks, such as backing up your computer. With shell scripts, you're basically using the shell's environment to run Unix commands—or other shell scripts—to automate tasks and processes.

If you want to learn more about the *bash* shell and how to program shell scripts with it, look to the venerable *Learning the bash Shell* by Cameron Newham and Bill Rosenblatt (O'Reilly). Don't let the age of this book fool you. And if you want to see what you can do with shell scripts, I'd recommend picking up a copy of *Wicked Cool Shell Scripts* (No Starch Press), authored by yours truly and still a timely and popular scripting reference.

The choice of shells in OS X includes: */bin/bash*, */bin/csh*, */bin/ksh*, */bin/tcsh*, */bin/zsh*, and */bin/sh*. Unix fans will no doubt find a shell to their liking, but if you're just learning, stick with *bash* (*/bin/bash*) and you'll be able to follow every example in this book without a hiccup.

Profiles

The Profiles pane (shown in Figure 2-3) shows lots of different appearance options, including nice visual thumbnails of the many different predefined color schemes available in the Terminal. The left side of the Profiles window shows the different color profiles, but the right side is where the action is. It's split into six sections: Text, Window, Tab, Shell, Keyboard, and Advanced.

The Text section is where you can specify what typeface you want to use: what size, what color, etc. You can see all of the options in Figure 2-4.

Figure 2-3. Terminal Preferences Profiles pane

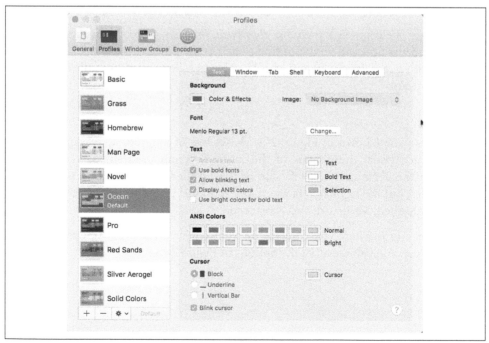

Figure 2-4. Terminal Profiles pane: Text preferences

If you use a predefined profile, of course, you don't have to tweak any of the color settings, but I know that some people can spend hours fiddling and tweaking to get it just so.

The most interesting section of the Profiles pane of the Preferences window is the Window section, shown in Figure 2-3. Here, you can add useful information to the Terminal window, change the background of the Terminal window to a graphic or photo (though I can't imagine why you would!), and change the default window size. The standard size is 25 lines by 80 characters, but that's just a historical artifact from the early Neolithic era of computing. Setting the size to 100 characters wide by 40 or 50 lines makes it considerably easier to work in the Terminal.

One really nice thing that the Terminal does is save the textual information that scrolls off the top of the screen so you can scroll up and review what's transpired earlier. In the old days, once it was off the top, it was off, gone, kaput. Now you can go back and review your command-line interaction from days or even weeks ago, depending on your available memory. You can also configure the size of the scroll-back buffer in the Window section; by default, it is unlimited.

Other sections of the Profiles pane are worth exploring too. In particular, the Shell section is useful for fine-tuning how your Terminal works. The most important setting here is under "Ask before closing." There are three options that let you choose whether or not the Terminal prompts you before closing its windows.

Set "Ask before closing" to "Always" if you'd like the Terminal to always ask before closing the window, or set it to "Never" to prevent it from ever asking. You can also use the "If there are processes other than the login shell and" setting (the default) to ignore the programs shown in the list (you can add items to or remove items from this list). If there's something still running in the window other than the programs defined in this list, a dialog box pops up asking if you're sure you want to quit. This feature is very helpful if you are prone to accidentally clicking the wrong window element or pushing the wrong key sequence.

The last two sections are Keyboard and Advanced. There's nothing there that you'll need to change or modify to fully explore all the capabilities of Unix on your Mac system, so we'll skip them.

Features of the Terminal

There are quite a few nifty Terminal features worth mentioning before I move further into the world of Unix.

Secure Keyboard Entry

While the vast majority of OS X users ignore this feature, the Terminal has a very nice security feature called Secure Keyboard Entry (enable it with Terminal→Secure Keyboard Entry). When enabled, Secure Keyboard Entry ensures that keyboard "sniffers" (or other applications that monitor your keystrokes) cannot see what you type within the Terminal. This means that the OS X utility that calculates whether your computer is in use or ready to sleep won't know you're working, for example, but that could be a small price to pay for the added security of circumventing possible spyware on your system.

More cool Terminal features

In addition to using the Secure Keyboard Entry option from the Terminal menu, some other features you'll find quite useful include:

Shell→New Command

If you need to run a Unix command but don't want to launch a new Terminal window or have its output appear in the current window (manpages are an excellent example), you'll appreciate knowing about the New Command option available on the Shell menu, shown in Figure 2-5. Choose that (or use the keyboard shortcut ⌘-Shift-N) and enter the command you'd like to run, and its output will be displayed in a new window that you can then easily close without affecting anything else.

Edit→Paste Escaped Text

One of the common challenges of working with Unix within the OS X environment is that while the Finder has no problems with spaces embedded in filenames, Unix can be rather testy about even a single space. When you're copying and pasting filenames, however, you don't have to worry about remembering to escape each and every space by preceding it with a backslash: just use Paste Escaped Text (^-⌘-V), and a filename like *taylor/Desktop/My Favorite Martian* is automatically pasted as *taylor/Desktop/My\ Favorite\ Martian*.

Edit→Paste Selection

If you want to copy and paste just what you've selected from a window, rather than everything visible in the Terminal window, use Paste Selection without a Copy, and it'll save you a step. The keyboard shortcut for this one is worth remembering, too: ⌘-Shift-V.

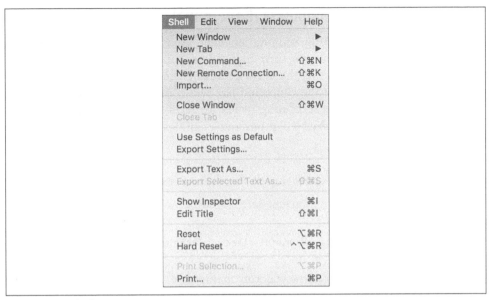

Figure 2-5. Shell menu options

Customizing Your Terminal Session

There are a number of different ways that you can customize your Terminal session beyond what's been shown so far in this chapter. These are more advanced techniques, and you can safely flip past them if they seem too complex (though I'd still encourage you to read through the material, just so you can see what capabilities are included within the Terminal application).

Setting the Terminal's Title

You can change the current Terminal title using the following cryptic sequence of characters:

```
echo '^[]2;My-Window-Title^G'
```

To type the ^[characters in *bash*, use the key sequence Control-V Escape (press Control-V and release, then press the Escape key). To type ^G, use Control-V Control-G. The *vi* editor supports the same key sequences.

Such cryptic sequences of characters are called *ANSI escape sequences*. An ANSI escape sequence is a special command that manipulates some characteristic of the Terminal, such as its title. ^[is the ASCII ESC character (which begins the sequence), and ^G is the ASCII BEL character. (The BEL character is used to "ring" the Terminal bell, but in this context, it terminates the escape sequence.)

Using AppleScript to Manipulate the Terminal

AppleScript is a powerful programming language used to automate OS X applications. The OS X Terminal is one such application. You can run AppleScript commands at the shell prompt using the *osascript* utility. The \ character at the end of an input line tells the shell that the command line will continue on the next input line and therefore not to start executing when it receives the subsequent Return key (when you use this, the shell will prompt you with a > character). The format is as follows:

```
osascript -e \
'tell app "Terminal" to set option of first window to value'
```

For example, to minimize your current Terminal window:

```
$ osascript -e \
> 'tell app "Terminal" to set miniaturized of first window to true'
$
```

For a complete list of properties you can manipulate with AppleScript, open the Script Editor (*/Applications/Utilities/Script Editor*) and select File→Open Dictionary. Open the Terminal dictionary and examine the properties available under *window*, as shown in Figure 2-6. If a property is marked r/o, it is read-only, which means you can't modify it on the fly.

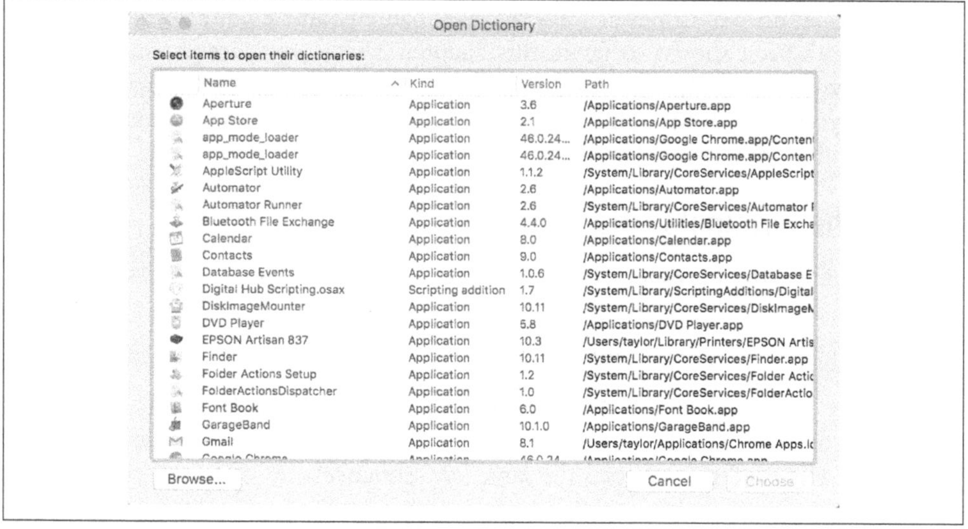

Figure 2-6. The Terminal's AppleScript dictionary

Working with .terminal Files

One useful feature of the Terminal is the ability for you to customize the appearance and behavior of a specific Terminal window, and then save that configuration as a *.terminal* file. Later, you can simply double-click on the *.terminal* file and you'll have your Terminal window back and ready to go, exactly as you set it up previously. Even better, you can set up multiple windows and have them all saved into a single *.terminal* file, then collectively relaunched when you restart the Terminal program.

As an example, suppose you set up the main Terminal window to display large, white text on a blue background. To save this configuration as a *.terminal* file, choose Shell→Export Settings, and you'll be prompted for a filename.

More interesting is a slight variation on this command that saves all the windows you've set up. To achieve this, choose Window→Save Windows as a Group. You'll be prompted for a filename, as shown in Figure 2-7.

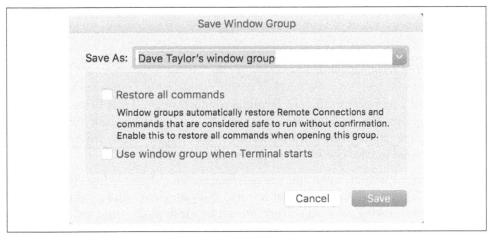

Figure 2-7. Saving a windows group .terminal file

Perhaps the most interesting option is the checkbox "Use window group when Terminal starts." Set things up the way you want, and you could find a half dozen different-sized and different-colored windows on your Desktop, all ready to go, every time you start up the Terminal. You can even have some windows start up running specific commands. A popular command to use is *top* or *tail -f /var/log/system.log*, to help you keep an eye on how your system is performing.

Working with the Terminal

To get into the Unix environment, launch the Terminal application. Hopefully you've already added it to your Dock, as explained earlier!

Once the Terminal is running, you'll see a window like the one in Figure 2-8.

Figure 2-8. The Terminal window

You can have a number of different Terminal windows open, if that helps your work-flow. Simply use ⌘-N to open each one, and ⌘-~ to cycle between them without removing your hands from the keyboard. Or you can have the different sessions neatly organized in tabs. Use ⌘-T to open new tabs as needed.

Once you have a window open and you're typing commands, it's helpful to know that regular OS X copy and paste commands work, so it's simple to send an email message to a colleague showing your latest Unix interaction, or to paste some text from a web page into a file you're editing with a Unix text editor such as *vi*.

If you have material in your scroll buffer that you want to find, use ⌘-F (or select Find→Find from the Edit menu) and enter the specific text. ⌘-G (Edit→Find→Find Next) lets you search down the scroll buffer for the next occurrence, and Shift-⌘-G (Edit→Find→Find Previous) lets you search up the scroll buffer for the previous occurrence. You can also search for material by highlighting a passage and entering ⌘-E (Find→Use Selection for Find), or jump to the selected material with ⌘-J (Find → Jump to Selection). You can save an entire Terminal session as a text file with Shell→Export Text As, and you can print the entire session with Shell→Print.

Study the menus in the Terminal too: there are symbols you might not have seen before in your OS X exploration. For example, the upward-facing diagonal arrow for View→Scroll to Top is the Top or Home key on your keyboard, and the downward-facing diagonal arrow for View→Scroll to Bottom is the End key. You can move up a page with View→Page Up (or ⌘-Page Up), and down a page with View→Page Down (or ⌘-Page Down). To move up or down lines, use ⌘-up arrow or ⌘-down arrow, as needed.

The Shell Prompt

When the system is ready to run a command, the shell outputs a *prompt* to tell you that you can enter a command.

The default prompt in *bash* is the computer name (which might be something automatically generated, such as dhcp-254-108, or a name you've given your system), the current directory (which might be represented by ~, Unix's shorthand for your home directory), your login name, and a dollar sign. For example, the complete prompt might look like this:

```
Dave-Taylors-MacBook-Pro:~ taylor$
```

The prompt can be customized, though, so your own shell prompt may be different. I'll show you how to customize your prompt later in this chapter.

A prompt that ends with a hash mark (#) usually means you're logged in as the *superuser*. The superuser doesn't have the protections for standard users that are built into the Unix system. If you don't know Unix well, you can inadvertently damage your system software when you are logged in as the superuser. In this case, I highly recommend that you stop work until you've found out how to access your personal Unix account.

The simplest solution is to open a new Terminal window (Shell→New Window) and work in that window. If you've still got the superuser prompt, it means that either you logged in to OS X as the superuser or your shell prompt has been customized to end with a #, even when you're not the superuser. To figure out which is the case, try logging out of OS X completely (Apple Menu→Log Out, or Shift-⌘-Q) and logging back in as yourself.

Entering a Command

Entering a command line at the shell prompt tells the computer what to do. Each command line includes the name of a Unix program. When you press Return, the shell interprets your command line and executes the program.

The first word that you type at a shell prompt is always a Unix command (or program name). Like most things in Unix, program names are case-sensitive; if the program name is lowercase (and most are), you must type it in lowercase. Some simple command lines have just one word, which is the program name.

date

An example of a single-word command is *date*. Entering the command *date* displays the current date and time:

```
$ date
Sat Oct  3 14:57:19 MDT 2015
```

As you type a command line, the system simply collects your keyboard input. Pressing the Return key tells the shell that you've finished entering text, and it can run the command.

who

Another simple command is *who*. It displays a list of each logged-on user's username, terminal number, and login time. Try it now, if you'd like.

The *who* program can also tell you which account is currently using the Terminal application, in case you have multiple user accounts on your Mac. The command line for this is *who am i*. This command line consists of the command (*who*, the program's name) and its arguments (*am i*). (Arguments are explained in "Syntax of a Unix Command" on page 14, earlier in this chapter.) For example:

```
$ who am i
taylor    ttys002   Oct  3 14:55
```

The response shown in this example says that:

- *taylor* is the username. The username is the same as the Short Name you define when you create a new user with System Preferences→Accounts→+.

- Virtual terminal *ttys002* is in use. The cryptic *ttys002* syntax is a holdover from the early days of Unix. All you need to know as a Unix beginner is that each time you open a new Terminal window, the number at the end of the name gets incremented by one. The first is *ttys001*, the second *ttys002*, and so on. The terminal ID can also be included in the title bar of the Terminal window, if desired.

- A new Terminal window was opened at 14:55 (or 2:55 p.m.) in the afternoon on Oct 3.

Recalling Previous Commands

Modern Unix shells remember commands you've typed previously. They can even remember commands from previous login sessions. This handy feature can save you a lot of retyping of common commands. As with many things in Unix, though, there are several different ways to do this; I don't have room to show and explain them all, but you can get more information from the sources listed in Chapter 10.

After you've typed and executed several commands, try pressing the up arrow key on your keyboard. You will see the previous command after your shell prompt, just as you typed it. Pressing the up arrow key again recalls the command before that one, and so on. Also, as you'd expect, the down arrow key will recall more recent commands.

To execute one of these remembered commands, just press the Return key. (Your cursor doesn't even have to be at the end of the command line.)

Once you've recalled a command, you can edit it as necessary, usually by moving left and right with the left or right arrow keys, then inserting or deleting characters as needed. If you don't want to execute any remembered commands, cancel the command shown either with the Mac-standard ⌘-. (Command-period) or with the Unix-standard Control-C.

Completing File and Directory Names

Most Unix shells can complete a partially typed file or directory name for you. If you're using the default shell in OS X (i.e., *bash*), just type the first few letters of the word, then press Tab. (Different shells have different methods.) If the shell finds just one way to complete the word, it will do so; your cursor moves to the end of the new word, where you can continue typing or just press Return to run the command.

You can also edit or erase the completed name by hitting the Delete key or moving the cursor back and forth with the left and right arrow keys.

What happens if more than one file or directory name matches what you've typed so far? In this case, the shell will beep at you to let you know that it couldn't find a unique match. To get a list of all possible completions, simply press the Tab key again and you will see a list of all names starting with the characters you've typed so far (you won't see anything if there are no matches). Here's an example from the *bash* shell:

```
$ cd /usr/bin
$ ma<Tab><Tab>
macbinary      machine    make              man
macerror       mail       makeinfo          manpath
macerror5.16   mailq      malloc_history
macerror5.18   mailx      malloc_history32
$ ma
```

At this point, you could type another character or two—an **i**, for example—and then press Tab once more to list only the *mail*-related commands.

Running Multiple Commands on the Command Line

An extremely helpful facet of working with the Unix system is the ability to specify more than one command on a single command line. Perhaps you want to run a command and find out how long it took to complete. This can be done by calling *date* before and after the command, or using the *time* command, but let's stick with *date* for this demonstration. If you hunt-and-peck out *date* each time, the timing is hardly going to be accurate. Much better is to put all three commands on the same line:

```
$ cd ~; date ; du -s . ; date
Sat Oct  3 15:04:38 MDT 2015
715163360    .
Sat Oct  3 15:06:03 MDT 2015
```

This example shows four different commands all strung together on a single command line, using the semicolon character (;) to separate each command. First, *cd ~* moves you into your home directory (as would *cd* by itself, as it happens), then *date* shows the current date and time. Next, the *du -s* command figures out how much disk space is used by the current directory, as denoted by the period (.). A second *date* command then shows the time after the *du* command has run.

Now you know it takes exactly 1 minute and 25 seconds to calculate the disk space used by your home directory—much more useful than knowing it takes 25 seconds for you to type the *date* command, for *du* to run, and for you to type *date* again.

Correcting a Command

What if you make a mistake in a command line? Suppose you type *dare* instead of *date* and press the Return key before you realize your error. If you haven't entered a command that happens to be a misspelled version of another command (which is theoretically possible, I suppose!), the shell displays the following error message:

```
$ dare
-bash: dare: command not found
```

Don't be too concerned about getting error messages. Sometimes you'll get an error even if it appears that you typed the command correctly. This can be caused by accidentally typing control characters that are invisible on the screen. Once the prompt returns, simply reenter your command.

As mentioned earlier, you can recall previous commands and edit command lines. Use the up arrow key to recall a previous command, then, to edit the command line, use the left and right arrow keys to move your cursor to the point where you want to make a change. You can use the Delete key to erase characters to the left of the cursor, and type in changes as needed.

If you have logged in to your Macintosh remotely from another system (see Chapter 8), your keyboard may be different. The erase character differs between systems and accounts, and can be customized. The most common erase characters are:

- Delete or Del
- Control-H

Control-C (or ⌘-.) interrupts or cancels a command, and can be used in many (but not all) cases when you want to quit what you're doing.

Other common control characters are:

Control-U
    Erases the whole input line; you can start over.

Control-S
    Pauses output from a program that's writing to the screen. This can be confusing, so I don't recommend using Control-S.

Control-Q
    Restarts output after a Control-S pause.

Control-D
    Signals the end of input for some programs (such as *cat*, explained in "Putting Text in a File" on page 137) and returns you to a shell prompt. If you type Control-D at a shell prompt, it quits your shell. Depending on your preferences, your Terminal window will either close or sit there, which is generally useless, until you manually close the window.

Ending Your Session

To end a Unix session, you must exit the shell. You should *not* end a session just by quitting the Terminal application or closing the Terminal window. It's possible that you might have started a process running in the background (see Chapter 7), and closing the window could therefore interrupt the process so it won't complete—or, worse, leave a program running stray, without a parent shell or terminal. Instead, type **exit** at the shell prompt and hit Return. The window will either close or simply not display any sort of prompt; you can then safely quit the Terminal application. If you've started a background process, you'll instead get one of the messages described in the next section.

Problem Checklist

The first few times you use OS X, you aren't likely to have the following problems. But you may encounter these problems later, as you do more advanced work:

You get another shell prompt, or the shell says "logout: not login shell."
    You've been using a subshell (a shell created by your original Terminal shell). Type **exit** (or just type Control-D) to close each subshell until the Terminal window closes.

The shell says "There are stopped jobs" or "There are running jobs."

OS X and many other Unix systems have a feature called *job control* that lets you suspend a program temporarily while it's running or keep it running separately in the "background." One or more programs you ran during your session has not ended but is stopped (paused) or in the background. Enter **fg** to bring each stopped job into the foreground, then quit the program normally. (See Chapter 7 for more information.)

The Terminal application refuses to quit, saying "Closing this window will terminate the following processes inside it," followed by a list of programs.

The Terminal tries to help by not quitting when you're in the middle of running a command. Cancel the dialog box and make sure you don't have any commands running that you've forgotten about. If need be, type *jobs* to see what's running.

Customizing the Shell Environment

The Unix shell reads a number of configuration files when it starts up. These configuration files are really *shell programs*, so they are extraordinarily powerful. Shell programming is beyond the scope of this book.

But let's look at what you can customize without having to become a full-fledged Unix geek, shall we?

Picking a Login Shell

The default login shell for OS X is the ever-popular *bash* shell, but many Unix fans prefer to use the Korn shell (*ksh*) instead. As mentioned earlier, OS X offers a host of different shells, including */bin/bash*, */bin/csh*, */bin/ksh*, */bin/tcsh*, */bin/zsh*, and */bin/sh*.

To change your login shell, you can either use the Unix *chsh* command (enter **chsh** on the command line and you'll be asked which shell you'd like, starting the next time you log in) or just change the shell setting in the Terminal Preferences, as shown earlier, in Figure 2-2.

Why Some Folks Love the Korn Shell

From the perspective of typing in commands and even working with command history or aliases, almost all shells are alike. In a rather old interview on the popular geek website SlashDot (*http://www.slashdot.org*), David Korn (author of the Korn shell) even says: "It is hard to argue that *ksh* is any better for interaction... but the scripting features in *ksh93* are far more advanced than any other shell."

If you spend a lot of time writing advanced shell scripts, *ksh* can be an excellent choice, because it offers some remarkably sophisticated capabilities—features that you'd only expect in a highly advanced programming environment like Java or C++.

The *bash* shell also has many sophisticated programming features, and it's my shell of choice, but in some Unix circles *ksh* is the preferred shell.

For more information on the Korn shell, see *Learning the Korn Shell*, by Bill Rosenblatt and Arnold Robbins (O'Reilly).

Changing the Command Prompt

The easiest customization you can make to the shell is to change your *command prompt*. By default, *bash* on OS X has a shell prompt made up of your computer's hostname, your current working directory, your account name, and a dollar sign. For example:

```
Dave-Taylors-MacBook-Pro:~ taylor$
```

If you'd rather have something shorter, like just the dollar sign ($), enter the following command:

```
Dave-Taylors-MacBook-Pro:~ taylor$ PS1="$ "
$
```

This command gives you a simple, sparse $ prompt, and nothing else. It isn't necessary to use the dollar sign as your prompt; you could use a colon (:), a greater than sign (>), or any character you like. Just remember to include a space after the character you've chosen to use as the prompt, because that helps you differentiate between the command prompt and the actual command you're typing in.

 If you want this change to take effect every time you start a shell, use the *vi* editor to create a file called *.profile* in your home directory (*/Users/your_name*), and then add the following to the end of the file: **export PS1="$ "**. (You can read more about the *vi* editor in Chapter 4.)

Of course, if that were all you could do to your command prompt, it wouldn't be very interesting. There are a number of special character sequences that, when used to define the prompt, cause the shell to print out various bits of useful data. Table 2-2 shows a partial list of these special character sequences for fine-tuning your prompt.

Table 2-2. Favorite escape sequences for bash prompts

Value	Meaning
\w	The current working directory
\W	The trailing element of the current working directory, with ~ substitution

Value	Meaning
\\!	The current command history number
\\H	The full hostname
\\h	The hostname up to the first dot
\\@	The time of day in 12-hour (a.m./p.m.) format
\\A	The time of day in 24-hour format
\\u	The username
\\$	A # if the effective user ID is zero (*root*), or a $ otherwise

Experiment and see what sorts of interesting Unix prompts you can create. For many years, a popular Unix prompt was:

```
$ PS1="Yes, Master? "
```

It might be a bit obsequious, but on the other hand, how many people in your life call you "Master"?

One prompt sequence that I like is:

```
$ PS1="\w \! \$ "
```

This prompt sequence shows the current working directory, followed by a space and the current history number, and then a $ or # to remind the user that this is *bash* and whether they're currently running as *root*. (The # is for when you're running as *root*, the administrator account, and the $ is for when you aren't *root*.) For example, the prompt might read:

```
~ 55 $
```

This tells you immediately that ~ (in my case, */Users/taylor*) is the current directory, and that this will be the 55th command you'll execute. Because you can use the up or down arrow keys to scroll back or forward, respectively, through your previous commands, as described in "Recalling Previous Commands" on page 28, this is not as important in the Terminal as it is in other command-line environments, but there is a very powerful command history syntax built into *bash* that allows you to recall a previous command by number. If you're familiar with this syntax, making the command history number part of the prompt can be handy.

On multiuser systems, it's not a bad idea to put the username into the prompt as well. That way, you'll always know who the system thinks you are. And if you routinely use more than one computer system, you should also consider including the hostname in the prompt so you'll always know which system you're logged in to.

Advanced Shell Customization

There's not much more you can do to customize the Terminal application than what's shown in this chapter, but there's an infinite amount of customization possible with the *bash* shell (or any other shell you might have picked). Remember, the Terminal is the program you're using to access the command line on your Mac system, and the shell is the actual program being run that lets you submit requests and have them processed.

Here are a few directions to get you started.

Shell Configuration Settings

Because Unix is a multiuser system, there are two possible locations for the configuration files: one applies to all users of the system and another to each individual user.

The system-wide setup files that are read by *bash*, the default shell for OS X, are found in */etc* (*profile* and *bashrc*). You only have permission to change these system-wide files if you use *sudo* (see "Superuser Privileges with sudo" on page 72, in Chapter 3). However, you can create another file called *.profile* in your home directory that will add additional commands to be executed whenever you start a new Terminal window. (If you configure the Terminal to use another shell, such as the Bourne shell, the C shell, or the Z shell, you'll need to set up different configuration files. See the manpage for your selected shell to learn the necessary details. To learn more about *csh*, for example, use the command *man csh*.)

The system-wide setup files are read first, then the user-specific ones, so commands in your *.profile* file can override those in the system-wide files. The system-wide *bashrc* file is succinct:

```
$ cat /etc/bashrc
# System-wide .bashrc file for interactive bash(1) shells.
if [ -z "$PS1" ]; then
   return
fi

PS1='\h:\W \u\$ '
# Make bash check its window size after a process completes
shopt -s checkwinsize

[ -r "/etc/bashrc_$TERM_PROGRAM" ] && . "/etc/bashrc_$TERM_PROGRAM"
```

Your own profile file—prefaced with a . to hide it from the Finder—can contain any shell command that you want to run automatically whenever you open a new Terminal window. Some typical examples include changing the shell prompt, setting environment variables (values that control the operation of other Unix utilities), setting aliases, or adding to the search path (where the shell searches for programs to be run). My *.profile* file looks like this:

```
PS1="\w (\!): " ❶

export PATH=$HOME/bin:/opt/local/bin:/opt/local/sbin:$PATH ❷

export SVN_EDITOR=/usr/bin/vi ❸

alias scale=~/bin/scale.sh ❹
alias ls="ls -F"
alias vps="ssh dtaylor@intuitive.com"

date ❺
```

❶ This line tells the shell to use a different prompt than the standard one. I explained the details of prompt setting in "Changing the Command Prompt" on page 33, earlier in this chapter. This particular sequence offers me a succinct prompt that's also informative: /bin (518):.

❷ This line sets a shell variable that the shell itself uses as its search path for finding commands that are typed in. Usually the default PATH is fine, but since I have some local programs and scripts I've written, this lets me use them without specifying their location in the filesystem each time.

❸ Similarly, this line specifies what editor the SVN command should use by default (*vi*). Not all commands recognize environment variables, but for those that do, this type of environment variable setting saves you the trouble of typing the options on every command line.

❹ These three lines define new custom commands that the shell will recognize just as if they were built-in Unix commands. Aliases are a great way to save shorthand names for long, complicated Unix command lines, or even to fix common mistakes you might make when typing command lines. These particular aliases create a command for launching my image-scaling shell script (*scale.sh*), add a favorite flag to the *ls* command, and let me invoke the secure shell utility (*ssh*) with the account information I need as a shortcut. A brief tutorial on creating aliases can be found in the next section.

❺ This line simply runs the *date* command to print the time and date when a new Terminal window is opened. You might not want to do this, but it's good for you to see that you can include any command that you could type at the shell prompt and have it automatically be executed whenever a new shell starts up.

By default, the *.profile* file doesn't yet exist in your home directory, and only the system-wide configuration files are read each time a Terminal window is opened. But if you create this file in your home directory, it will be read and its contents executed the next time you start a shell. You can create or change this file with a text editor such as *vi* (see Chapter 4).

Don't use a word processor like Microsoft Word that breaks long lines or puts special nontext codes into the file. TextEdit can work if you really insist, but you need to ensure that you chose Format→Make Plain Text (Shift-⌘-T) before you save the file to ensure that no additional formatting information is added by the application.

Any changes you make to your shell setup files will take effect when you open a new Terminal window. Unfortunately, it's not always easy to know which shell setup file you should change, and an editing mistake in your shell setup file can interfere with the normal startup of the Terminal window itself. It is recommended that beginners get help from experienced users before tweaking these files. Also, you shouldn't make changes to these files at all if you're about to do some critical work with your account, unless there's some reason you have to make the changes immediately.

You can execute any customization command discussed here from the command line as well, rather than making a more permanent change by editing *.profile*. In this case, the changes remain in effect only until you close the window you're using or quit the Terminal.

For example, to change the default options for the other *less* command so it clears the Terminal window before showing each new page of text, you could add the *-c* option to the LESS environment variable. The command looks something like this:

```
$ export LESS='eMqc'
```

If you don't want some of the *less* options shown here, you can leave those options out.

Unix has many other configuration commands to learn about; the books and websites listed in Chapter 10 can help you identify which modifications you can make and how they can help you produce an optimal computing environment for yourself.

Just as you can execute the setup commands from the command line, you can specify that any command that you can execute from the command line be executed automatically when you log in by placing it in your setup file. (Running interactive commands such as *vi* or *ftp* from your setup file isn't a good idea, though, in case you ever log in from a system that can't display a full-screen editor window. That would leave you rather stuck.)

Creating Aliases

The flexibility of Unix is simultaneously its greatest strength and greatest downfall; the operating system can do just about anything you can imagine (the command-line interface is certainly far more flexible than the Finder!), but it's very difficult to remember every single option to every command. That's where shell aliases can be a real boon. A shell alias is a simple mechanism that lets you create your own command names that act exactly as you desire.

For example, I like the *-a* and *-F* options to be included every time I list a directory with *ls*, so I created the following alias:

```
$ alias ls="/bin/ls -aF"
```

Now every time I enter *ls* in the shell, the command is run and the *-a* and *-F* options are specified automatically. To have this available in your next session, make sure you remember to also add the alias to your *.profile* file.

You can also have aliases that let you jump quickly to common locations, a particularly helpful trick in OS X. For example:

```
$ alias desktop="cd ~/Desktop"
```

With that alias in place, all you need to do is enter **desktop** at the command prompt, and you're taken to your *Desktop* directory. The shell looks at its *.profile* file, sees that *desktop* is an alias, and runs the commands found in the quotes (in this case, *cd ~/Desktop*).

Another set of useful aliases is to automatically set the *rm*, *cp*, and *mv* commands into interactive mode, using their *-i* option. (Chapter 4 describes the *cp*, *mv*, and *rm* commands, which copy, move, and remove files, respectively.) Each of these supports the *-i* option, which prompts you before overwriting or deleting a file. You can use aliases to always enable this option:

```
$ alias rm="rm -i"
$ alias cp="cp -i"
$ alias mv="mv -i"
```

You can list all active aliases by typing **alias** without any arguments:

```
$ alias
alias cp='cp -i'
alias desktop='cd ~/Desktop'
alias ls='/bin/ls -a'
```

Have an alias you want to get rid of? You can use the *unalias* command for that. For example, *unalias ls* removes the *-aF* options added earlier. To remove them permanently, however, you'll likely have to delete that line from your *.bashrc* or *.profile* file.

The Unresponsive Terminal

During your Unix session, your terminal may fail to respond when you type a command, or the display on your screen may stop at an unusual place. That's called a "hung" or "frozen" terminal or session. Note that most of the techniques in this section apply to a Terminal window, but not to non-Terminal windows, such as a web browser.

A session can hang for several reasons. For instance, your computer can get too busy, and the Terminal application has to wait its turn. In that case, your session will resume after a few moments. Do *not* try to "un-hang" the session by entering extra commands, because those commands will all take effect after the Terminal comes back to life.

If your display becomes garbled, press Control-L. In the shell, this will clear the screen and display the prompt. In a full-screen program, such as a text editor, this keyboard shortcut redraws the screen.

If the system doesn't respond for quite a while (how long that is depends on your individual situation; if you're not sure, ask other users about their experiences), the following solutions usually work. Try these steps in the order shown until the system responds:

Press the Return key once
> You may have typed text at a prompt (for example, a command line at a shell prompt) but not yet pressed Return to say that you're done typing and your text should be interpreted.

Try job control (see Chapter 7); type Control-Z
> This suspends the program running in the foreground and gives you a new shell prompt.

Press Control-C or ⌘.
> This interrupts a program that may be running. (Unless the program is run in the background; as described in Chapter 7, the shell waits for a background program to finish before giving a new prompt. A long-running background program may thus appear to hang the Terminal.) If this doesn't work the first time, try it once more; doing it more than twice usually won't help.

Type Control-Q

If output has been stopped with Control-S, this restarts the previously paused process. Note that some systems automatically issue a Control-S if they need to pause output; this sequence may not have been typed from the keyboard.

Type Control-D once at the beginning of a new line

Some programs (such as *mail*) expect text from the user. A program may be waiting for an end-of-input character from you to tell it that you've finished entering text. Typing Control-D may cause you to log out, so you should try this only as a last resort.

If all else fails, close your Terminal window (⌘-W) and open a new one.

## CHAPTER 3

Exploring the Filesystem

Once you launch the Terminal, you can use the many facilities that OS X provides at the command line—an environment that's quite a bit more powerful than the graphical interface you may be used to viewing. As a user, you have an account that gives you:

- A place in the filesystem where you can store your files
- A username that identifies you and lets you control access to files
- An environment you can customize

In this chapter, you'll see how all the thousands of files on your Mac are organized, how to learn more details about any given file, and how to move around through OS X's filesystem. You'll see that the Finder has been hiding quite a lot of information from you: there are entire directories with thousands of files that are invisible from the Finder but easily found and explored within the Terminal.

The OS X Filesystem

A *file* is the unit of storage in OS X. A file can hold anything: text (a report you're writing, a to-do list), a program, digitally encoded pictures or sound, and so on. All of those are just sequences of raw data until they're interpreted by the right program.

Files are organized into *directories* (more commonly referred to as *folders* on the Aqua side of the Mac). A directory is actually a special kind of file where the system stores information about other files. You can think of a directory as a place, so that files are said to be contained *in* directories, and you work *inside* a directory. It's important that you realize that *everything is a file in Unix*. Whether you're working with a directory (perhaps moving files around) or editing a document, Unix fundamentally looks at everything as the same sort of container of information.

A *filesystem* includes all the files and directories on a mounted volume, such as your system's hard disk, Dropbox, Google Drive, or your iCloud account (all of which you *mount* on your system with a little help from WebDAV). This section introduces OS X's filesystem, showing you how all the files on your Mac are organized and how to use Unix commands to explore your Mac's filesystem. Later sections show how you can look in files and protect them. Chapter 4 has more information about file management.

Your Home Directory

When you launch the Terminal, you're placed in a directory called your *home directory*. This directory, which can also be viewed in the Finder by clicking the Home icon, contains personal files, application preferences, and application data such as Safari's bookmarks. In your home directory, you can create your own files, create other subdirectories, and so on. Like folders in a file cabinet, directories offer a way for you to organize your files.

You can find out where your home directory is at any time by typing the following command:

```
$ echo $HOME
/Users/taylor
```

As you can see, this tells me that my home directory (*taylor*) is found within the *Users* directory (*/Users*). In Unix, a forward slash (/) is used to separate directory names, with just a single slash signifying the very top, or *root level*, of your Mac's filesystem. For example, to change directories to the root level of your hard drive, use the following command:

```
$ cd /
```

For more information on the filesystem's structure and the root directory, see "The Directory Tree" on page 43.

Your Working Directory

Your *working directory* (also called your current directory) is the directory in which you're currently working. Every time you open a new Terminal window, your home directory is your working directory. When you change to another directory, the directory you move to becomes your working directory, and so on.

Unless you specify otherwise, all commands that you enter apply to the files in your working directory. In the same way, when you create files, they're created in your working directory unless you specify another directory. For instance, if you type the command *vi report*, the *vi* editor starts and a file named *report* is created in your working directory once you've saved your changes. (Unless, of course, a *report* file already exists there, in which case that file will be opened in *vi*.) But if you enter the following command:

```
$ vi /Users/john/Documents/report
```

a *report* file is created in your *Documents* directory—all without your having to change from your current working directory. You'll learn more about this when we cover pathnames, later in this chapter.

Here's something that's important for you to recognize: if you have more than one Terminal window open, each shell has its own working directory. Changing the working directory in one shell doesn't affect other Terminal windows.

You can find out your working directory at any time by entering the *pwd* command:

```
$ pwd
/Users/taylor
```

The Directory Tree

All directories in OS X are organized into a hierarchical structure that you can imagine as a family tree. The parent directory of the tree (the directory that contains all other directories) is known as the *root directory* and is written as a forward slash (/). The root directory is what you see if you open a new Finder window, click the Computer icon, and then open your hard disk.

The root directory contains several other directories. Figure 3-1 shows a visual representation of the top of OS X's filesystem tree: the root directory and some directories under the root.

Applications, *Library*, *System*, and *Users* are some of the *subdirectories* (child directories) of the root directory. There are several other directories that are invisible in the Finder but visible at the shell prompt (you can see them if you use the *ls /* command). These subdirectories are standard Unix directories *bin*, *dev*, *etc*, *sbin*, *tmp*, *usr*, and *var*; they contain Unix system files. For instance, *bin* contains many Unix programs (also known as *binaries*, hence the "bin" directory name).

In a Figure 3-1, the parent directory of *Users* (one level above) is the root directory. *Users* has two subdirectories (one level below), *john* and *carol*. On an OS X system, each directory has only one parent directory, but it may have one or more subdirectories. The root directory at the top of the tree is *its own* parent and is just known as "slash." A subdirectory (such as *carol*) can have its own subdirectories (such as *Documents* and *Music*).

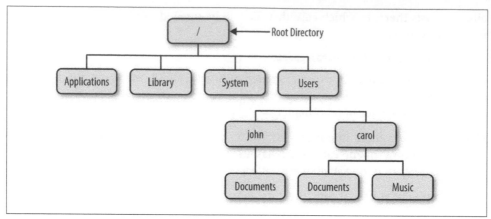

Figure 3-1. Example of a directory tree

To specify a file or directory location, write its *pathname*. A pathname is essentially the address of the directory or file in the filesystem. For more on pathnames, see the upcoming sections "Absolute Pathnames" and "Relative Pathnames".

On a basic OS X system, all files in the filesystem are stored on disks connected to your computer. OS X also has a way to access files on other computers: a *networked filesystem*. Networked filesystems make a remote computer's files appear as if they're part of your computer's directory tree. You can also mount shared directories from other Macs, Windows machines, or even Unix and Linux servers (from the Finder's menu bar, select Go→Connect to Server). These also appear in the */Volumes* directory, as will other disks, including any external drives plugged directly into your Mac and any removable media (CDs, DVDs) you have available.

Absolute Pathnames

As you saw earlier, the Unix filesystem organizes its files and directories in an inverted tree structure with the root directory at the top. An *absolute pathname* tells you the path of directories through which you must travel to get from the root to the directory or file you want. In a pathname, slashes (/) are used between the directory names.

For example, */Users/john* is an absolute pathname. It identifies one (*only* one!) directory. Here's how:

- The root directory is the first slash (/).
- The directory *Users* (a subdirectory of the root directory) is second.
- The directory *john* (a subdirectory of *Users*) is last.

Be sure that you do not type spaces anywhere in the pathname. If there are spaces in one or more of the directory names, you need to either quote the entire directory pathname, or preface each space with a backslash (\) to ensure that the shell understands that the spaces are part of the pathname itself. The backslash is known as an *escape character* for just this reason.

In Figure 3-2, you'll see that the directory *john* has a subdirectory named *Documents*. Its absolute pathname is */Users/john/Documents*.

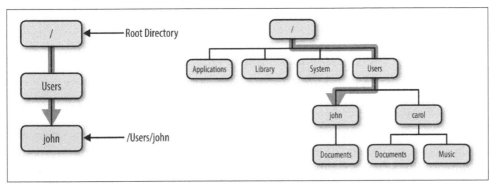

Figure 3-2. Absolute path of directory john

 The root directory is always indicated by the slash (/) at the start of the pathname. In other words, an absolute pathname always starts with a slash.

Relative Pathnames

You can also locate a file or directory with a *relative pathname*. A relative pathname gives the location relative to your working directory.

Unless you use an absolute pathname (a path that starts with a slash), Unix assumes that you're using a relative pathname. Like absolute pathnames, relative pathnames can go through more than one directory level by naming the directories along the path.

For example, if you're currently in the */Users* directory (see Figure 3-2), the relative pathname to the *carol* directory is simply *carol*:

```
$ pwd
/Users
$ cd carol
$ pwd
/Users/carol
```

If *carol* wanted to move from her home directory to the *Music* directory, the relative pathname to the *Music* directory would be as follows:

```
$ cd Music
$ pwd
/Users/carol/Music
```

Or, she could just use the following command to get from */Users* to *carol/Music*:

```
$ cd carol/Music
$ pwd
/Users/carol/Music
```

In these examples, notice that none of the pathnames we are specifying to the *cd* command start with a slash. That's what makes them relative pathnames! Relative pathnames start at the working directory, not the root directory. Just remember, a relative pathname never starts with a slash.

Relative pathnames up

You can go up the tree with the Unix shorthand .. (two periods, commonly referred to in Unix lingo as "dot dot") for the parent directory. As you saw earlier, you can also go down the tree by using subdirectory names. In either case (up or down), separate each level by a forward slash (/).

Figure 3-3 shows part of Figure 3-1. If your working directory in the figure is *Documents*, then there are two pathnames you can use to navigate to the *Music* subdirectory of *carol*. You already know how to write the absolute pathname, */Users/carol/Music*. You can also go up one level (with ..) to *carol*, then go down the tree to *Music*. Figure 3-3 illustrates this.

The relative pathname would be *../Music*. It would be wrong to give the relative address as *carol/Music*. Using *carol/Music* would say that *carol* is a subdirectory of your working directory instead of what it is in this case: the parent directory.

 Absolute and relative pathnames are interchangeable. Unix programs simply follow whichever path you specify to wherever it leads. If you use an absolute pathname, the path starts from the root. If you use a relative pathname, the path starts from your current working directory. Choose whichever is easier at the moment.

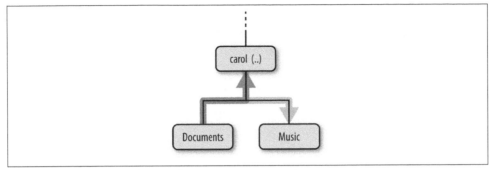

Figure 3-3. Relative pathname from Documents to Music

Pathname Puzzle

Here's a short but important question. The previous examples explain the relative pathname *carol/Music*. What do you think Unix would say about the pathname */carol/Music*? (Look again at Figure 3-1.)

Unix would say "No such file or directory." Why? (Please think about that a little bit; this is very important, and it's one of the most common mistakes made by Unix newbies.) The answer is because the path starts with a slash. The pathname */carol/Music* is an absolute pathname that starts from the root. It says to look in the root directory (/) for a subdirectory named *carol*. But since the root directory has no subdirectory named *carol*, the pathname is wrong. The only absolute pathname to the *Music* directory is */Users/carol/Music*.

Changing Your Working Directory

Once you know the absolute or relative pathname of a directory where you'd like to work, you can move up and down the OS X filesystem to reach it. The following sections explain some helpful commands for navigating through a directory tree.

pwd

To find which directory you're currently in, use *pwd* (print working directory), which prints the absolute pathname of your working directory. The *pwd* command takes no arguments:

```
$ pwd
/Users/john
```

cd

You can change from your present working directory to any directory (including another user's directory, if you have permission) with the *cd* (change directory) command, which has the form:

```
cd pathname
```

The argument is an absolute or a relative pathname (whichever is easier) for the directory you want to change to:

```
$ cd /Users/carol
$ pwd
/Users/carol
$ cd Documents
$ pwd
/Users/carol/Documents
```

 The command *cd*, with no arguments, takes you to your home directory from wherever you are in the filesystem. It's identical to typing in *cd $HOME* and also identical to typing in *cd ~*, as shown earlier.

Note that you can only change to another directory that you have permission to access. If you try to change to a directory that you're otherwise shut out of, you'll see an error:

```
$ cd /Users/john
-bash: cd: /Users/john: Permission denied
```

You also cannot *cd* to a filename. If you try, your shell (in this example, *bash*) gives you an error message:

```
$ cd /etc/aliases
-bash: cd: /etc/aliases:  Not a directory.
```

 If you're curious, */etc/aliases* is a file that contains system-level email aliases for your Mac system.

One neat trick worth mentioning is that you can quickly give the Terminal a file or directory path by dragging a file or folder icon from the Finder onto the Terminal window. This is particularly helpful for those times when you'd have to type an extra-long pathname. For example, if you wanted to change directories to an album in your iTunes collection, you'd have to type something like the following:

```
$ cd /Users/taylor/Music/iTunes/iTunes\ Media/Music/Maroon\ 5/Hands\ All\ Over
```

Sure, like you're going to remember that pathname off the top of your head!

To make this easier, you could just type *cd* followed by a space in a Terminal window, and then drag the folder in question from a Finder window onto the Terminal window, as shown in Figure 3-4. When you let go of the file or folder you're dragging into the Terminal window, the pathname gets added to the command prompt.

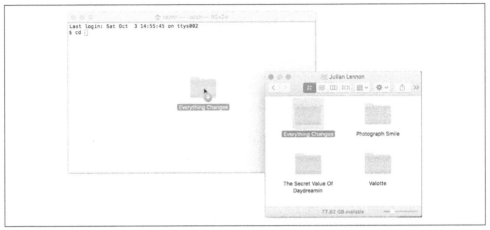

Figure 3-4. Dragging a folder from the Finder to a Terminal window saves you from having to type long and complex paths

Files in the Directory Tree

A directory can hold subdirectories. And, of course, a directory can hold files. Figure 3-5 is a close-up of the filesystem around *john's* home directory. Six directories are shown, along with the *mac-rocks* file created by using the *touch* command, as explained in the sidebar "Two Ways to Explore Your Filesystem" on page 50.

Pathnames to files are constructed the same way as pathnames to directories. As with directories, file pathnames can be absolute (starting from the root directory) or relative (starting from the working directory). For example, if your working directory is */Users*, the relative pathname to the *Documents* directory would be *john/Documents*. The relative pathname to the *mac-rocks* file would be *john/mac-rocks*.

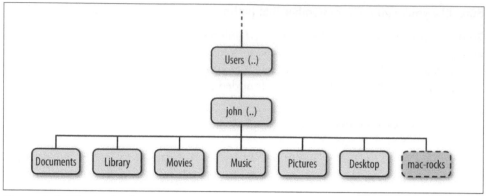

Figure 3-5. Files in the directory tree

Unix filesystems can also hold things that aren't directories or files, such as symbolic links (similar to aliases in OS X), devices (the */dev* directory contains entries for devices attached to the system), and sockets (network communication channels). You may see some of them as you explore the filesystem. These advanced topics aren't covered in this little book, however, because they're more complex, and overloading you with advanced stuff right now just wouldn't be fair.

Two Ways to Explore Your Filesystem

Every file and folder that you view from the Finder is also accessible from the Unix shell. Changes made in one environment are reflected (almost) immediately in the other. For example, the *Desktop* folder is also the Unix directory */Users/your_name/Desktop*.

Just for fun, open a Finder window, move to your home folder, and keep it visible while you type these commands at the shell prompt:

```
$ cd
$ touch mac-rocks
```

Switch back to the Finder (you can click on the Desktop) and watch a file called *mac-rocks* appear magically. (The *touch* command creates an empty file with the name you specify, unless it already exists, in which case it updates the last modified time.)

Now type:

```
$ rm mac-rocks
```

Return to the Finder, and watch the file disappear. The *rm* command removes the file.

Listing Files and Directories

To use the *cd* command, you must know which entries in a directory are subdirectories and which are files. The *ls* command lists entries in the directory tree and can also show you which are which.

The All-Powerful ls Command

When you enter the *ls* command, you get a list of the files and subdirectories contained in your working directory. The syntax is:

```
ls options directory-and-filenames
```

If you've just moved into an empty directory, entering *ls* without any arguments may seem to do nothing. This isn't surprising; if you have no files, nothing is displayed. Instead, you'll simply get a new shell prompt:

```
$ ls
$
```

But if you're in your home directory, *ls* displays the names of the files and directories in that directory. The output depends on what's in your directory. The screen should look something like what I see in my own home directory:

```
$ ls
Applications    Downloads    Movies      Presentations    bin
Desktop         Dropbox      Music       Public
Documents       Library      Pictures    VirtualBox VMs
```

Sometimes *ls* might display filenames in a single column. If yours does, you can make a multicolumn display with the *-C* option (multicolumn, sorted down) or the *-x* option (multicolumn, sorted across). *ls* has a lot of options that change the information and display format.

The *-a* (all) option is guaranteed to show you some more files, as in the following example:

```
$ ls -a
.                        .profile        Movies
..                       .ssh            Music
.CFUserTextEncoding      .viminfo        Pictures
.DS_Store                Applications    Presentations
.Trash                   Desktop         Public
.bash_history            Documents       VirtualBox VMs
.bash_sessions           Downloads       bin
.cups                    Dropbox
.dropbox                 Library
```

When you use *ls -a*, you'll always see at least two entries named . (dot) and .. (dot, dot). As mentioned earlier, .. is always the relative pathname to the parent directory. A single . always represents the current directory; believe it or not, this is useful with commands such as *cp* (see Chapter 4). There may also be other files, such as *.bash_history* or *.Trash*. Any entry whose name begins with a dot is a hidden file—it's listed only if you add the *-a* flag to the *ls* command and is always hidden from the Finder.

Trying Out the ls Command

Since the *ls* command is such an important part of the Terminal, let's practice using some of the different options.

Open the Terminal application, and then type along to see what your system shows you:

```
$ ls
Applications    Downloads    Movies      Presentations    bin
Desktop         Dropbox      Music       Public
Documents       Library      Pictures    VirtualBox VMs
$ ls -1
Applications
Desktop
Documents
Downloads
Dropbox
Library
Movies
Music
Pictures
Presentations
Public
VirtualBox VMs
bin
```

The *-1* option (that's the number one, not a lowercase "L") causes *ls* to output the list of files in one-file-per-line format, which can be useful if you're going to paste the list into a Word document or other material.

One problem with *ls* is that, unlike the Finder with its helpful icons, the output from *ls* doesn't let you differentiate between files and directories. That's where the helpful *-F* option comes in handy:

```
$ ls -F
Applications/    Downloads/    Movies/      Presentations/    bin/
Desktop/         Dropbox/      Music/       Public/
Documents/       Library/      Pictures/    VirtualBox VMs/
```

The *-F* option shows you which entries are directories by appending a forward slash (/) to the end of their names. If there were any executable programs or scripts in this directory, *-F* would append an asterisk (*) after their filenames; an at symbol (@) would denote a symbolic link.

The *-s* option indicates the size of each file, in units of 512 bytes. Why 512 bytes? Well, that's what the original Unix filesystem used as its block size all those years ago, and since then that's just what the *ls -s* command uses. If you really want to use *-s* but aren't interested in 512-byte blocks, you can set the environment variable BLOCKSIZE to 1024 to make the resultant listings use the more logical 1-kilobyte size. The results of this command may be somewhat unexpected.

```
$ ls -s
total 0
0 Applications    0 Library        0 Public
0 Desktop         0 Movies         0 VirtualBox VMs
0 Documents       0 Music          0 bin
0 Downloads       0 Pictures
0 Dropbox         0 Presentations
```

Directories and empty files are always shown as having zero blocks used. You need to use the *du* (disk usage) command, as discussed a bit later in this chapter, to find out the size of a directory.

Truth be told, most Unix users skip the *-s* flag to *ls* in favor of using *du*. Let's try this again on a directory that we know contains files that aren't empty (*Library/Preferences*):

```
$ ls -sF Library/Preferences/
total 43672
      8 2BUA8C4S2C.com.agilebits.onepassword4-helper.plist
      0 ByHost/
     72 CD Info.cidb
      0 Epson/
      8 Lingsoft
      0 Macromedia/
      0 Microsoft/
      8 MobileMeAccounts.plist
     32 QuickTime Preferences
      8 SafariCloudHistoryPushAgent.plist
      0 VMware Fusion/
      8 callservicesd.plist
      8 com.884e51b2-8cd1-4d52-88a3-df0ac5fcc4db.plist
      8 com.Echostar.Sling.plist
      8 com.TechSmith.Snagit.LSSharedFileList.plist
   2720 com.TechSmith.Snagit.plist
...
      8 org.bitcoin.Bitcoin-Qt.plist
      8 org.cups.PrintingPrefs.plist
      8 org.m0k.transmission.LSSharedFileList.plist
      8 org.m0k.transmission.plist
      0 org.videolan.vlc/
     24 org.videolan.vlc.LSSharedFileList.plist
     16 org.videolan.vlc.plist
      8 org.virtualbox.app.VirtualBox.plist
```

This is much more useful. You can see that the directories *Microsoft, VMware Fusion, ByHost*, etc., are all zero size, as expected, but notice that some of the preference files, notably *CD Info.cidb* and *SnagIt.plist*, are bigger than the other files. The difference? Some applications have quite a bit of information that they store as preferences, while others save only preference settings that are different from the default configuration.

A more interesting place to look is your logfile directory, */var/log*:

```
$ ls -s /var/log
total 17232
    8 CDIS.custom
    0 CoreCapture
    0 DiagnosticMessages
  336 SleepWakeStacks.bin
    8 accountpolicy.log
    8 accountpolicy.log.0.gz
    8 accountpolicy.log.1.gz
    8 accountpolicy.log.2.gz
    0 alf.log
    0 apache2
    8 appfirewall.log
    0 asl
   48 authd.log
    8 authd.log.0.gz
    8 authd.log.1.gz
   16 bluetooth.pklg
    0 com.apple.clouddocs.asl
    0 com.apple.revisiond
    0 com.apple.xpc.launchd
  536 commerce.log
   16 corecaptured.log
...
```

Notice that the first line of output with the *-s* option is always a sum of the size of all files in the specified directory. This shows that there are 17,232 512-byte blocks, which you can easily divide by 2 to get kilobytes (8,616 KB). The largest file in this directory is *install.log*, which was created after you installed OS X.

Now let's see if there's a directory called *Library* in the current working directory:

```
$ ls Library
Accounts                Fonts               Preferences
Address Book Plug-Ins    Fonts Disabled      Printers
Application Scripts      GameKit             PubSub
Application Support      Google              Safari
Assistants               Group Containers    Saved Application State
Audio                    IdentityServices    Screen Savers
Autosave Information      Input Methods       Services
Caches                   Internet Plug-Ins   Social
Calendars                Keyboard Layouts    Sounds
ColorPickers             Keychains           Spelling
Colors                   LanguageModeling    StickiesDatabase
```

```
Compositions          LaunchAgents         Suggestions
Containers            Logs                 SyncedPreferences
Cookies               Mail                 VirtualBox
CoreData              Messages             Voices
Dictionaries          Metadata             WebKit
Favorites             Mobile Documents     com.apple.nsurlsessiond
Filters               Network              iMovie
FontCollections       PreferencePanes      iTunes
```

This is a classic conundrum with the *ls* command; you want to see whether a folder exists or not, but you don't actually want to see what's inside the folder. To accomplish this, you can't just specify the name of the folder because, as shown, you end up seeing what's inside. Instead, use the *-d* option to indicate that it's the directory information you want, not its contents:

```
$ ls -d Library
Library
$ ls -d
.
```

That second example is interesting because it confirms that the current directory is indeed the period (.) shorthand, as explained earlier.

Using the -l Option

To get more information about each item that *ls* lists, add the *-l* option (that's a lower-case "L" for "long"). This option can be used alone, or in combination with *-a*, as shown in Figure 3-6.

```
                                    taylor — -bash — 92×31
~ 504 $ ls -al
total 120
drwxr-xr-x+   25 taylor   staff     850 Oct  3 14:55 .
drwxr-xr-x     6 root     admin     204 Sep 30 14:31 ..
-r--------     1 taylor   staff       7 Jun 19 01:07 .CFUserTextEncoding
-rw-r--r--@    1 taylor   staff   30724 Oct  3 15:38 .DS_Store
drwx------  1036 taylor   staff   35224 Oct  3 15:47 .Trash
-rw-------     1 taylor   staff    9712 Oct  3 14:55 .bash_history
drwxr-xr-x    23 taylor   staff     782 Oct  3 15:38 .bash_sessions
drwx------     3 taylor   staff     102 Jun 20 07:02 .cups
drwx------     9 taylor   staff     306 Oct  2 18:27 .dropbox
-rw-r--r--     1 taylor   staff     119 Oct  3 14:55 .profile
drwx------     3 taylor   staff     102 Jul 12 08:13 .ssh
-rw-------     1 taylor   staff    7989 Oct  3 14:55 .viminfo
drwx------     5 taylor   staff     170 Sep 27 19:24 Applications
drwxr-xr-x+   35 taylor   staff    1190 Oct  3 15:47 Desktop
drwx------+   82 taylor   staff    2788 Sep 24 11:07 Documents
drwx------+   14 taylor   staff     476 Oct  2 23:38 Downloads
drwx------@   18 taylor   staff     612 Oct  2 18:27 Dropbox
drwx------@   61 taylor   staff    2074 Oct  1 11:02 Library
drwx------+   19 taylor   staff     646 Jun 19 12:30 Movies
drwx------+    7 taylor   staff     238 Sep 20 10:54 Music
drwx------+   44 taylor   staff    1496 Sep 22 08:36 Pictures
drwxrwxrwx@   74 taylor   staff    2516 Sep 22 20:15 Presentations
drwxr-xr-x+    5 taylor   staff     170 Jun 19 01:06 Public
drwxr-xr-x     4 taylor   staff     136 Jun 20 16:35 VirtualBox VMs
drwxr-xr-x    17 taylor   staff     578 Oct 13  2014 bin
~ 505 $
```

Figure 3-6. Output from ls -al

The long format provides the following information about each item:

Total n

> States the amount of storage space (*n*) used by everything in this directory. This is measured in blocks. On OS X, blocks are 512 bytes in size. If you want to know the total size of everything in a directory, however, the *du* command is more accurate.

Type

> Tells whether the item is a directory (d) or a plain file (-). (There are other less common types as well.)

Access modes

> Specifies whether or not the file owner, any members of the group associated with the file, and all other users are allowed to read (r), write (w), or execute (x) the listed files and directories. We'll talk more about access modes in the next section.

Links

> Lists the number of files or directories linked to this file or directory. (This isn't the same as a web page link, as you'll see in "Working with Links" on page 103 in Chapter 4.)

Owner

> States the user who owns this file or directory.

Group

> Lists the group that owns the file or directory (usually the group that the file or directory owner belongs to, but group ownership can be changed as needed).

Size (in bytes)

> States the size of the file or directory. (A directory is actually a special type of file. Here, the "size" of a directory is that of the directory file itself, not the total of all the files in that directory.)

Modification date

> States the date when the file was last modified or when the directory contents last changed (when something in the directory was added, renamed, or removed). If an entry was modified more than six months ago, *ls* shows the year instead of the time.

Name

> Gives the name of the file or directory.

File Permissions

In Figure 3-6, notice especially the columns that list the owner and group of the files, and the access modes (also called *permissions*). Unless changed afterward, the person who creates a file is its owner; if you've created any files, this column should show your short username. You also belong to a group. Files you create are marked either with the name of your group or, in some cases, the group that owns the directory.

The file mode indicates what type of file the item is (such as a directory or a regular file), as well as who can read, write, or execute the file or directory. The file mode has 10 characters, as shown in Figure 3-7. The first character shows the file type (d for directory or - for a plain file). The other characters come in sets of three.

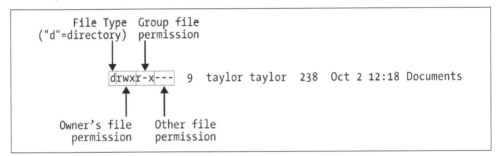

Figure 3-7. A detailed look at file permissions

The first set, characters 2 through 4, shows the permissions for the file's owner (which is you, if you created the file). The second set, characters 5 through 7, shows permissions for other members of the group that is associated with the file, such as all people in the marketing team or everyone on Project Alpha in your firm. The third set, characters 8 through 10, shows permissions for all other users on the system.

The Finder shows directory permissions in the Get Info dialog box. Figure 3-8 shows the Get Info permissions information for the *Documents* directory. Compare this to the *ls -l* output shown in Figure 3-7.

For example, the permissions for *.DS_Store* in Figure 3-6 are -rw-r--r--. The first hyphen, -, indicates that it's a plain file. The next three characters, rw-, mean that the owner, *taylor*, has both read (r) and write (w) permissions, but cannot execute the file, as noted by the hyphen following the rw. The next two sets of permissions are both r--, which means that other users who belong to the file's group, *taylor*, as well as all other users of the system, can only read the file; they don't have write or execute permissions, which means they can't make changes to the file, and if it's a program (such as a shell script), they can't execute it either.

Figure 3-8. The Finder's Get Info window shows directory permissions much differently from how they appear in the Terminal

In the case of directories, x means the permission to access the directory—for example, to run a command that reads a file there or to access a subdirectory. Notice that the first directory shown in Figure 3-6, *Desktop*, is executable (accessible) by *taylor*, but completely closed off to everyone else on the system. A directory with write (w) permission allows deleting, renaming, or adding files within the directory. Read (r) permission allows listing the directory with *ls*.

You can use the *chmod* command to change the permissions of your files and directories (see "Protecting and Sharing Files" on page 64).

If you need to know only which files are directories and which are executable files, you can use the -F option with *ls*. If you give the pathname to a directory, *ls* lists the directory but does *not* change your working directory. The *pwd* command, shown here, illustrates this:

```
$ cd /Applications
$ ls -F ~
Applications/   Downloads/   Movies/      Presentations/    bin/
Desktop/        Dropbox/     Music/       Public/
Documents/      Library/     Pictures/    VirtualBox VMs/
$ pwd
/Applications
```

As noted earlier, the *ls -F* command places a slash (/) at the end of each directory name displayed in the output. (The directory name doesn't really have a slash in it; that's just the shorthand *ls -F* uses to identify a directory.) In this example, every entry other than the hidden "dot" files is a directory. You can verify this by using *ls -l* and noting the d in the first field of the output. Files with an execute status (x), such as programs, are marked with an asterisk (*).

The *ls -R* (recursive) command lists a directory and all its subdirectories. This gives you a very long list, especially when you list a directory near the root! (Piping the output of *ls* to a pager program—such as *more* or *less*—solves this problem. There's an example in "Pipes and Filters" on page 141.) You can combine other options with -R; for instance, *ls -RF* marks each directory and file type, while recursively listing files and directories.

Calculating File Size and Disk Space

You can find the size of a file with the *du* (disk usage) command:

```
$ du Documents/Outline.doc
300     Documents/Outline.doc
```

The size is reported in 512-byte blocks, so *Outline.doc* is 150 KB in size.

If you give *du* the name of a directory, it calculates the sizes of everything inside that directory, including any subdirectories and their contents:

```
$ du Library
5920 Library/Accounts
24 Library/Address Book Plug-Ins/SkypeABDialer.bundle/Contents/MacOS
16 Library/Address Book Plug-Ins/SkypeABDialer.bundle/Contents/Resources/bg.lproj
```

```
16 Library/Address Book Plug-Ins/SkypeABDialer.bundle/Contents/Resources/ca.lproj
16 Library/Address Book Plug-Ins/SkypeABDialer.bundle/Contents/Resources/cs.lproj
16 Library/Address Book Plug-Ins/SkypeABDialer.bundle/Contents/Resources/da.lproj
...
```

 This means that it's not a great idea to type *du /*, unless you want to see a lot of information stream past your screen at a lightning pace!

If you want the total for the directory, use *-s* (summarize):

```
$ du -s Library
91704304    Library
```

If you'd like separate totals for all directories and files, including hidden ones, use a wildcard pattern that ignores the current (.) and parent (..) directories, as discussed earlier in this chapter:

```
$ du -s * .[^.]*
1704        Applications
6976480     Desktop
113934056   Documents
2410512     Downloads
34819944    Dropbox
91704048    Library
77745816    Movies
181162848   Music
...
57900360    .Trash
24          .bash_history
192         .bash_sessions
8           .cups
542088      .dropbox
8           .profile
8           .ssh
16          .viminfo
```

To gain information about the size of the standard user applications in OS X, use the pattern */Applications/*.app*:

```
$ du -s /Applications/*.app
135352      /Applications/1Password 5.app
262440      /Applications/Amazon Music.app
1633400     /Applications/Aperture.app
3808        /Applications/App Store.app
20192       /Applications/Automator.app
49688       /Applications/Bitcoin-Qt.app
5104        /Applications/Calculator.app
29816       /Applications/Calendar.app
...
```

```
24464     /Applications/Transmission.app
224168    /Applications/VLC.app
1515904   /Applications/VMware Fusion.app
487368    /Applications/VirtualBox.app
53520     /Applications/iBooks.app
4100200   /Applications/iMovie.app
384056    /Applications/iTunes.app
```

Notice that the output is in alphabetical order, but all the uppercase filenames are sorted before the lowercase filenames (that is, VLC appears before iMovie in a case-sensitive sort).

One option that's worth keeping in mind when using *du -s* is *-h*, which produces more human-readable output:

```
$ du -sh Library/*
2.9M Library/Accounts
672K Library/Address Book Plug-Ins
4.0K Library/Application Scripts
 36G Library/Application Support
 0B Library/Assistants
 0B Library/Audio
 0B Library/Autosave Information
1.1G Library/Caches
176M Library/Calendars
...
 20K Library/Spelling
4.0K Library/StickiesDatabase
 23M Library/Suggestions
748K Library/SyncedPreferences
 72K Library/VirtualBox
 0B Library/Voices
 0B Library/WebKit
132K Library/com.apple.nsurlsessiond
 0B Library/iMovie
 48K Library/iTunes
```

While this is a bit more readable, the enormous *Library/Application Support*, at 36 GB, doesn't jump out as it would if the *-h* flag wasn't used and the output of 74488432 blocks was shown instead. It's probably best to include the *-h* flag, but remember to scan the suffix letters to see if anything jumps out as being ridiculously large.

 You can also sort the largest directories to the top of the results with a command sequence like *du -s /Library/* | sort -rn*, or, better, only view the top 10 results with *du -s /Library/* | sort -rn | head*. I'll explain command pipes and the tremendously useful *sort* command a bit later.

Calculating Available Disk Space

You can calculate your system's free disk space with *df -h* (the *-h* produces more user-friendly output):

```
$ df -h
Filesystem     Size   Used   Avail  Capacity  iused       ifree      %iused
/dev/disk1     446Gi  383Gi  63Gi   86%       100398174   16481408   86%
devfs          188Ki  188Ki  0Bi    100%      649         0          100%
map -hosts     0Bi    0Bi    0Bi    100%      0           0          100%
map auto_home  0Bi    0Bi    0Bi    100%      0           0          100%
/dev/disk2s2   118Gi  32Gi   86Gi   27%       8324429     22589863   27%
```

Here's the breakdown for the output from the command:

- The first column (`Filesystem`) shows the Unix device name for the volume.

- The second column (`Size`) shows the total disk size, and it's followed by the amount of disk space used up (`Used`) and the amount that's available (`Avail`).

- The `Capacity` column shows the percentage of disk space used. Many devices are shown at 100% because they're not regular disks, but special Unix devices. All you really need to pay attention to is your main hard drive (mine is */dev/disk0s2*).

- Filesystems are built from chained sets of blocks of data: the larger the file, the more blocks are connected in the chain. Each block on a filesystem is referred to as an inode, and you can see that for each filesystem, *df* shows `iused`, `ifree`, and `%iused`. You can safely ignore these values.

- The `Mounted on` column displays the paths for the volumes mounted on your computer. The / is the root of your filesystem (a volume that is named *Macintosh HD* by default). */dev* contains files that correspond to hardware devices, and */.vol* exposes some internals of the OS X filesystem called the *HFS+ file ID*.

Notice that I have one hard disk on my system, */dev/disk1* (which is 446 GB in size, of which 383 GB are used and 63 GB are still available).

The *df* command has a second, more friendly output that uses the more common divide-by-10 rule for calculating sizes, rather than the more mathematically precise divide-by-2 rule of the *-h* flag:

```
$ df -H
Filesystem     Size  Used  Avail  Capacity  iused       ifree      %iused
/dev/disk1     479G  411G  67G    86%       100406706   16472876   86%
devfs          192k  192k  0B     100%      649         0          100%
map -hosts     0B    0B    0B     100%      0           0          100%
map auto_home  0B    0B    0B     100%      0           0          100%
/dev/disk2s2   127G  34G   93G    27%       8324429     22589863   27%
```

These figures make more sense because I know that the hard disk mounted at */dev/ disk1* is actually 500 GB in size (note that it shows up as 479 instead of 500 GB because the filesystem itself consumes some of the space for housekeeping). You might prefer the more accurate *-h* output, but many people prefer *-H* since the reported disk sizes are more in line with drive capacity expectations.

Yet another way to look at the data is to use the *-m* flag to have *df* show you 1 MB blocks, which rounds down all the tiny OS partitions like *devfs* and *.vol* to zero:

```
$ df -m
Filesystem     1M-blocks Used   Available Capacity  iused       ifree     %iused
/dev/disk1     456560    391971 64339     86%       100408782   16470800  86%
devfs          0         0      0         100%      649         0         100%
map -hosts     0         0      0         100%      0           0         100%
map auto_home  0         0      0         100%      0           0         100%
/dev/disk2s2   120758    32517  88241     27%       8324429     22589863  27%
```

Finally, in addition to raw disk space, another factor to keep track of with your OS X system is the number of inodes available. Inodes are the fundamental disk blocks that are grafted together to make space for all the different-sized files in your filesystem. A given disk in Unix has a finite number of files and directories that can be created, and even if there's additional disk space available, running out of inodes effectively stops the disk from being used. This unusual event can happen if you have lots and lots (I'm talking millions and millions) of tiny files.

The *-i* flag to *df* shows how you're doing with inodes, providing details on how many inodes are allocated and available on each filesystem.

Generally disks have plenty of unused inodes, so there's nothing to worry about. For example, as you can see here, disk *0s2* has 20,315,203 available inodes:

```
$ df -i
Filesystem     512-blocks Used      Available Capacity iused      ifree     %iused
/dev/disk1     935036672  802769344 131755328 86%      100410166  16469416  86%
devfs          375        375       0         100%     649        0  100%     /dev
map -hosts     0          0         0         100%     0          0  100%     /net
map auto_home  0          0         0         100%     0          0  100%     /home
/dev/disk2s2   247314352  66595448  180718904 27%      8324429    22589863 27%
```

Exercise: Exploring the Filesystem

Now that you're equipped with some basic commands, it's time to explore the filesystem with *cd*, *ls*, and *pwd*. Take a tour of the directory system, as detailed in Table 3-1, hopping one or many levels at a time, with a mixture of *cd* and *pwd* commands.

Table 3-1. Take this guided tour of your filesystem; read each task (left column) and then enter the Unix command (right column) to see where you go

Task	Command
Go to your home directory.	*cd*
Find your working directory.	*pwd*
Change to a new working directory with its absolute pathname.	*cd /bin*
List files in the new working directory.	*ls*
Change directory to root and list it in one step. (Use the command separator: a semicolon.)	*cd /; ls*
Find your working directory.	*pwd*
Change to a subdirectory; use its relative pathname.	*cd usr*
Find your working directory.	*pwd*
Change to a subdirectory.	*cd lib*
Find your working directory.	*pwd*
Give a wrong pathname.	*cd xqk*
List files in another directory.	*ls /bin*
Find your working directory (notice that *ls* didn't change it).	*pwd*
Return to your home directory.	*cd*

Protecting and Sharing Files

OS X makes it easy for users on the same system to share files and directories. For instance, all users in a group can read documents stored in one of their manager's directories without needing to make their own copies (if the manager has allowed such access). The advantage of this is that you don't need to send files via email as attachments. Instead, if the files and directories have open permissions, anyone can access them with a little help from the Unix filesystem.

Here's a brief introduction to file security and sharing. If you have critical security needs, or you just want more information, talk to your system staff, or see a book on Unix security such as *Practical Unix and Internet Security*, by Simson Garfinkel, Gene Spafford, and Alan Schwartz (O'Reilly).

Any user with admin privileges can use the *sudo* command (see "Superuser Privileges with sudo" on page 72 to do anything to any file at any time—regardless of what its permissions are. Access permissions won't keep your private information safe from *everyone*, although let's hope that you can trust the other folks who share your Macintosh! This is one reason that you'll want to be thoughtful about those directory access permissions.

A directory's access permissions help to control access to the files and subdirectories in that directory:

- A user who has read permission (r) for a directory can run *ls* to see what's in the directory and use wildcards to match files in it.

- A user who has write permission (w) for a directory can add, rename, and delete files in the directory.

- To access a directory (that is, to read or write the files in the directory or to run the files if they're programs), a user needs execute permission (x) for that directory. The user must *also* have execute permission for all of the directory's parent directories—all the way up to the root.

 OS X includes a shared directory for all users: */Users/Shared*. Any user can create files in this directory and modify files they put there. However, you cannot modify a file that's owned by another user. Instead, you'll have to copy that file from */Users/Shared* to another directory in which you have write permissions (such as your *Documents* directory).

In practice, there are three directory permissions you'll see in Unix:

- - - - means that the user cannot access the directory.

- r-x means that the user can access the directory with read-only permission, but cannot add or delete files, or modify the directory.

- rwx means that the user has read, write, and access permission.

For example, here are the default permissions for a home directory, courtesy of *ls -l*:

```
$ ls -ld $HOME
drwxr-xr-x  25 taylor  staff  850 Oct  3 14:55 /Users/taylor
```

This shows that the owner, *taylor*, has read, write, and access permission for this directory, while the group, *staff*, and everyone else on the system are restricted to read-only access. To be candid, OS X doesn't really use groups much, so you can safely ignore them in most instances.

In contrast, the following example shows that user *taylor* has complete access, but everyone else is shut out from browsing the *Documents* directory:

```
$ ls -ld $HOME/Documents
drwx------  51 taylor  staff  1734 13 Dec 14:46 /Users/taylor/Documents/
```

The Finder shows directory permissions in the Get Info dialog box. Figure 3-9 shows the Get Info permissions information for both *$HOME* and *$HOME/Documents*.

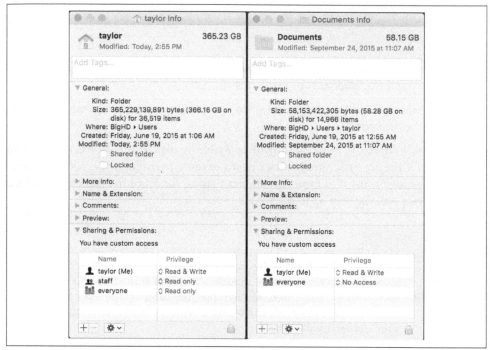

Figure 3-9. The Finder's Get Info window shows directory permissions differently

File Access Permissions

The access permissions on a file control what can be done to the file's *contents*. Likewise, the access permissions on the directory where the file is kept control whether the file can be renamed or removed. If this seems confusing, think of it this way: the directory is actually a list of files. Adding, renaming, or removing a file changes the contents of the directory. If the directory isn't writable, you can't change that list.

Read permission controls whether you can read a file's contents. Write permission lets you change a file's contents. A file shouldn't have execute permission unless it's a program or a script.

Let's have a look at a few file permissions examples. First, a "dot file" in my home directory:

```
$ cd ~
$ ls -l .viminfo
-rw-------  1 taylor  staff  2159 27 Dec 11:07 .viminfo
```

This shows that user *taylor* can read from the file or write to the file, but everyone else is prevented from touching, or even seeing, its contents.

Next, let's look at the operating system "kernel," the program that really contains the heart of the operating system itself. It's rather hidden, but that's okay—we can find it:

```
$ ls -l /System/Library/Kernels/kernel
-rwxr-xr-x  1 root  wheel  10705248 Aug 26 18:00 kernel
```

This file, a part of the operating system core (known in Unix-geek circles as the *kernel*), is owned by *root*, who has read, write, and execute permission. Everyone else has read and execute permission.

Finally, consider this security database file that belongs to the operating system. The owner, *root*, has read-only permission, as does anyone in the *wheel* group, but the file is off-limits to anyone else on the computer:

```
$ ls -l /etc/sudoers
-r--r-----  1 root  wheel  2299   Aug 22 16:39 /etc/sudoers
```

Setting Permissions with chmod

Once you know what permissions a file or directory needs, provided you're the owner (listed in the third column of *ls -l* output), you can change the permissions with the *chmod* program. If you select a file or folder in the Finder and then choose File→Get Info (⌘-I), you can also change the permissions using the Sharing & Permissions section of the Get Info dialog (see Figure 3-9). One reason to use the Finder method is because changing the permissions of files and directories *inside* the directory is easy to accomplish by clicking the "Apply to Enclosed Items" button (this can be done on the command line using the *find* command or the *-R* flag to *chmod*, but they're both beyond the scope of this book).

There are two ways to change permissions: by specifying the permissions to add or delete, or by specifying the exact permissions to apply. For instance, if a directory's permissions are almost correct, but you also need to make it writable by its group, tell *chmod* to add group-write permission. But if you need to make more than one change to the permissions—for instance, if you want to add read and execute permission but delete write permission—it's easier to set all the permissions explicitly instead of changing them one by one. The syntax is:

```
chmod permissions directory_or_filename(s)
```

Let's start with the rules, followed by some examples a little later. The `permissions` argument has three parts, which you must give in order, with no spaces in between:

1. The category of permissions you want to change. There are three: the owner's permissions (which *chmod* calls "user," abbreviated *u*), the group's permissions (*g*), or others' permissions (*o*). To change more than one category, string the letters together, such as *go* for "group and others," or simply use *a* to mean "all" (same as *ugo*).

2. Whether you want to add (+) the permission, delete (-) it, or specify it exactly (=).

3. What permissions you want to affect: read (*r*), write (*w*), or execute (*x*). To change more than one permission, string the letters together—for example, *rw* for "read and write."

Some examples should make this clearer. In the following command lines, you can replace *dirname* or *filename* with the pathname (absolute or relative) of the directory or file. An easy way to change permissions on the working directory is by using its relative pathname, . (dot), as in *chmod o-w .*.

You can combine two permission changes in the same *chmod* command by separating them with a comma (,), as shown in the final example in the following list:

- To protect a file from accidental editing, delete everyone's write permission with the command:

      chmod a-w *filename*

- On the other hand, if you own an unwritable file that you want to edit, but you don't want to change other people's write permissions, you can add "user" (owner) write permission with:

      chmod u+w *filename*

- To keep yourself from accidentally removing files (or adding or renaming files) in an important directory of yours, delete your own write permission with the command:

      chmod u-w *dirname*

- If other users have that permission, too, you could delete everyone's write permission with:

      chmod a-w *dirname*

- If you want you and your group to be able to read and write all the files in your working directory—but those files have various permissions now, so adding and deleting the permissions individually would be a pain—this is a good place to use the = operator to set the exact permissions you want. Use the filename wildcard *, which means "everything in this directory" (explained in "File and Directory Wildcards" on page 78 in Chapter 4), and type:

```
chmod ug=rw *
```

- If your working directory has any subdirectories, though, that command would be wrong; it would take away execute permission from the subdirectories, so they couldn't be accessed anymore. In that case, you could try a more specific wildcard, or simply list the filenames whose permissions you want to change, separated by spaces, as in:

```
chmod ug=rw filename1 filename2 filename3
```

- To protect the files in a directory and all its subdirectories from everyone else on your system, but still keep the access permissions *you* have there, you could use:

```
chmod go-rwx dirname
```

to delete all "group" and "others" permissions to read, write, and execute. A simpler way is to use the command:

```
chmod go= dirname
```

to set "group" and "others" permissions to nothing.

- Finally, suppose you want full access to a directory. Other people on the system should be able to see what's in the directory (and read or edit the files if the file permissions allow it), but not rename, remove, or add files. To do that, give yourself all permissions, but give "group" and "others" only read and execute permissions. Use the command:

```
chmod u=rwx,go=rx dirname
```

After you change permissions, it's a good idea to check your work with *ls -l filename*, *ls -ld dirname* (without the *-d* option, *ls* lists the contents of the directory instead of its permissions and other information), or by using the Finder's Get Info window.

Problem checklist

Here are some problems you might encounter while working with *chmod*, along with some solutions:

I get the message "chmod: Not owner."
    Only the owner of a file or directory (or the superuser) can set its permissions. Use *ls -l* to find the owner, or use superuser privileges (see "Superuser Privileges with sudo" on page 72).

A file is writable, but my program says it can't be written.

Check the file permissions with *ls -l* and be sure you're in the category (user, group, or others) that has write permission.

The problem may also be in the permissions of the file's directory. Some programs need permission to write more files into the same directory (for example, temporary files) or to rename files (for instance, making a file into a backup) while editing. If it's safe to add write permission to the directory (if other files in the directory don't need protection from removal or renaming), try that. Otherwise, copy the file to a writable directory (with *cp*), edit it there, and then copy it back to the original directory.

Changing the Group and Owner

Group ownership lets a certain group of users have access to a file or directory. But sometimes you'll need to let a different group have access. The *chgrp* program sets the group owner of a file or directory. You can set the group to any of the groups to which you belong. Because you're likely to be administering your system, you can control the list of groups you're in. (If this isn't the case, the system administrator will control the list of groups you're in.) The *groups* program lists your groups.

For example, if you're a designer creating a directory named *images* for several illustrators, the directory's original group owner might be *admin*. Suppose you'd like the illustrators, all of whom are in the group named *staff*, to be able to access the directory, but members of other groups should have no access. To achieve this, you can use commands such as the following:

```
$ groups
gareth admin
$ mkdir images
$ ls -ld images
drwxr-xr-x    2 gareth  admin        68 Oct  3 16:45  images
$ chgrp staff images
$ chmod o= images
$ ls -ld images
drwxr-x---    2 gareth  staff        68 Oct  3 16:45  images
```

 OS X also lets you set a directory's group ownership so that any files you later create in that directory will be owned by the same group that owns the directory. Try the command *chmod g+s dirname*. The permissions listing from *ls -ld* should now show an s in place of the second x, as in drwxr-s---.

The *chown* program changes the owner of a file or directory. Only the superuser can use *chown* (see "Superuser Privileges with sudo" on page 72):

```
$ chown eric images
chown: changing
```

```
ownership of `images': Operation not permitted
$ sudo chown eric images
Password:
```

If you have permission to read another user's file, however, you can make a copy of it (with *cp*; see "Copying Files" on page 98 in Chapter 4), and you'll own the copy.

Changing Your Password

The ownership and permissions system described in this chapter depends on the security of your username and password. If others get hold of your username and password, they can log in to your account and do anything you can, and if you have admin privileges, that could be *anything*—including deleting all your files. They'll be able to read private information, corrupt or delete important files, send email messages as if they came from you, and more. If your computer is connected to a network—whether to the Internet or a local network inside your organization—intruders may also be able to log in without sitting at your keyboard! See "Remote Logins" on page 169 in Chapter 8 for one way this can be done.

Anyone may be able to get your username—it's often part of your email address, for instance, and it will show up for any files you own in a long directory listing. Your password is what keeps others from logging in as you. Don't leave a written record of your password anywhere around your computer. Don't give your password to anyone who asks you for it, unless you're sure he'll preserve your account security. Also, don't send your password by email; it can be stored, unprotected, on other systems and on backup tapes, where other people may find it and then break in to your account.

If you think that someone knows your password, you should probably change it right away—although if you suspect that a computer "cracker" (or "hacker") is using your account to break in to your system, you should ask your system administrator for advice first, if possible. You should also change your password periodically. Every few months is recommended.

A password should be easy for you to remember but hard for other people (or password-guessing programs) to guess. Here are some guidelines. A password should be between six and eight characters long. It should not be a word in any language, a proper name, your phone number, your address, or anything anyone else might know or guess that you'd use as a password. It's best to mix upper- and lowercase letters, punctuation, and numbers. A good way to come up with a unique but memorable password is to think of a phrase that has personal significance to you, and use the first letters of each word (and punctuation) to create the password. For example, consider the password *MlwsiF!* ("My laptop was stolen in Florence!").

To change your password, you can use Apple Menu→System Preferences→Users & Groups, but you can also change it from the command line using the *passwd* command. After you enter the command, you're prompted to enter your old password. If the password is correct, you're asked to enter a new password—twice, to be sure there is no typing mistake:

```
$ passwd
Changing password for taylor.
Old password:
New password:
Retype new password:
```

For security, neither the old nor the new passwords appear as you type them.

Superuser Privileges with sudo

Most OS X user accounts run with restricted privileges; there are parts of the filesystem to which you don't have access, and there are certain activities that are prohibited until you supply a password. For example, when you run the Software Update utility from System Preferences, OS X may ask you for your password before it proceeds. This extra authentication step allows Software Update to run installers with superuser privileges.

You can invoke these same privileges at the command line by prefixing a command with *sudo* (short for "superuser do"), a utility that prompts you for your password and executes the command as the superuser. You must be an administrative (or *admin*, for short) user to use *sudo*. The user you created when you first set up your Mac is an admin user. You can add new admin users or grant admin status to a user in System Preferences→Accounts, as shown in Figure 3-10.

You may need to use *sudo* when you install certain Unix utilities, or if you want to modify a file you don't own. Suppose you accidentally created a file in the */Users* directory while you were doing something else as the superuser. You won't be able to modify it with your normal privileges, so you'll need to use *sudo*:

```
$ ls -l logfile.out
-rw-r--r--    1 root     wheel      1784064 Nov  6 11:25 logfile.out
$ rm logfile.out
override rw-r--r--  root/wheel for logfile.out? y
rm: logfile.out: Permission denied
$ sudo rm logfile.out
Password:
$ ls -l logfile.out
ls: logfile.out: No such file or directory
```

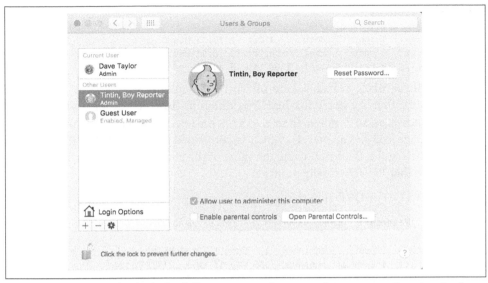

Figure 3-10. When checked, the "Allow user to administer this computer" option in the Accounts preference panel gives a user administrative privileges and allows use of the sudo command

If you use *sudo* again within five minutes, it won't ask for your password. Be careful using *sudo*, since it gives you the ability to modify protected files, all of which are protected to ensure the system runs properly.

I commonly find myself using *sudo* when I want to search across the entire filesystem without worrying about disk permissions. For example, suppose *makewhatis* was once in */usr/sbin*, but looking in that directory reveals it has been moved somewhere else. To find it, I can search the entire filesystem using the *find* command (as discussed in Chapter 5) with *sudo*:

```
$ sudo find / -name makewhatis -print
Password:
/usr/libexec/makewhatis
```

Without the use of *sudo*, I would see hundreds of error messages as the command tried to peek into directories that, I as a regular user, don't have permission to visit.

Exploring External Volumes

Earlier I mentioned that additional hard disks on your system and any network-based disks are all mounted onto the filesystem under the */Volumes* directory. Let's take a closer look to see how this works:

```
$ ls /Volumes
BigHD    MobileBackups red
```

```
$ ls -l /Volumes
total 8
lrwxr-xr-x   1 root     admin       1 Oct  1 10:02 BigHD -> /
drwxrwxrwx   0 root     wheel       0 Oct  3 16:51 MobileBackups
drwxrwxr-x@ 38 taylor   staff    1360 Sep  5 20:08 red
```

There are three disks available, one of which is actually the root (or boot) disk:
BigHD. Notice that the entry for *BigHD* is different from the others, with the first
character shown as an l rather than a d. This means it's a link (see "Working with
Links" on page 103 in Chapter 4), which is confirmed by the fact that it's shown as
BigHD in the regular *ls* output, while the value of the alias is shown in the long listing
(you can see that *BigHD* actually points to /).

If you insert a CD or DVD into the system, it also shows up in */Volumes*:

```
$ ls -l /Volumes
total 12
lrwxr-xr-x   1 root     admin       1   Oct  1 10:02 BigHD -> /
dr-xr-xr-x   4 unknown  nogroup   136 Aug 17 2015  CITIZEN_KANE
drwxrwxrwx   0 root     wheel       0   Oct  3 16:51 MobileBackups
drwxrwxr-x@ 38 taylor   staff    1360   Sep  5 20:08 red
```

Plugging in an iPhone and a digital camera produces the following results:

```
$ ls -l /Volumes
total 44
lrwxr-xr-x   1 root     admin         1   Oct  1 10:02 BigHD -> /
dr-xr-xr-x   4 unknown  nogroup     136 Aug 17 2015  CITIZEN_KANE
drwxrwxrwx   0 root     wheel         0 Oct  3 16:51 MobileBackups
drwxrwxrwx   1 taylor   admin     16384 Aug 17 20:54 NIKON D100
drwxr-xr-x  15 taylor   unknown     510 Apr 17 09:37 Zephyr
drwxrwxr-x@ 38 taylor   staff      1360 Sep  5 20:08 red
```

Here, *Zephyr* is the name of the iPod, and *NIKON D100* is the camera.

## CHAPTER 4

File Management

The previous chapter introduced the Unix filesystem, including an extensive discussion of the directory structure, the *ls* command for seeing what files are on your system, and how to move around using *cd* and *pwd*. This chapter focuses on Unix filenaming schemes—which aren't the same as those used in the Finder, as you'll see —and how to view, edit, rename, copy, and move files.

File and Directory Names

As Chapter 3 explained, both files and directories are identified by their names. A directory is really just a special kind of file, so the rules for naming directories are the same as the rules for naming files.

Unix filenames may contain almost any character except /, which is reserved as the separator between files and directories in a pathname. Filenames are usually made up of upper- and lowercase letters, numbers, dots (.), and underscores (_). Other characters (including spaces) are legal in a filename, but they can be hard to use because the shell gives them special meanings or otherwise forces you to constantly be changing how you work with these filenames on the command line.

Spaces are a standard part of Macintosh file and folder names, so while I recommend using only letters, numbers, dots, and underscores in filenames, the reality is that you will probably have to work with spaces in file and directory names because Mac people are used to including them. That is, rather than naming a file *myFile.txt*, as a Unix person would, most Mac folks would call it *my file.txt*. Also be aware that the Finder dislikes colons (which older versions of OS X used as a directory separator, just as Unix uses the forward slash). If you display a file called *test:me* in the Finder, the name is shown as *test/me* instead. (The reverse is also true: if you create a file in the Finder whose name contains a slash, it will appear as a colon in the Terminal.)

Though it may be tempting to include spaces in filenames as you do in the Finder, if you're planning on doing any substantial amount of work on the Unix side, get used to using dashes or underscores in place of spaces in your filenames. It's 99 percent as legible, and considerably easier to work with.

Further, in the interest of having files correctly identified in both the Finder and Unix, you'd be wise to get into the habit of using the appropriate file extensions (i.e., *.doc* for Microsoft Word documents, *.txt* for text files, *.xls* for Excel spreadsheets, and so on). As an added bonus, this makes life easier for your less fortunate (Windows-using) friends when you send them files.

If you have a file with a space in its name, that space confuses the shell if you enter it as part of the filename. That's because the shell breaks commands into separate words with spaces as delimiters, just as we do in English. To tell the shell not to break an argument at spaces, you can either put quotation marks around a filename that includes spaces (for example, *"my file.txt"*), or escape the spaces by prefacing each one with a backslash (\).

For example, the *rm* program, covered later in this chapter, removes Unix files. To remove a file named *a confusing name*, the first *rm* command in the following snippet doesn't work, but the second does. The third example illustrates how to avoid the shell incorrectly interpreting the filename *another odd name* by escaping the spaces with backslashes:

```
$ ls -l
total 2
-rw-r--r--  1 taylor  staff   324 Feb  4 23:07 a confusing name
-rw-r--r--  1 taylor  staff    64 Feb  4 23:07 another odd name
$ rm a confusing name
rm: a: no such file or directory
rm: confusing: no such file or directory
rm: name: no such file or directory
$ rm "a confusing name"
$ rm another\ odd\ name
```

You also need to escape any of the following characters with a backslash, because they have special meaning to the shell:

```
* # ` " ' \ $ | & ? ; ~ ( ) < > ! ^
```

My recommendation is to simply avoid using any of these characters in your filenames—along with spaces—to make your life easier. Indeed, that's why most Unix file and directory names are composed exclusively of lowercase letters, dashes, and underscores.

Open a Terminal window and change directories to your *Library* directory. You'll see files with names that contain spaces, though the other punctuation characters are more unusual components of filenames:

```
$ cd Library
$ ls
Accounts              Fonts                Preferences
Address Book Plug-Ins Fonts Disabled       Printers
Application Scripts   GameKit              PubSub
Application Support   Google               Safari
Assistants            Group Containers     Saved Application State
Audio                 IdentityServices     Screen Savers
Autosave Information  Input Methods        Services
Caches                Internet Plug-Ins    Social
Calendars             Keyboard Layouts     Sounds
ColorPickers          Keychains            Spelling
Colors                LanguageModeling     StickiesDatabase
Compositions          LaunchAgents         Suggestions
Containers            Logs                 SyncedPreferences
Cookies               Mail                 VirtualBox
CoreData              Messages             Voices
Dictionaries          Metadata             WebKit
Favorites             Mobile Documents     com.apple.nsurlsessiond
Filters               Network              iMovie
FontCollections       PreferencePanes      iTunes
$ cd App<TAB>
$ cd Application\ S
```

The last example shows a useful trick: hitting the Tab key after entering a few characters of the filename invokes the shell's filename completion feature. When you hit the Tab key, the shell automatically includes the backslashes required to escape any spaces as it completes the file or directory name. Darn handy!

One place where you can find all sorts of peculiar filenames is within your iTunes library, because iTunes uses the song titles as the filenames for the corresponding MP3- or AAC-encoded files. Here are a few examples of filenames from my own library that would be incredibly difficult to work with on the command line:

```
The Beatles/Sgt. Pepper's /Being For The Benefit of Mr. Kite!.mp3
The Art of Noise/In No Sense? Nonsense!/How Rapid?.mp3
Joe Jackson/Look Sharp!/(Do The) Instant Mash.mp3
```

True Unix diehards are undoubtedly cringing at those filenames, which include specific wildcard characters and other elements that are important to the shell, all of which would have to be escaped. Those filenames are ugly enough now, but just imagine them like this:

```
The\ Beatles/Sgt\.\ Pepper\'s\ /Being\ For\ The\ Benefit\ of\ Mr\.\ Kite\!.mp3
The\ Art\ of\ Noise/In\ No\ Sense\?\ Nonsense\!/How\ Rapid\?\.mp3
Joe\ Jackson/Look\ Sharp\!/\(Do\ The\)\ Instant\ Mash\.mp3
```

Not pretty.

One more thing: a filename must be unique inside its directory, but other directories can have files with the same name. For example, you may have files called *chap1.doc* and *chap2.doc* in the directory */Users/carol/Documents* and also have different files with the same names in */Users/carol/Desktop*.

This can cause confusion for people who are used to just having all their files on their Desktop or in the topmost level of the *Documents* directory. In that situation, an attempt to save a file as *chap1.doc* would just generate a warning that the file already exists, but if you create different directories for different projects, it's quite feasible that you'll end up with a dozen or more files with the exact same name.

File and Directory Wildcards

When you have a number of files named in series (for example, *chap1.doc* to *chap12.doc*) or filenames with common characters (such as *aegis*, *aeon*, and *aerie*), you can use wildcards to save yourself lots of typing and match multiple files at the same time. These special characters are the asterisk (*), question mark (?), square brackets (*[ ]*), and curly braces (*{ }*). When used in a file or directory name given as an argument in a command line, the characteristics detailed in Table 4-1 are true.

Table 4-1. Shell wildcards

Notation	Definition
*	An asterisk stands for any number of characters in a filename. For example, *ae** matches any filename that begins with "ae" (such as *aegis*, *aerie*, *aeon*, etc.) if those files are in the same directory. You can use this to save typing for a single filename (for example, *al** for *alphabet.txt*) or to choose many files at once (as in *ae**). An asterisk by itself matches all file and subdirectory names in a directory, with the exception of any starting with a period. To match all your dot files, try *.** as your pattern.
?	A question mark stands for any single character (so *h?p* matches *hop* and *hip*, but not *hp* or *help*).
[]	Square brackets can surround a choice of single characters (i.e., one digit or one letter) you'd like to match. For example, *[Cc]hapter* would match either *Chapter* or *chapter*, but *chap[12]* would match *chap1* or *chap2*. Use a hyphen (*-*) to separate a range of consecutive characters. For example, *chap[1-3]* matches *chap1*, *chap2*, or *chap3*.
{}	Curly braces are used to provide a list of two or more subpatterns, separated by commas, that are matched as alternatives. The pattern *a{b,c,d}e* would match *abe*, *ace*, and *ade*, but not *aee* because the middle *e* isn't inside the curly braces. This is most commonly used to reference multiple files within a subdirectory, as in *Mail/{drafts,inbox}*, which is functionally identical to typing both *Mail/drafts* and *Mail/inbox*.

The following examples show how to use wildcards. The first command lists all the (nonhidden) entries in a directory, and the rest use wildcards to list just some of the entries. The second-to-last one is a little tricky; it matches files whose names contain two (or more) a's:

```
$ ls
chap0.txt        chap2.txt        chap5.txt        cold.txt
chap1a.old.txt   chap3.old.txt    chap6.txt        haha.txt
chap1b.txt       chap4.txt        chap7.txt        oldjunk
$ ls chap?.txt
chap0.txt        chap4.txt        chap6.txt
chap2.txt        chap5.txt        chap7.txt
$ ls chap[3-7]*
chat3.old.txt    chap4.txt        chap5.txt        chap6.txt    chap7.txt
$ ls chap??.txt
chap1b.txt
$ ls *old*
chap1a.old.txt   chap3.old.txt    cold.txt         oldjunk
$ ls *a*a*
chap1a.old.txt   haha.txt
$ ls chap{3,6}.txt
chap3.txt        chap6.txt
```

Wildcards are useful for more than listing files. Most Unix programs accept more than one filename, and you can use wildcards to name multiple files on the command line. For example, both the *cat* and *less* programs display files on the screen. *cat* streams a file's contents until end of file, while *less* shows the contents one screen at a time. (By "screen," I'm referring to what the *less* command actually shows inside the Terminal window—this term stems from the early days of Unix when you didn't have any windows and had only one screen.) Let's say you want to display the files *chap3.old.txt* and *chap1a.old.txt*. Instead of specifying these files individually, you could enter the command as:

```
$ less *.old.txt
```

Which is equivalent to:

```
$ less chap1a.old.txt chap3.old.txt
```

Wildcards match directory names, too. You can use them anywhere in a pathname—absolute or relative—though you still need to remember to separate directory levels with forward slashes (/). For example, let's say you have subdirectories named *Jan, Feb, Mar*, and so on. Each has a file named *summary*. You could read all the *summary* files by typing *less */summary*. That's almost equivalent to *less Jan/summary Feb/summary Mar/summary...* However, there's one important difference when you use *less */summary*: the names will be alphabetized, so *Apr/summary* will be first in the list, not your January summary.

Using wildcards can also be useful if you have lots of files to match. A classic example of where the shell is way more powerful than the Finder is when it comes to moving a subset of files in a directory that match a specific pattern. For instance, if all the JPEG image files in a directory should be moved to a new subdirectory called *JPEG Images*, while the TIFF and PNG image files should remain in the current directory, the fast command-line solution is:

```
$ mv *.{jpg,JPG} JPEG\ Images
```

Compare this to a tedious one-by-one selection process in the Finder!

Looking Inside Files

By now, you're probably tired of looking at files from the outside. It's like visiting a bookstore and never getting to open a book and read what's inside. Fortunately, it doesn't have to be this way. In this section, we'll look at three different programs for looking inside text files.

Why "text files" rather than "all files"? Since Unix treats everything as a file, it'll let you "look at" image data, executable programs, and even the actual bits of the directory structure itself. It's not really useful to look at any of these, though, and while there is a program called *strings* that helps you snoop around in these datafiles, it's not at all commonly used in the world of OS X and Terminal.

cat

The most rudimentary of the programs that let you look inside a file is called *cat*, not for any sort of feline, but because that's short for *concatenate*, a fancy word for "put a bunch of stuff together." The *cat* command is useful for peeking at short files, but because it doesn't care how long the file is or how big your Terminal window is, using *cat* to view a long file results in the top lines scrolling right off the screen before you can even read them.

In its most basic form, you list one or more files, and *cat* displays the contents on the screen:

```
$ cd /etc
$ cat notify.conf
#
# Notification Center configuration file
#

reserve com.apple.system. 0 0 rwr-r-
monitor com.apple.system.timezone /etc/localtime
monitor com.apple.system.info:/etc/hosts /etc/hosts
monitor com.apple.system.info:/etc/services /etc/services
monitor com.apple.system.info:/etc/protocols /etc/protocols
```

In this case, I've moved to the */etc* administrative directory and used *cat* to display the contents of the *notify.conf* configuration file.

Using a wildcard pattern (shown earlier), I can look at a couple of different configuration files with a single invocation of *cat*:

```
$ cat {syslog,nfs,ftpd}.conf
# Note that flat file logs are now configured in /etc/asl.conf

install.*                                        @127.0.0.1:32376
#
# nfs.conf: the NFS configuration file
#
# match umask from OS X Server ftpd
umask all 022
```

One serious drawback of using *cat* to view more than one file in this manner should be obvious: there's no indication of where one file ends and the next begins. The previous listing is actually three different files, all just dumped to the screen.

There are a couple of useful options for the *cat* command: most notably, *-n* to add line numbers, and *-v*, which ensures that everything displayed is printable (though not necessarily readable).

The split between files is more obvious when the *-n* option adds line numbers to the output. For example:

```
$ cat -n {syslog,nfs,ftpd}.conf
     1  # Note that flat file logs are now configured in /etc/asl.conf
     2
     3  install.*                                        @127.0.0.1:32376
     1  #
     2  # nfs.conf: the NFS configuration file
     3  #
     1  # match umask from OS X Server ftpd
     2  umask all 022
```

Here you can see that the line numbers for each file are printed to the left of the file's contents. So, to find out where a file begins, just look for the number 1, as that's the first line of a file. This output shows us that *syslog.conf* is three lines long, *nfs.conf* has three lines, and *ftpd.conf* is just two lines long.

less

If you want to "read" a long plain-text file in a Terminal window, you can use the *less* command to display one "page" (a Terminal window filled from top to bottom) of text at a time.

Or, if you don't like *less*, you can use a program named *more*. In fact, the name *less* is a play on the name of *more*, which came first (but *less* has more features than *more*). Here's an OS X secret, though: *more* is *less*. Really. The *more* utility is actually the very same program, just with a different name and slightly different default behavior. The *ls* command shows the truth:

```
$ ls -l /usr/bin/{more,less}
-rwxr-xr-x  1 root  wheel  129152 Sep 17 01:07 /usr/bin/less
-rwxr-xr-x  1 root  wheel  129152 Sep 17 01:07 /usr/bin/more
```

To avoid confusion, I'll just stick with *less*. The syntax for *less* is:

```
less options files
```

less lets you move forward or backward in the files that you're viewing by any number of pages or lines; you can also move back and forth between two or more files specified on the command line. When you invoke *less*, the first "page" of the file appears, and a prompt appears at the bottom of the Terminal window, as in the following example:

```
$ less ch03
A file is the unit of storage in Unix, as in most other systems.
A file can hold anything: text (a report you're writing,
  .
  .
  .
:
```

The basic *less* prompt is a colon (:), although for the first screen, *less* displays the file's name as a prompt. The cursor sits to the right of this prompt as a signal for you to enter a *less* command to tell *less* what to do. To quit, type **q**.

Like almost everything about *less*, the prompt can be customized. For example, using the *-M* starting flag on the *less* command line makes the prompt show the filename and your position in the file (as a percentage) at the end of each page.

 If you want this to happen every time you use *less*, you can set the LESS environment variable to M (without a dash) in your shell setup file. See "Shell Configuration Settings" on page 35 for details.

You can set or unset most options temporarily from the *less* prompt. For instance, if you have the short *less* prompt (a colon), you can enter -M while *less* is running. *less* responds `Long prompt (press Return)`, and for the rest of the session *less* prompts with the filename, line number, and percentage of the file viewed.

To display the *less* commands and options available on your system, press **h** (for "help") while *less* is running. Table 4-2 lists some simple (but quite useful) commands.

Table 4-2. Useful less commands

Command	Description
Space bar	Display next page
v	Start the *vi* editor
Return	Display next line
Control-L	Redisplay current page
n f	Move forward *n* lines
h	Display help
g	Go to beginning of file
G	Go to end of file
b	Move backward one page
:n	Go to next file on command line
n b	Move backward *n* lines
:p	Go back to previous file on command line
/word	Search forward for *word*
q	Quit *less*
?word	Search backward for *word*

I quite commonly use the /word search notation, for instance, when using the *man* command, which uses *less* behind the scenes to display information one page at a time. For example, instead of flipping through *bash*'s manpage for information on file completion, typing **/file completion** at the colon prompt while reading the *bash* manpage lets you skip straight to what you seek. Gone too far? Use **b** to go back to the previous page.

grep

Instead of having the entire contents of the file dumped to your screen or having to step through a file one line at a time, you will undoubtedly find it useful to be able to search for specific patterns within a file or set of files. This is done with the oddly named *grep* command.

 grep gains its name from an old line-editor command, global/regular expression/print, which was used to list only the lines in the file being edited that matched a specified pattern. With the name *g/re/p*, it wasn't much of a stretch to end up with *grep*, and the programmer who created the command actually imagined it'd be mnemonic for his user community. Imagine!

grep uses a different pattern language than the filename patterns shown earlier in this chapter: a more sophisticated pattern language called *regular expressions*. Regular expressions are discussed in the next chapter; for now, let's just look at how to use *grep* to find word fragments or specific words in a set of files.

Since we're already in the */etc* directory, let's look to see if there's any mention of firewalls by using *grep*:

```
$ grep firewall *conf
asl.conf:# Facility com.apple.alf.logging gets saved in appfirewall.log
asl.conf:? [= Facility com.apple.alf.logging] file appfirewall.log file_max=5M
all_max=50M
```

Within the set of configuration files, there were two matches, as shown. In the output, the matching filename is shown, followed by a colon, followed by the actual matching line in the file.

You can search a lot more than just the configuration files by changing the filename pattern. If you broaden this search, though, you'll inevitably get error messages about *grep* trying to search directory entries rather than files, "operation not permitted" errors, along with "permission denied" errors for files that you don't have permission to search in the first place (remember *sudo* from the last chapter?). To sidestep the "operation not permitted" problem, *grep*'s *-s* option causes it to be quieter in its operation:

```
$ grep firewall *
grep: aliases.db: Permission denied
grep: apache2: Is a directory
grep: asl: Is a directory
asl.conf:# Facility com.apple.alf.logging gets saved in appfirewall.log
asl.conf:? [= Facility com.apple.alf.logging] file appfirewall.log file_max=5M
all_max=50M
...
$ grep -s firewall *
asl.conf:# Facility com.apple.alf.logging gets saved in appfirewall.log
asl.conf:? [= Facility com.apple.alf.logging] file appfirewall.log file_max=5M
all_max=50M
pf.os:# the case that X is a NAT firewall. While nmap is talking to the
```

```
pf.os:# device itself, p0f is fingerprinting the guy behind the firewall
pf.os:# caused by a commonly used software (personal firewalls, security
pf.os:# KEEP IN MIND: Some packet firewalls configured to normalize outgoing
pf.os:# system (and probably not quite to the firewall either).
services:csccfirewall     40843/udp    # CSCCFIREWALL
services:csccfirewall     40843/tcp    # CSCCFIREWALL
```

We'll look at *grep* in much greater detail in Chapter 5.

Creating and Editing Files

There are lots of ways to create and edit files when you're working on a Macintosh. You can use TextEdit, BBEdit, Microsoft Word, and any number of other applications within the Aqua graphical environment. Or, if you'd like to stick to the command line, it turns out that there are a bunch of text-only, Terminal-friendly editors included with OS X.

Chief among these options is an editor called *vi* that can be a bit tricky to learn but is powerful, fast, and available on a wide range of Unix and Linux systems, too. Because *vi* is so powerful and ubiquitous across all *nix systems, that's what we'll focus on in this section; however, we'll take a quick look at a few alternatives too.

Text Editors and Word Processors

A text editor lets you add, change, and rearrange text easily. Three popular Unix editors included with OS X are *vi* (pronounced "vee-eye"), *Pico*, ("pea-co"), and *Emacs* ("e-max"; no relation to Apple's eMac). By contrast, a word processor has all sorts of fancy layout and presentation capabilities, typically built around a "what you see is what you get" (WYSIWYG, or "wizzy-wig") model similar to Microsoft Word. They work great for lots of things but are useless for creating files within the Terminal.

You should choose an editor you're comfortable with. *vi* is probably the best choice, because all Unix systems have it, but Emacs is also widely available and is preferred by many developers because of the features it offers. If you'll be doing simple editing, you should also consider Pico: although it's much less powerful than *vi* or Emacs, it's a lot easier to learn. I'll focus on the rudiments of *vi* here, since it's the most widely available Unix editor, and there's a terrific version included with OS X called *vim*.

None of these plain-text editors has the same features as popular word-processing software, but *vi* and Emacs are sophisticated, extremely flexible editors for all kinds of plain-text files: programs, email messages, and so on. By "plain text," I mean a file with only letters, numbers, and punctuation characters, and no formatting such as point size, bold and italics, or embedded images. Unix systems use plain-text files in many places: in the redirected input and output of Unix programs (see Chapter 6), as shell setup files (see Chapter 2), for shell scripts, for system configuration, and more.

Of course, you can opt to use a graphical text editor such as BBEdit (*http://www.barebones.com*) or TextEdit (*/Applications*) with good results, too, if you'd rather just sidestep editing while within the Terminal application. If you do, try using the *open* command within the Terminal to launch TextEdit with the proper file already loaded. For example, the following command opens the specified file in TextEdit:

```
open -e myfile.txt
```

It's critical that you select Format→Make Plain Text (Shift-⌘-T) within TextEdit to ensure that no extraneous formatting characters or information is included in the text file when you save your changes.

Text editors edit these plain-text files without a hitch. When you use a word processor, though, while on the screen it may look as if the file is only plain text, it will inevitably have some hidden codes in it, too. That's often true even if you tell the word processor to "Save as plain text."

One easy way to check for nontext characters in a file is by reading the file with *less*; look for characters in reversed colors, codes such as <36>, and so on.

Fixing Those Pesky Carriage Returns

Switching between Finder applications and Unix tools for editing can be a hassle, because you might end up having to translate file formats along the way. Fortunately, this is easy with the Unix command line.

One of the more awkward things about Apple putting a Mac graphical environment on top of a Unix core is that the two systems use different end-of-line sequences. If you ever open up a file in a Finder application and see lots of little boxes at the end of each line, or if you try to edit a file within Unix and find that it's littered with ^M sequences, you've hit the end-of-line problem.

To fix it, create the following command aliases:

```
alias m2u="tr '\015' '\012'"
alias u2m="tr '\012' '\015'"
```

Now, whenever you're working with Unix editing tools and you need to fix a Mac-format file, simply use *m2u* (Mac to Unix), as in:

```
$ m2u < mac-format-file > unix-friendly-file
```

And if you find yourself in the opposite situation, where you're editing a Unix file in a Mac tool and it has some carriage-return weirdness, use the reverse *u2m* (Unix to Mac) within the Terminal before opening the file for editing:

```
$ u2m < unix-friendly-file > mac-format-file
```

You can add these aliases to your future login sessions by copying the two alias definition lines into your *.profile* file.

Also worthy of note is the helpful *tr* command, which makes it easy to translate all occurrences of one character to another. Use *man tr* to learn more about this powerful utility.

If you need to do word processing—making documents, address labels, and so on—your best bet is to work with a program designed for that purpose. While TextEdit is surprisingly powerful (it can read and write Word files), you might want to opt for something more powerful, such as Pages (*http://www.apple.com/mac/pages*) (which comes with Apple's iWork), Microsoft Office 2016, or NeoOffice (*http://www.neoof fice.org*), an open source suite of applications similar to Microsoft Office.

The vi Text Editor

The *vi* editor, originally written by Bill Joy at the University of California, Berkeley, is easy to use once you master the fundamental concept of a modal editor. OS X actually includes a version of *vi* called *vim* that has many useful new features. We'll focus on *vi*'s basic commands here, but if you become a *vi* master you'll enjoy *vim*'s powerful extensions.

To learn more about *vi*, I'd recommend picking up a copy of *Learning the vi and Vim Editors*, by Arnold Robbins, Elbert Hannah, and Linda Lamb (O'Reilly), or the *vi and Vim Editors Pocket Reference*, by Arnold Robbins (O'Reilly). These books are packed with useful information about *vi*, and the *Learning* book includes a handy quick-reference card of commands you can use with *vi*. Though focused on *vi*, they offer extensive information about *vim* as well, and will get you up to speed in no time. Or, if you have a Safari account (*http://safari.oreilly.com*), you can read the books online.

Before we start looking at what you can do with *vi*, however, let's talk about *modality*. Modes can best be explained by analogy to your car stereo. When you have a CD in, the "1" button does one task, but if you are listening to the radio, the very same button does something else (perhaps jumping to preprogrammed station number 1). The *vi* editor is exactly the same: in `Command mode`, pressing the i key on the keyboard switches you into *Insert mode*, but in Insert mode, the very same keystroke inserts an "i" into the text itself. The handiest key on your keyboard while you're learning *vi* is unquestionably the Escape key (Esc), located at the upper-left corner of your keyboard. If you're in Insert mode, Esc switches you back to Command mode, and if you're in Command mode, it'll beep to remind you that you're already in Command mode. Use Esc often, until you're completely comfortable keeping track of what mode you're in.

 Jump-start your learning by using OS X's included *vimtutor*: just type in **vimtutor** on the command line for a guided tour of the *vi* editor.

Start *vi* by typing its name; the argument is the filename you want to create or edit. For instance, to edit your shell's *.profile* setup file, you would *cd* to your home directory and enter:

```
$ vi .profile
```

The Terminal fills with a copy of the file (and, because the file is short, some empty lines, too, as denoted by the ~ at the beginning of these lines), as shown in Figure 4-1.

```
 ● ● ●                    taylor — vi .profile — 80×24
# my .profile file

cd $HOME/Desktop

alias ls="/bin/ls -F"
alias grep="grep --color=always"
alias vps="ssh dtaylor@intuitive.com"

# PS1="(\W) : "; export PS1

export SVN_EDITOR=/usr/bin/vi

echo ""
~
~
~
~
~
~
~
~
~
~
```

Figure 4-1. vi display while editing

At the bottom of the window is the status line, which indicates what file you're editing: ".profile" 14L, 210C. This indicates that the file has 14 lines (14L) with a total of 210 characters (210C). Quit the program by typing :q and pressing Return while in Command mode.

vi Basics

Let's take a tour through *vi*. In this example, you'll create a new text file. You can call the file anything you want, but it's best to use only letters and numbers in the file-name. For instance, to make a file named *sample*, enter the following command:

```
$ vi sample
```

Now, let's start the tour...

Your screen should look something like Figure 4-1, but the cursor should be on the top line and the rest of the lines will have the tilde character (~) at the start to denote that they are blank. The bottom status line indicates the following:

```
"sample" [New File]
```

To start entering text in the file, press **i** to switch from Command mode to Insert mode. Now type something. Make some lines too short (press Return before the line gets to the right margin). Make others too long; watch how *vi* wraps long lines. If you have another Terminal window open with some text in it, or if you have an application like Word or TextEdit open, you can use your mouse to copy text from another window and paste it into the Terminal window where you're working with *vi*. (Always make sure you're in Insert mode before you do this, however, or you could irrevocably mess up your file since the text will be interpreted as a sequence of relatively random commands.) To get a lot of text quickly, paste the same text more than once.

Figure 4-2 shows how the *sample* file looks after I copied and pasted the previous paragraph into *vi*'s buffer.

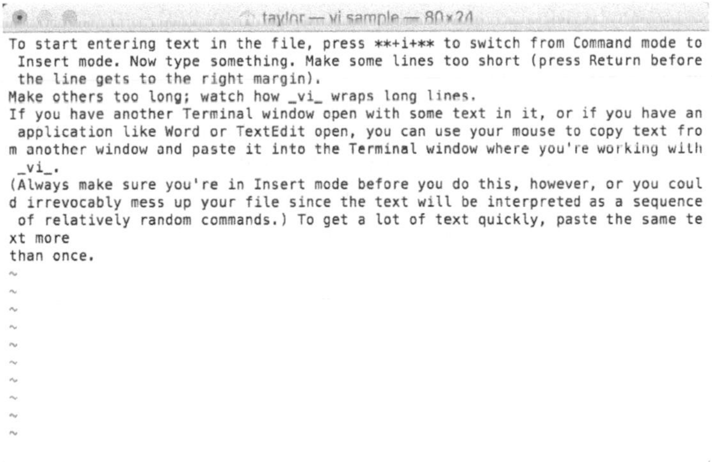

Figure 4-2. vi with some text pasted into the buffer

To move the cursor around in the file, you'll need to leave Insert mode by pressing Esc once. Press it again and you'll hear a beep, reminding you that you are already in Command mode.

 In Command mode, press Control-G to produce a useful status line that shows the filename, the number of lines in the file, and where the cursor is relative to the file buffer.

You can use the arrow keys on your keyboard to move around the file, but most *vi* users have taught themselves to move around with the h, j, k, and l motion keys (left, down, up, and right, respectively). They may seem unintuitive, but not having to move your hand off the main keyboard area can produce a dramatic increase in editing speed as you get more used to them.

 Unless you have enabled "Option click to position cursor" in the Terminal's preferences, *vi* ignores your mouse if you try to use it to move the cursor.

If you've entered a lot of text, you can experiment with some additional movement commands: H to jump to the first line on the screen, and G to jump to the very last line of the file. You should also try the w and b commands to move forward and backward one word at a time (for example, to move forward three words, press the w key three times), and 0 (zero) to jump to the beginning of the line, and $ to jump to the end.

Searching in vi

While *vi* is proving to be a worthy text editor, you're probably thinking that it's lacking one feature that many graphical text editors have: the ability to use ⌘-F to search through the file for some text. Actually, you can search for text strings in *vi*; it's just a little different. *vi*'s search command is accessed by typing a forward slash (/) while in Command mode, followed by the pattern you want to search for. It's handy even in a short file, where it can be quicker to type / and a word than it is to use the cursor-moving commands. For example, if you wanted to search through a text file for the word "cheese," you would first press the Esc key twice (just to make sure you're out of Insert mode and in Command mode) and then type:

```
/cheese
```

You'll see this string appear at the bottom of your Terminal window. When you hit Return, *vi* searches through the file, starting at the current cursor location, for the word "cheese." If it finds it, *vi* places the cursor at the beginning of the word. You can then press the n key to repeat the search; if *vi* finds another occurrence of that word, it moves the cursor to that word.

Invoking external Unix commands

One fabulous feature of *vi* is that it's easy to invoke Unix commands and have their output included in the file you're editing. That said, *vi* also makes it easy to send some of the text in its buffer to a Unix command, ultimately replacing that text with the output of the command. Sound confusing? It's really not so bad.

For example, to include the current date in your file, type **o** in Command mode to open up a blank line immediately below the line that the cursor is sitting on, hit the Esc key to get out of Insert mode, and then enter **!!date**. As you type this, the cursor drops to the bottom of the screen and shows :.!date there. Press Return, and the blank line is replaced by the output from the *date* command.

What if you want to justify a paragraph of text? You can do this by feeding it to the external Unix *fmt* command. Make sure you're in Command mode (hit Esc just to be safe), then use the arrow keys to move the cursor to the beginning of the paragraph and type **!}fmt**. (*vi*'s status line won't change until you press the } character.) Now the lines of the paragraph should flow and fit neatly between the margins. Figure 4-3 shows what happened when I moved to the top of the file (using the H command) then typed in !}fmt to reflow the text in the document.

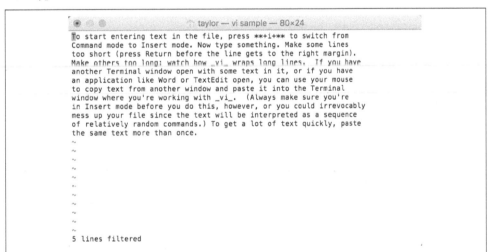

Figure 4-3. Reformatted text using the Unix fmt command

More powerful capabilities

You can delete text in a file by using x to delete the character that's under the cursor, or use the powerful d command:

dd

    Deletes lines

dw

    Deletes individual words

d$

    Deletes to the end of the line

d0

    Deletes to the beginning of the line

dG

    Deletes to the end of the file (if you're seeing a pattern and thinking that it's d +
    motion key, you're absolutely correct)

To undo the deletion, press **u**. You can also paste the deleted text with the p command.

The first step to copying text is to position your cursor at the beginning of the word or line (or series of lines) you want to copy. In *vi*, you don't copy, you "yank" the text. The yw command copies ("yanks") one word, yy yanks the line, yy*n* yanks *n* lines (for example, yy5 yanks five lines), y1 yanks a single character, and y*n*w yanks *n* words (y5w yanks five words, for example). Move the cursor to the line you want to copy and press **yy**. After repositioning your cursor to the line below which you'd like the text copied, press **p** to paste the text.

Yanking does not cut the text; it only copies it to *vi*'s paste buffer. If you want to move the text, you'll have to go back to the lines you've yanked (copied) and delete them with the aforementioned d commands.

As with any text editor, it's a good idea to save your work from *vi* every 5 or 10 minutes. That way, if something goes wrong on the computer or network, you'll be able to recover the edited buffer from the last time you saved it.

If the editor, the Terminal, or the computer does crash, you can recover the saved temporary edit buffer by using the *-r* option when you next launch the program. If there is a file that can be recovered, *vi* shows specific information about it:

```
$ vi -r
Swap files found:
   In current directory:
1.    .sample.swp
            owned by: taylor   dated: Mon May  7 23:06:23 201r
         file name: ~taylor/sample
```

```
        modified: YES
       user name: taylor     host name: Dave-Taylors-MacBook-Pro.local
      process ID: 8085
In directory ~/tmp:
   -- none --
In directory /var/tmp:
   -- none --
In directory /tmp:
   -- none --
```

To recover this file, just type **vi -r sample** and you'll move into the *vi* editor with the recovered version of the file.

In *vi*, to save your work to disk, you use the write command by typing :w followed by Return. The bottom of the display shows the filename saved and the number of lines and characters in the file.

For some reason, saving the edited file sometimes confuses *vi* beginners. It's really very simple: if you want to save the file with the same name it had when you started, just press :w and Return. That's all! If you'd rather use a different filename, type :w followed by the new filename (for example, :w new.sample). Press Return, and it's saved.

Finally, if you try to exit *vi* when you have unsaved changes with the usual :q command, the program will beep, warning you that the modified file has not been saved. If you want to override the warning and discard the changes that you've made since the last time the file was saved, type :q!. If you want to save the changes and don't need to rename the output file, you can use a shortcut: :wq writes out your changes and quits *vi*. In fact, there's a shortcut for that shortcut, too. Type ZZ (uppercase, and no : needed) and you'll write and quit if the file's been modified, or just quit without disturbing the file if it hasn't been changed. That's it!

Of course, there's a lot more to learn about *vi*. In Table 4-3, you'll find a handy listing of some of the most common *vi* commands and their descriptions.

Table 4-3. Common vi editing commands

Command	Meaning
/ *pattern*	Search forward for specified pattern. Repeat search with n.
:q	Quit the edit session.
:q!	Quit, discarding any changes.
:w	Write (save) any changes out to the file.
:wq or ZZ	Write out any changes, then quit (shortcut).

Command	Meaning
a	Move into Append mode (like Insert mode, but you enter information after the cursor, not before).
b	Move backward one word.
w	Move forward one word.
d1G	Delete from the current point back to the beginning of the file.
dd	Delete the current line.
dG	Delete through end of file.
dw	Delete the following word.
Esc	Move into Command mode.
h	Move backward one character.
l	Move forward one character.
i	Switch to Insert mode (Esc switches you back to Command mode).
j	Move down one line.
k	Move up one line.
O	Open up a line above the current line and switch to Insert mode.
o	Open up a line below the current line and switch to Insert mode.
P	Put (paste) deleted text before the cursor.
p	Put (paste) deleted text after the cursor.
X	Delete the character to the left of the cursor.
x	Delete the character under the cursor.
yw	Yank (copy) from the cursor to the end of the current word. You can then paste it with p or P.
yy	Yank (copy) the current line. You can then paste it with p or P.

A Simpler vi Alternative: Pico

If the section on *vi* has left you longing for the safety and logic of the graphical world, you might want to explore the simple editing alternative of Pico. Originally written as part of a text-based email system called Pine (which itself was based on an email program called Elm that I wrote in the mid-1980s), Pico has taken on a life of its own and is included in many Unix distributions, including OS X. Figure 4-4 shows the sample file from the earlier example opened in Pico.

 The GNU *nano* editor is actually included with OS X as a fully functional free software version of Pico. You can type **nano** instead of **pico** if you'd like.

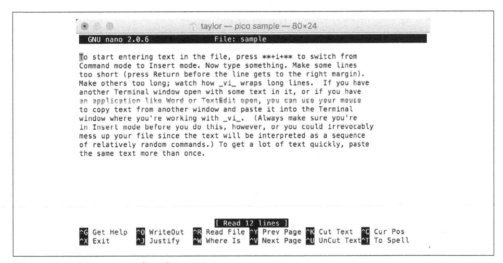

Figure 4-4. Pico, a simpler alternative to vi

Pico offers a menu-based approach to editing, with on-screen help. It's a lot friendlier than *vi*, whose primary way to tell you that you've done something wrong is to beep. Pico offers a comfortable middle ground between text editors such as TextEdit and hardcore Unix text editors such as *vi*. It's a friendly editor that you can launch from the command line and never have to take your hands off the keyboard to use. To learn more about Pico, type Control-G while within the editor, or use *man pico* to read the manpage.

The More Complex Option: Emacs

If Pico is the simpler alternative to *vi*, then Emacs is the more complex alternative. Originally written as part of an artificial intelligence environment and including its own powerful programming language built atop LISP, Emacs is one of the most powerful editors available on any computer system. Indeed, hardcore Emacs users never leave the editor, and there are Emacs extensions for browsing the Web (albeit in text-only mode), reading and responding to email, chatting via an instant messaging system, and more. Figure 4-5 shows Emacs with the sample file in the edit buffer.

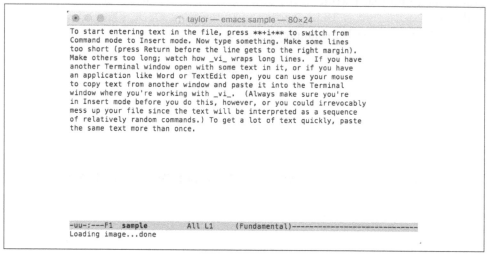

Figure 4-5. Emacs is the Ferrari of Unix text editors

But with great power comes great complexity, and Emacs not only is built upon a completely different paradigm—it's a *nonmodal* editor—but requires you to memorize dozens of different Control, Meta, and Option key sequences.

 If you are interested in trying out the Emacs editor, it's now included with OS X, so you can launch it by typing **emacs** on the command line. It's not easy to figure out, however, so I'd recommend you consider picking up the book *Learning GNU Emacs* by Debra Cameron, James Elliott, Marc Loy, Eric S. Raymond, and Bill Rosenblatt (O'Reilly).

Managing Files

The tree structure of the Unix filesystem makes it easy to organize your files. After you create and edit some files, you may want to copy or move files from one directory to another, or rename files to distinguish different versions. You may even want to create new directories each time you start a different project. To save typing, it's worth knowing that if you copy a file into a directory, the shell is smart enough to use the same filename for the new file.

In addition to its efficiency, the command line is much more precise, offering greater control than the Finder's drag-and-drop interface. For example, if you want to create a new folder in the Finder, you need to mouse up to the File menu and choose New Folder or use a nonmnemonic keystroke combination. On the command line, it's just *mkdir* to create a new directory. Even more to the point, if you have a folder full of hundreds of files and want to move just those that have *temp* in their filenames into the Trash, that's a tedious and error-prone Finder task, while the command-line equivalent is the simple *rm *temp**.

A directory tree can get cluttered with old files you don't need. If you don't need a file or a directory, delete it to free storage space on the disk. The following sections explain how to make and remove directories and files.

Creating Directories with mkdir

It's handy to group related files in the same directory. If you were writing a spy novel and reviewing restaurants for a local newspaper, for example, you probably wouldn't want your intriguing files mixed with restaurant listings. You could create two directories: one for all the chapters in your novel (*spy*, for example) and another for restaurants (*boston.dine*).

To create a new directory, use the *mkdir* program. The syntax is:

```
mkdir dirname(s)
```

where *dirname* is the name of the new directory. To make several directories, put a space between each directory name. To continue this example, you would enter:

```
$ mkdir spy boston.dine
```

This means that if you want to create a directory with a space in the name, you'll need to escape the space just as you had to earlier when you referenced filenames with spaces in them. To create the directory *My Favorite Music*, you'd use:

```
$ mkdir "My Favorite Music"
```

Another trick is that you can create a new directory and include a bunch of subdirectories within that directory, all from a single command. For example, your spy novel most likely has a few chapters in it, and let's say that you need separate directories for each chapter to hold the chapter file itself, any illustrations you want to add, research notes, whatever. You could use the following command to create the spy novel's main directory and individual subdirectories for the various chapters:

```
$ mkdir -p spy/ch{01,02,03,04,05,intro,toc,index,bio}
```

The curly braces ({ }) are used to specify the names of the subdirectories: in this case, each name will consist of the string *ch*, with one of the values in the comma-delimited list in the enclosed set of curly braces appended to it. Run the following command to see the list of directories and subdirectories you've created:

```
$ ls -F spy
ch01/          ch03/          ch05/          chindex/          chtoc/
ch02/          ch04/          chbio/         chintro/
```

Try doing *that* in the Finder! You'd have to first create a folder named *spy*, open that, and then create and rename all those subfolders. Talk about time-consuming! But here, the power of Unix goes into action and saves the day.

Copying Files

If you're about to edit a file, you may want to save a copy of it first. That makes it easy to get back the original version should the edit go haywire. To copy files, use the *cp* program.

The *cp* program can put a copy of a file into the same directory or into another directory. *cp* doesn't affect the original file, so it's a good way to keep an identical backup of a file.

To copy a file, use the command:

```
cp old new
```

Here, `old` is the pathname to the original file and `new` is the pathname you want for the copy. For example, to copy the */etc/passwd* file into a file called *password* in your home directory, you would enter:

```
$ cp /etc/passwd ~/password
```

You can also use the form:

```
cp old dir
```

This puts a copy of the original file `old` into an existing directory, `dir`. The copy has the same filename as the original.

If there's already a file with the same name as the copy, *cp* replaces the old file with your new copy. This is handy when you want to replace an old copy of a file with a newer version, but it can cause trouble if you accidentally overwrite a copy you wanted to keep. To be safe, use *ls* to list the directory before you make a copy there.

Also, *cp* has an *-i* (interactive) option that asks you before overwriting an existing file. It works like this:

```
$ cp -i master existing-file.txt
overwrite existing-file.txt? no
```

(You have to either type **yes** or **no** to respond to the question; you can also just type **y** or **n** and press Return.)

You can copy more than one file at a time to a single directory by listing the pathnames of each file you want copied, with the destination directory at the end of the command line. You can use relative or absolute pathnames (see "Absolute Pathnames" on page 44 and "Relative Pathnames" on page 45), as well as simple filenames. For example, let's say your working directory is */Users/carol* (from the filesystem diagram in Figure 3-3). To copy three files called *ch1.doc*, *ch2.doc*, and *ch3.doc* from */Users/john* to a subdirectory called *Documents* (that's */Users/carol/Documents*), assuming you have the appropriate access permissions, enter:

```
$ cp ../john/ch1.doc ../john/ch2.doc ../john/ch3.doc Documents
```

Or you could use wildcards and let the shell find all the appropriate files. This time, let's add the *-i* option for safety:

```
$ cp -i ../john/ch[1-3].doc Documents
cp: overwrite ../john/ch2.doc ? n
```

This tells you that there is already a file named *ch2.doc* in the *Documents* directory. When *cp* asks, answer **n** to prevent copying *ch2.doc*. Answering **y** overwrites the old *ch2.doc*. As you saw in Chapter 3, the shorthand form . (a single dot or period) refers to the working directory, and .. (dot, dot) refers to the parent directory. For example, the following puts the copies into the working directory:

```
$ cp ../john/ch[1-3].doc .
```

One more possibility: when you're working with home directories, you can use the convenient shorthand *~account* to represent John's and Carol's home directories (and ~ by itself to represent your own). So here's yet another way to copy those three files:

```
$ cp ~john/ch[1-3].doc Documents
```

cp can also copy entire directory trees with the help of the *-R* (recursive) option. There are two arguments after the option: the pathname of the top-level directory from which you want to copy, and the pathname of the place where you want the top level of the copy to be.

As an example, let's say that a new employee, Asha, has joined John and Carol. She needs a copy of John's *Documents/work* directory in her own home directory. (See the filesystem diagram in Figure 3-3.) Her home directory is */Users/asha*. If Asha's own *work* directory doesn't exist yet (this is important!), she could type the following commands:

```
$ cd /Users
$ cp -R john/Documents/work asha/work
```

Or, from her home directory, she could use:

```
$ cp -R ~john/Documents/work work
```

Either way, Asha now has a new subdirectory, */Users/asha/work*, that contains copies of all the files and subdirectories in */Users/john/Documents/work*.

If you give *cp -R* the wrong pathnames, it could end up copying a directory tree into itself and running forever until your filesystem fills up!

When *cp* copies a file, the new copy has its ownership changed to the user running the *cp* command, too, so not only does Asha have the new files, but they're also owned by her. This doesn't always work in your favor, depending on directory permissions, so remember that *cp* also has the *-p* flag to retain original permissions and ownership, as needed. In this case, however, it's good. Here's an example of how that works:

```
$ ls -l /etc/shells
-rw-r--r--  1 root   wheel  179 Aug 22 15:35 /etc/shells
$ cp /etc/shells ~
$ ls -l ~/shells
-rw-r--r--   1 taylor  staff  179 Oct  3 07:59 /Users/taylor/shells
```

Notice that the ~ shortcut for the home directory can also be used as a target directory with a *cp* command. Very helpful!

Problem checklist

The following tips should help you diagnose any error messages *cp* throws your way:

The system says something like "cp: cannot copy file to itself."
If the copy is in the same directory as the original, the filenames must be different.

The system says something like "cp: filename: no such file or directory."
The system can't find the file you want to copy. Check for a typing mistake. If a file isn't in the working directory, be sure to use its pathname.

The system says something like "cp: permission denied."
You may not have permission to copy a file created by someone else or to copy it into a directory that does not belong to you. Use *ls -l* to find the owner and the permissions for the file, or use *ls -ld* to check the destination directory. If you feel that you should be able to copy a file, ask the file's owner or use *sudo* (see "Superuser Privileges with sudo" on page 72 in Chapter 3) to change its access modes.

Renaming and Moving Files with mv

To rename a file, use *mv* (move). The *mv* program can also move a file from one directory to another.

The *mv* command has the same syntax as the *cp* command:

```
mv old new
```

Here, *old* is the old name of the file and *new* is the new name. *mv* writes over existing files, which is handy for updating old versions of a file.

If you don't want to overwrite an old file, be sure that the new name is unique. Like *cp*, *mv* also has an *-i* option for moving and renaming files interactively, which can help you avoid accidentally overwriting files that you want to keep:

```
$ mv chap1.doc intro.doc
$ mv -i chap2.doc intro.doc
mv: overwrite `intro.doc'? n
```

The previous example changed the name of the file *chap1.doc* to *intro.doc*, and then tried to do the same with *chap2.doc* (answering **n** canceled the last operation). If you list your files with *ls*, you'll see that the filename *chap1.doc* has disappeared, but *chap2.doc* and *intro.doc* are intact.

The *mv* command can also move a file from one directory to another. As with the *cp* command, if you want to keep the same filename, you need only give *mv* the name of the destination directory. For example, to move the *intro.doc* file from its present directory to your Desktop, use the following command:

```
$ mv intro.doc ~/Desktop
```

Or, to move the file to your Desktop and rename it at the same time, use a command like this:

```
$ mv intro.doc ~/Desktop/preface.doc
```

Removing Files and Directories

You may finish work on a file or directory and see no need to keep it, or the contents may become obsolete. Periodically removing unwanted files and directories frees storage space and saves you from getting confused when there are too many versions of files on your disk.

rm

The *rm* program removes files. One important thing to point out here, though, is that *rm* permanently removes the file from the filesystem. It doesn't move the file to the Trash, from which it can be recovered (at least until you select "Empty Trash" from the Finder menu). Once you hit Return, that file is gone, so make darn sure that the file you're deleting with *rm* is something you really want to get rid of. Let me say that again: *rm* does *not* offer a way to recover deleted files.

The syntax is simple:

```
rm filename(s)
```

rm removes the named files, as the following example shows:

```
$ ls
chap10        chap2        chap5        cold
chap1a.old    chap3.old    chap6        haha
chap1b        chap4        chap7        oldjunk
$ rm *.old chap10
$ ls
chap1b    chap4    chap6    cold        oldjunk
chap2     chap5    chap7    haha
$ rm c*
$ ls
haha      oldjunk
```

When you use wildcards with *rm*, be sure you're deleting the right files! If you accidentally remove a file you need, you can't recover it unless you have a copy in another directory or in your backups.

Do not enter *rm* * carelessly. It deletes all the files in your working directory.

Here's another easy mistake to make: you want to enter a command such as *rm c** (remove all files with names starting with "c"), but instead enter *rm c** (remove the file named *c* and all the other files in the current directory!).

It's good practice to list the files with *ls* before you remove them. Or, if you use *rm*'s *-i* (interactive) option, *rm* asks you whether you want to remove each file.

If you're security-conscious, *rm*'s *-P* option might appeal to you: it causes files to be overwritten three times, with zeros, ones, and then zeros again, before they're removed. This makes it just about impossible for the data to be recovered, even by the most earnest malicious user. The flag doesn't produce any additional output or confirm that it's done a safe delete, however:

```
$ ls
haha    oldjunk
$ rm -P haha
```

rmdir

Just as you can create new directories with *mkdir*, you can remove them with the *rmdir* program. As a precaution, *rmdir* won't let you delete directories that contain any files or subdirectories; the directory must first be empty. (The *rm -r* command removes a directory and everything in it, but use the *-r* flag with caution: it can be dangerous.)

The syntax is:

```
rmdir dirname(s)
```

If you try to remove a directory that contains files, you'll get the following message:

```
rmdir: dirname not empty
```

To delete a directory that contains files or subdirectories:

1. Enter **cd *dirname*** to get into the directory you want to delete.

2. Enter **rm *** to remove all files in that directory.

3. Enter **cd ..** to go to the parent directory.

4. Enter **rmdir *dirname*** to remove the unwanted directory.

One error you might encounter when using *rmdir* is that you still get the *dirname* not empty message, even after you've deleted all the files inside. If this happens, use *ls -a* to check that there are no hidden files (names that start with a period) other than . and .. (the working directory and its parent). The following command is good for cleaning up hidden files (which aren't matched by a simple wildcard such as *). It matches all hidden files except for . (the current directory) and .. (the parent directory):

```
$ rm -i .[^.]*
```

Working with Links

If you've used the Mac for a while, you'll be familiar with *aliases*, which are empty files that point to other files on the system. A common use of aliases is to have a copy of an application on the Desktop, or to have a shortcut in your home directory. Within the graphical environment, you make aliases by Control-clicking on an item (a file, folder, application, whatever), and then choosing Make Alias from the context menu. This creates a file with a similar name in the same directory. The only difference is that the alias has the word *alias* at the end of its filename. For example, in the Terminal, you might see something like the following:

```
$ ls -l *3*
-rw-r--r--  1 taylor  taylor  1546099  Oct  3 20:58 fig0403.pdf
-rw-r--r--  1 taylor  taylor        0  Oct  3 08:34 fig0403.pdf alias
```

In this case, the file *fig0403.pdf alias* is an alias pointing to the actual file *fig0403.pdf* in the same directory. Opening this file will display the same contents as the original file, even though it appears to be an empty file: the size is shown as zero bytes.

 If you have a tendency to delete the *alias* part of a filename, as I do, one quick technique for identifying whether a file is an alias or not is to check out its file size: if it's size 0 but there's actually content when you look at it with *less*, it's an alias. Failing that, check out its directory in the Finder—use *open .* as a shortcut—and look for the telltale arrow on the icon.

Unix works with aliases differently; on the Unix side, we talk about *links*, not aliases. There are two types of links possible in Unix, *hard links* and *symbolic links*, and both are created with the *ln* command.

The syntax is:

```
ln [-s] source target
```

The *-s* option indicates that you're creating a symbolic link, so to create a second file that links to the file *fig0403.pdf*, the command would be:

```
$ ln -s fig0403.pdf neato-pic.pdf
```

and the result would be:

```
$ ls -l *pdf
-rw-r--r--  1 taylor  taylor  1532749  Oct  3 20:47 fig0401.pdf
-rw-r--r--  1 taylor  taylor  1539493  Oct  3 20:52 fig0402.pdf
-rw-r--r--  1 taylor  taylor  1546099  Oct  3 20:58 fig0403.pdf
lrwxr-xr-x  1 taylor  taylor       18  Oct  4 08:40 neato-pic.pdf -> fig0403.pdf
```

One way to think about symbolic links is that they're akin to notes saying "the info you want isn't here, it's in file *X*." This also implies a peculiar behavior of symbolic links (and Aqua aliases): move, rename, or remove the item being pointed to, and you have an orphan link. The system doesn't automatically remove or update symbolic links.

The other type of link is a hard link, which creates a second name for the exact same contents. That is, if you create a hard link to *fig0403.pdf*, you can then delete the original file using *rm*, and its contents will remain accessible through the second filename. Essentially, they're different doors into the same room (as opposed to a note taped on a door telling you to go to the second door, as would be the case with a symbolic link). Hard links are also created with the *ln* command, except you omit the *-s* option:

```
$ ln mypic.pdf copy2.pdf
$ ls -l mypic.pdf copy2.pdf
-rw-r--r--  2 taylor  staff  1546099  Oct  3 08:45 copy2.pdf
-rw-r--r--  2 taylor  staff  1546099  Oct  3 08:45 mypic.pdf
$ rm mypic.pdf
$ ls -l copy2.pdf
-rw-r--r--  1 taylor  staff  1546099  Oct  3 08:45 copy2.pdf
```

Notice that both files are exactly the same size when the hard link is created. This makes sense because they're both names pointing to the same underlying set of data, so they should be identical. Then, when the original is deleted, the data survives with the second name now as its only name. The only difference is that the second field in the preceding output, the link count, shows 2 when there are two filenames pointing to the same data, but when the original is deleted, the link count of the second entry, *copy2.pdf*, goes back to 1.

Compressing and Archiving Files

Aqua users commonly use the ZIP archive capability of OS X itself (Control-click and choose "Compress *filename*" from the context menu, and your Mac promptly creates a *.zip* archive), but Unix users have many other options worth exploring when it comes to compressing and archiving files and directories.

Even though OS X is far superior to Windows 8, we unfortunately live in a Windows world, which means you're going to occasionally send email attachments to and receive them from Windows users. It's also not uncommon to download shareware from a web or FTP site that's been zipped (a file with a *.zip* extension). OS X gives you many ways to create your own ZIP archives (and to unzip the ones you receive, too). And if you're interacting with other Unix users (such as Linux, FreeBSD, or even OS X users), OS X offers a suite of command-line utilities for batching and unbatching files.

There are three compression programs included with OS X, though the most popular is *gzip* (the others are *compress* and *bzip2*; read their manpages to learn more about how they differ). There's also a very common Unix archive format called *tar* that I'll cover briefly.

gzip

Though it may initially confuse you into thinking that it's part of the ZIP archive tool-set, *gzip* has nothing to do with the ZIP archive files created by OS X's Make Archive capability. Instead, *gzip* is actually a compression program that does a very good job of shrinking down individual files for storage and transmission. If you're sending a file to someone with a slow Internet connection, for example, running the file through *gzip* can significantly reduce its size and make it much more portable. Just as importantly, it can help save space on your disk by letting you compress files you want to keep but aren't using currently. *gzip* works particularly well with *tar*, too, as you'll see.

The syntax is:

```
gzip [-v] file(s)
```

The *-v* flag offers verbose output, letting the program indicate how much space it saved by compressing the file. Very useful information, as you may expect! Here's an example:

```
$ ls -l ch06.doc
-rwxr-xr-x  1 taylor   staff  138240  Oct  4 08:52 ch06.doc
$ gzip -v ch06.doc
ch06.doc:                 75.2% -- replaced with ch06.doc.gz
$ ls -l ch06.doc.gz
-rwxr-xr-x 1 taylor staff 34206 24  Oct  4 08:52 ch06.doc.gz
```

You can see that *gzip* did a great job compressing the file, reducing its size by over 75 percent. Notice that it has automatically appended a *.gz* filename suffix to indicate that the file is now compressed. To uncompress the file, just use *gunzip*:

```
$ gunzip ch06.doc.gz
$ ls -l ch06.doc
-rwxr-xr-x  1 taylor  staff  138240  Oct  4 08:52 ch06.doc
```

The amount of space saved by compression varies significantly based on the format of the original data in the file. Some file formats lend themselves to compression, but with others, the compressed version ends up being just as big as the original file:

```
$ ls -l 10*.m4a
-rw-r--r--   1 taylor  staff  4645048 Oct  4 21:29 10 Serpentine Lane.m4a
$ gzip -v 10*.m4a
10 Serpentine Lane.m4a:   0.9% -- replaced with 10 Serpentine Lane.m4a.gz
$ ls -l 10*
-rw-r--r--  1 taylor  staff  4603044 Oct  4 21:29 10 Serpentine Lane.m4a.gz
```

This example resulted in a space savings of less than one percent of the file size.

tar

In the old days, Unix system backups were done to streaming tape devices (today you can only see these units in cheesy 1960s sci-fi films, the huge round tape units that randomly spin as data is accessed). The tool of choice for creating backups from Unix systems onto these streaming tape devices was *tar*, the *tape archiver*. Fast-forward to OS X, and *tar* continues its long tradition as a useful utility, but now it's used to create files that contain directories and other files within them, as an archive. It's similar to the ZIP format, but *tar* differs from *gzip* because its job is to create a file that contains multiple files and directories. *gzip*, by contrast, makes an existing file shrink as much as possible through compression.

The *tar* program is particularly helpful when combined with *gzip*, actually, because it makes creating archive copies of directories simple and effective. Even better, if you use the *-z* flag to *tar*, it automatically invokes *gzip* to compress its output without any further work. Here's a fun bit of jargon, too: compressed *tar* archives are known in the Unix community as *tarballs*.

The syntax is:

```
tar [c|t|x] [flags] files_and_directories_to_archive
```

The *tar* program is too complex to fully explain here (as always, *man tar* produces lots more information about *tar*'s options), but in a nutshell, *tar -c* creates archives, *tar -t* shows what's in an existing archive, and *tar -x* extracts files and directories from an archive. The *-f file* flag is used to specify the archive name, and the *-v* flag offers verbose output to let you see what's going on:

```
$ du -s Masters\ Thesis
6704    Masters Thesis
$ tar -czvf masters.thesis.tgz "Masters Thesis"
Masters Thesis/
Masters Thesis/.DS_Store
Masters Thesis/analysis.doc
...
Masters Thesis/Web Survey Results.doc
Masters Thesis/web usage by section.doc
$ ls -l masters.thesis.tgz
-rw-r--r--  1 taylor  staff  853574  Oct  4 09:20 masters.thesis.tgz
```

 Notice that we gave *tar* the directory name, rather than a list of files. This ensures that when the directory is unpacked, the files are placed in a new directory (*Masters Thesis*), rather than filling the current directory. This is a good habit for people who make lots of archives.

In this example, the directory *Masters Thesis* is 6.7 MB in size, and hasn't been accessed in quite a while. This makes it a perfect candidate for a compressed *tar* archive. This is done by combining the following options: -c (create), -z (compress with *gzip*), *v* (verbose), and *f file* (output filename; notice that we added the *.tgz* suffix to avoid later confusion about the file type). In under 10 seconds, a new archive file is created that is less than 1 MB in size, yet contains all the files and directories in the original archive. To unpack the archive, use the following command:

```
$ tar -xvzf masters.thesis.tgz
```

Files on Other Operating Systems

Chapter 8 explains ways to transfer files across a network—possibly to non-Unix operating systems. OS X has the capability of connecting to a variety of different filesystems remotely, including Microsoft Windows, other Unix systems, and even web-based filesystems.

If the Windows-format filesystem is mounted with your other filesystems, you'll be able to use its files by typing a Unix-like pathname. For instance, if you've mounted a remote Windows system's *C:* drive over a share named *winc*, you can access the Windows file *C:\WORD\REPORT.DOC* through the pathname */Volumes/winc/word/report.doc*. Indeed, most external volumes are automatically mounted within the */Volumes* directory.

## CHAPTER 5

Finding Files and Information

One of the fundamental challenges of using modern computers is finding files and information with ever-larger storage systems. Whether you're highly organized and use wonderfully mnemonic names for every file and directory you create or you have lots of *letter1*, *letter2*, and *work* files and directories scattered around your filesystem, there will undoubtedly come a time when you need to find something on your computer based on its contents, filename, or some other attribute.

It turns out that there are four different ways in Unix to search for—and hopefully find—what you seek. To look inside files, you need to use the *grep* command, introduced briefly in the previous chapter. To find files by filename, the fastest solution is the *locate* command. A more sophisticated filename and attribute search can be done with the Unix power user's *find* command. And finally, OS X includes a search system called *Spotlight* that has a powerful command-line component that's worth exploring.

Searching Inside Files with the grep Command

The *grep* program searches the contents of files for lines that match the specified pattern. The syntax is:

```
grep pattern [file(s)]
```

The simplest use of *grep* is to search for lines within files that contain a particular word by feeding *grep* a pattern and a list of files in which to search. For example, let's search all the files in the working directory (using the wildcard *) for the word "Unix":

```
$ grep "Unix" *
ch01:Unix is a flexible and powerful operating system
ch01:When the Unix designers started work, little did
ch05:What can we do with Unix?
```

Note that *grep* understands plain text—and that's all. Feeding it nontext files can produce puzzling and peculiar results. For example, Word files (and those created by other WYSIWYG editors) contain characters that, when sent to the Terminal, mess up your display in strange and occasionally interesting ways.

 One way to search such files from the command line is to extract only the printable characters using the *strings* program (see *man strings* for details).

grep can be used in a *pipe*, which enables *grep* to scan the output of a different command. This makes it so only those lines of the input stream containing a given pattern are sent to the output stream in the pipe. Pipes are denoted with the | symbol (which can be found above the \ on a standard Apple keyboard layout) and are a method of joining the output of one command to the input of another (in the following example, the output of the *ls* command to the input of the *grep* command), flowing data between them just as a plastic pipe transports water from a water main to a sprinkler head in your garden.

When *grep* searches multiple files, it shows the name of the file where it finds each matching line of text. Alternatively, if you don't give *grep* a filename to read, it reads its standard input; that's the way all filter programs work (standard input and output are discussed in Chapter 6):

```
$ ls -l | grep "Aug"
drwxr-xr-x+  5 taylor   staff    170 Aug 11  2015 Public/
drwxr-xr-x+  5 taylor   staff    170 Aug 11  2015 Sites/
```

First, this example runs *ls -l* to list your working directory. The standard output of *ls -l* is piped to *grep*, which outputs only lines that contain the string "Aug" (that is, files or directories that were last modified in August and any other lines that contain the pattern "Aug").

Useful grep Options

Table 5-1 lists some of *grep*'s options, which you can use to modify your searches.

Table 5-1. Some grep options

Option	Description
-A n	Show n lines after the matching line.
-B n	Show n lines before the matching line.
-C n	Show n lines before and after the matching line.

Option	Description
-v	Print only lines that do *not* match the pattern.
-n	Print the matched line and its line number.
-l	Print only the names of files with matching lines (this is the lowercase letter "L").
-c	Print only the count of matching lines.
-i	Match either upper- or lowercase.

In the previous search, a file named *aug-finances.xls* wouldn't have matched, because by default, *grep* is case-sensitive. That means a search for "aug" wouldn't match "Aug", either. To make the search case-insensitive, add *grep*'s *-i* option.

Though it may seem odd, being able to invert the search logic with the *-v* flag and show lines that don't match the given pattern can be quite useful. You can also make it so the *grep* command outputs only matching filenames (rather than the lines in those files that contain the search pattern) by adding the *-l* option. To find all the files in the current directory that *don't* mention Jane, for example, the command would be:

```
$ grep -lv Jane *
sample
diary.txt
myprogram.c
```

This has the same potential case-sensitivity issues, though, so an even better set of command flags would be *-lvi*, which would also match "jane" and possibly filter out even more files.

Matching context

When searching for specific lines in a file, you may actually want to also see a line or two above or below the matching line, rather than just the matching line itself. This can be accomplished in three ways, depending on whether you want lines above, lines below, or both, by using *-A*, *-B*, and *-C*, respectively.

For example, to show one additional line above and below the matching line (and add line numbers too, by using the *-n* option), you could use a command like this:

```
$ grep -n -C1 Aqua sample
3-watch how vi wraps long lines.  If you have another Terminal window
4:open with some text in it, or if you have an Aqua application open,
5-you can also use your mouse to copy text from another window and
```

Notice that the line that has a match has a colon after the line number, while the other context lines are preceded with a dash. Very subtle, but knowing what to look for helps you find your match instantly!

Matches in color

One great feature of OS X's *grep* command is that it automatically highlights the matching passage in each line if you use the verbose *--color=always* option. Here's how it looks (well, it's not in color here because we're in a book, but try this example yourself to see how it shows the results in an interesting manner!):

```
$ grep --color=always text sample
Enter some lines of text. Make some lines too short (press Return
open with some text in it, or if you have an Aqua application open,
you can also use your mouse to copy text from another window and
your file.) To get a lot of text quickly, paste the same text more
```

In this command, you're searching for the word "text" within the *sample* file. Because you've added the *--color=always* option, any instances of the word "text" are highlighted in bold red text in the output. To take permanent advantage of this feature, you can create a new *grep* alias that includes the *--color=always* option, or set an environment variable in your *.profile* or *.login* file, depending on your shell. For example, if you use *bash*, you could add the following to your *.profile* file:

```
GREP_OPTIONS="--color=always";export GREP_OPTIONS
```

Now whenever you use *grep*, your results will come back in cheery color.

Counting matches rather than showing matching lines

When you're going through a large file and have a lot of matches, it's often quite useful to just get a report of how many lines matched rather than having all the output stream past on your screen. This is accomplished with the *-c* option:

```
$ grep -c "kernel" /var/log/system.log
160
```

You can also accomplish this result by piping the output to the *wc* command, as shown in "wc" on page 142, but this is considerably faster!

Working with Regular Expressions

You can use simple patterns with the *grep* program—patterns like "Jane" or "hot key"—but *grep* actually has the ability to match incredibly complex and sophisticated patterns because it uses regular expressions, an entire language for specifying patterns. Let's spend some time talking about regular expressions so you can see how powerful they are.

A word of warning, though: regular expressions are not the same as file-matching patterns in the shell, and some patterns are interpreted quite differently in regular expressions than they are at the command line. This can be confusing when you have a command like *grep* `regexp filematchpattern`, with two different styles of patterns on the same line.

The fundamental building blocks of regular expressions are symbols and sequences that are intended to match a specific character. Almost all characters automatically match themselves, so the pattern `Jane` is a regular expression that matches `J`, `a`, `n`, and `e`. Some characters are more powerful, however. For example, a `.` (a period) matches any single character.

To specify any one of a range of characters, use the set operator (brackets) to group them: `[Jj]ane` matches both `Jane` and `jane`, for example. You can also do ranges within brackets, so `J[aeiou]ne` and `j[a-z]ne` are both valid expressions; the first matches `Jane`, `Jene`, `Jine`, `Jone`, and `June`, and the second matches any occurrence of `j` followed by a lowercase letter, followed by `ne`.

Many classes of characters are already predefined for your currently set language (remember, your Mac and the underlying Unix system work with dozens of languages), so `[:alnum:]`, which is Unix shorthand for "alphanumeric," is equivalent to `[a-zA-Z0-9]` in English, `[:digit:]` is the same as `[0-9]`, `[:upper:]` is the same as `[A-Z]`, and so on.

The big reason for using named character ranges is that by using them you ensure that your regular expression will work in other languages in addition to English. Specifically, `[a-z]` won't include the Spanish ñ, for example, but `[:lower:]` will, if the locale is set to Spanish. Table 5-2 lists the most important named character ranges.

Table 5-2. Named character ranges in regular expressions

Option	Matches
`[:alnum:]`	Upper- and lowercase letters and numeric digit values (0–9)
`[:alpha:]`	Upper- and lowercase letters
`[:digit:]`	Numeric digit values (0–9)
`[:lower:]`	Lowercase letters
`[:print:]`	Printable (visible) characters
`[:punct:]`	Punctuation characters

Option	Matches
[:space:]	The set of characters that can serve as a space, including the space, tab, and carriage return
[:upper:]	Uppercase letters
[:xdigit:]	Hexadecimal digit values (0–9, plus a–f and A–F)

Named character ranges are considered an element in a range expression, so the earlier pattern j[a-z]ne is correctly written as j[[:lower:]]ne. You can also negate the value of a range by prefacing it with the caret symbol (^), which you get with Shift-6. So, j[^aeiou]ne matches everything that has a j, followed by any letter that *isn't a vowel*, followed by ne.

The period matches any single character, and the \w expression denotes a word that's a sequence of letters—almost synonymous with :alnum:, but it also matches underscores. When not used in a character range, the ^ matches the beginning of the line, and the $ matches the end of the line.

If you want to find blank lines that have no content, the pattern ^$ does the trick. Lines that begin with a digit? Start the pattern with ^ followed by a set operator, followed by a named character range, like this: ^[[:digit:]].

Each expression can be followed by what's called a *repetition operator*, which indicates how often the pattern can or should occur for a match to be found. For example:

- ? means that the preceding is optional and may be matched at most one time.
- * matches zero or more times.
- + matches one or more times.
- {*n*} matches exactly *n* times.
- {*n,m*} matches between *n* and *m* times.

To put these to the test, here's a pattern that matches exactly five digits followed by the letter M:

    [[:digit:]]{5}M

And here's a pattern that matches J, followed by any number of lowercase letters (including none at all), followed by a period:

    J[[:lower:]]*\.

Notice you need to escape the period (.) with the backslash so it's not seen as a request to match any single character.

The pattern `jpe?g` matches both `jpeg` and `jpg`, while `jpe*g` matches both of those words, also matching sequences like `jpeeeg` and `jpeeeeeeeeeg`.

You can list multiple patterns in an `OR` configuration by separating them with a pipe (`|`). This is almost always done by grouping the expression in parentheses. For example, `(cat|dog)house` matches both `cathouse` and `doghouse`, and `[[:digit:]]+(am|pm)` matches any one-or-more-digit value followed by `am` or `pm`.

Quite a complex language, isn't it?

Let's use a few regular expressions to see how they work in practice. This one tells *grep* to find lines containing `root`, followed by zero or more other characters (abbreviated in a regular expression as `.*`), followed by Aug:

```
$ ls -l | grep "root.*Aug"
drwxr-xr-x@  3 root   admin       102 Aug  1  2015 opt/
```

Next, let's look at the logfile for my Q&A website, *http://www.AskDaveTaylor.com*. Visitors who enter data and submit questions on the site invoke what's called an HTTP `POST` action when they use the contact form, which is differentiated from the `GET` of most page retrieval transactions in the Hypertext Transport Protocol (HTTP). Finding all the `POST` transactions in the logfile is therefore simple:

```
$ grep POST access_log
178.73.212.114 - - [06/May/2015...] "POST /how_do_i_get..." "...Firefox/3.0.14"
78.47.115.26 - - [06/May/2015...] "POST /tag/latino.tra..." "...Firefox/3.0.1"
78.47.115.26 - - [06/May/2015...] "POST /tag/latino.zim..." "...Firefox/3.0.1"
62.212.85.36 - - [06/May/2015...] "POST /RPC2 HTTP/1.1"..." "...Safari/535.11"
```

If you look closely at that output, you'll see that an identification string from the actual browser that the visitor is using is included near the end of each line. The first match is Firefox running on Windows, the second and third are Firefox running on a Linux system, and the last is Safari.

By using *grep* with a regular expression, we can identify those queries originating from Firefox or Apple's Safari (use the -E flag, as shown, to force proper regular expressions):

```
$ grep -E "POST.*(Safari|Firefox)" access_log
178.73.212.114 - - [06/May/2015...] "POST /how_do_i_get..." "...Firefox/3.0.14"
178.73.212.114 - - [06/May/2015...] "POST /whats_a_goog..." "...Firefox/3.0.14"
178.73.212.114 - - [06/May/2015:...] "POST /how_can_i_a..." "...Firefox/3.0.14"
78.47.115.26 - - [06/May/2015...] "POST /tag/latino.tra..." "...Firefox/3.0.1"
```

What's more, it's possible to figure out how many forms were submitted and then break them down into MSIE (Internet Explorer) and non-MSIE submissions with just a few *grep* queries, coupled with a simple pipe and the *wc* word count program (both of which are discussed in more detail in Chapter 6):

```
$ grep -E POST access_log | wc -l
     272
$ grep -E "POST.*MSIE" access_log | wc -l
       3
$ grep -E "POST.*(Firefox)" access_log | wc -l
       9
$ grep -E "POST.*(Safari)" access_log | wc -l
     258
```

This shows that of the 272 submissions, 3 were done with MSIE, 9 were done with Firefox, and 258 were done with Safari.

Of course, while having to enter all of those commands separately is fine if you're only doing this occasionally, if you're going to need this sort of information more often, you should consider pulling the commands together in a shell script. That way, all you'll need to do is execute the shell script, and it will run the commands separately and provide you with output that shows the results.

 There's a lot more to regular expressions than I can fit into a few pages in this book. If you really want to become a regular expression maven, I suggest that you read the book *Mastering Regular Expressions*, by Jeffrey E. F. Friedl (O'Reilly).

If you'd like to learn more about shell scripts, I invite you to start with my own book *Wicked Cool Shell Scripts (http://shop.oreilly.com/product/9781593276027.do)* (No Starch).

Finding Files with locate

Sometimes, you'll create a file, save it someplace, and forget about it. Then, when you need that file six months later, you can't remember where you saved it. For situations like this, OS X includes the *locate* program to help you find files quickly. You can use *locate* to search part or all of a filesystem for a file with a certain name. *locate* doesn't actually search the filesystem, though; rather, it searches through a prebuilt index of every single file and directory on the system. This is a good thing, because the command doesn't have to traverse each and every directory in your filesystem. This makes *locate* very fast. However, it's also a potential problem because the *locate* database can get old and out of sync with the actual files on your system.

The first step, therefore, is to build the *locate* database. To learn how to do that on your OS X system, check the manpage: *man 8 locate.updatedb*.

Fast Filename Search with locate

Once you have updated the database, you can search it with the *locate* command. For instance, if you're looking for a file named *alpha-test*, *alphatest*, or something like that, try this:

```
$ locate alpha
/Users/alan/Desktop/alpha3
/usr/local/projects/mega/alphatest
/usr/share/man/man3/alphasort.3
/usr/share/man/man3/isalpha.3
/usr/share/man/man3/iswalpha.3
/Volumes/Hello/Applications/Cool Stuff/Mail.app/Contents/Resources/
alphaPixel.tiff
/Volumes/Hello/sw/fink/10.1/unstable/main/finkinfo/editors/
emacs-alpha-21.1-3.info
/Volumes/Hello/sw/share/doc/tar/README-alpha
/Volumes/Hello/usr/share/man/man3/alphasort.3
/Volumes/Hello/usr/share/man/man3/isalpha.3
/Volumes/Hello/usr/share/man/man3/iswalpha.3
```

You'll get the absolute pathnames of any files and directories with *alpha* in their names. (If you get a lot of output, add a pipe to *less*. See "Pipes and Filters" on page 141 in Chapter 6.) *locate* may or may not list protected, private files.

Unfortunately, you can't specify regular expressions with *locate*. For example, the following command doesn't return any results:

```
$ locate "/man/.*alpha"
```

You instead need to use a series of *grep* commands in a pipeline to pick through the *locate* output.

Note that a *pipeline* is where the output of one command is used as the input to the next, as denoted by the "|" symbol and shown in the following example.

To accomplish the task of identifying which matches to the pattern *alpha* are from the */man/* directory, do this:

```
$ locate alpha | grep "/man/"
/usr/share/file/magic/alpha
/usr/share/man/man3/alphasort.3
/usr/share/man/man3/isalpha.3
/usr/share/man/man3/isalpha_l.3
/usr/share/man/man3/iswalpha.3
/usr/share/man/man3/iswalpha_l.3
```

This ability to combine commands is at the heart of Unix's great power. You aren't constrained to just the specific commands that others have written; you can combine them with pipes to create exactly the function or capability you seek. We'll spend a lot more time on this powerful concept later in the book, so stay tuned!

Using find to Explore Your Filesystem

Reading about the limitations of the *locate* command undoubtedly caused you to wonder if there was a more powerful option: a command that could let you search through the actual, live filesystem to find what you seek. The *find* command lets you search for files not only by filename patterns, but by a remarkable number of additional criteria, too—though since it's not using a previously saved filename database, as *locate* does, it is definitely going to be slower.

find has a completely different syntax than any of the Unix commands we've examined to this point in the book, so the best place to start is with the *find* command syntax itself:

```
find flags pathname expression
```

Expressions are where the complexity shows up, because a typical expression is a "primary" followed by a relevant value, and there are dozens of different primaries that can be combined in thousands of different ways. For example, to match files that end with *.html*, you would use something like:

```
find -name "*.html"
```

To search for all HTML files starting at the current directory on an OS X system, here's how the command would look:

```
$ find . -name "*.html" -print
./Documents/Books/Learning OSX Unix/lumch04A.html
./Library/Mail Downloads/Aéropostale - Checkout.html
./Library/Mail Downloads/Mail Attachment.html
./Library/PreferencePanes/MusicManager.prefPane/Contents/Resources/
thirdparty.html
./Library/Widgets/Local Weather.wdgt/index.html
./Sites/index.html
```

Notice that the pathname specified is the current working directory (.), so *find* only searches that directory and anything within it, not the entire filesystem. Change this to your home directory (*$HOME*), and the *find* command traverses everything within that directory looking for matches. Rather than listing all the matches, however, I'm going to feed the output of the command to the ever-helpful *wc* (word count) program to just get a count of matching entries:

```
$ find $HOME -name "*.html" -print | wc -l
    1291
```

As you can see, I have a lot of web content in my home directory—there are over a thousand files that match the filename pattern **.html*. That's a lot of web pages!

Matching by File Size

Another primary that can be tested is the file size, using *-size*. This is a typically complex *find* primary in that the default unit for specifying size is 512-byte blocks, so *-size 10* matches files that are 10*512 bytes, or 5,120 bytes, in size. To match a specific number of bytes, append a *c*; for example, *-size 10c* matches files that are exactly 10 bytes in size. That's not particularly useful, but it turns out you can specify "more than" or "less than" by prefacing the number with a + or -, respectively. Now that is useful!

For example, to match only files that are greater than 5 KB in size, you can use either *-size +10* or *-size +5120c*, and to find files that are less than 100 bytes, you can use *-size -100c*.

Let's look at the executable commands in */bin* to see which are greater than 30 KB in size:

```
$ find /bin -size +30k -print
/bin/bash
/bin/chmod
/bin/csh
/bin/dd
/bin/ed
/bin/ksh
/bin/launchctl
/bin/ls
/bin/pax
/bin/ps
/bin/sh
/bin/stty
/bin/sync
/bin/tcsh
/bin/zsh
```

This is just the tip of the iceberg with *find* primaries, however, so let's have a closer look. The most useful primaries are listed in Table 5-3. This isn't an exhaustive list; if you want to know about every single possible primary, check the manpage for *find*.

Table 5-3. The most useful find primaries

Option	Description
-cmin time	True if the file has been modified within the last *time* minutes.
-ctime time	Same as *-cmin*, but for units of hours, not minutes.
-delete	Delete matching files. Use with caution!
-exec	Invoke the specified command for matching filenames.
-group name	True if the file is owned by group *name* (which can be specified as a group name or group ID).
-iname pattern	Identical to *-name* except tests are case-insensitive.
-iregex regex	Identical to *-regex*, but the regular expression is evaluated as case-insensitive.
-ls	Produces *ls -l* output for matching files.

Option	Description
-name pattern	True if the filename matches the specified *pattern*.
-newer file	True if the file is newer than the specified reference *file*.
-nouser	True if the file belongs to an unknown user (that is, a user ID that doesn't appear in either */etc/passwd* or *NetInfo*).
-perm mode	True if the file matches the specified permission. This complex primary is explained later in this chapter.
-print	Prints the full pathname of the current file.
-print0	Special version of *-print* that compensates for spaces and other nonstandard characters in filenames. An important addition for OS X *find* usage.
-regex regex	Same as *-name*, but allows full regular expressions rather than just simple filename pattern matches.
-size n	True if the file's size matches the specified size. Default unit is 512-byte blocks; append *c* for bytes, and prepend + for "more than" or - for "less than" tests.
-type t	True if the file is of the specified type. Common types are *d* for directories, and *f* for regular files.
-user name	True if the file is owned by the specified user. *name* can be a username or user ID number.

One of the more useful options listed in Table 5-3 that most Unix users ignore is *-ls*. Here's a more complex *find* command that uses this very primary, along with a test to ensure that the matching files are regular files, not symbolic links and so on:

```
$ find /bin -size +60 -type f -ls
21849474      688 -r-xr-xr-x    1 root     wheel       628496 Sep 17 01:07 /bin/bash
21849476       24 -rwxr-xr-x    1 root     wheel        33904 Sep 17 01:07 /bin
/chmod
21849478      408 -rwxr-xr-x    1 root     wheel       378624 Sep 17 01:07 /bin/csh
21849480       24 -rwxr-xr-x    1 root     wheel        31856 Sep 17 01:07 /bin/dd
21849484       56 -rwxr-xr-x    1 root     wheel        53872 Sep 17 01:07 /bin/ed
21849488     1496 -r-xr-xr-x    1 root     wheel      1394432 Sep 17 01:07 /bin/ksh
21849489       88 -rwxr-xr-x    1 root     wheel       119936 Sep 17 01:07 /bin
/launchctl
21849492       32 -rwxr-xr-x    1 root     wheel        38512 Sep 17 01:07 /bin/ls
21849495      112 -rwxr-xr-x    1 root     wheel       110800 Sep 17 01:07 /bin/pax
21849496       40 -rwsr-xr-x    1 root     wheel        51008 Sep 17 01:07 /bin/ps
21849501      688 -r-xr-xr-x    1 root     wheel       632672 Sep 17 01:07 /bin/sh
21849503       24 -rwxr-xr-x    1 root     wheel        32048 Sep 17 01:07 /bin
/stty
21849504       16 -rwxr-xr-x    1 root     wheel        42320 Sep 17 01:07 /bin
/sync
21849505      408 -rwxr-xr-x    1 root     wheel       378624 Sep 17 01:07 /bin
```

```
/tcsh
21849509        680 -rwxr-xr-x   1 root     wheel      573600 Sep 17 01:07 /bin/zsh
```

This output is slightly different from a regular *ls -l* listing, but it does show the file permissions, owner and group information, file size, and last modification date.

Exploring find Permission Strings

find lets you search for files that match specific permission settings, but this is one of the most confusing primaries for Unix neophytes. To try to keep you from sinking into the mire, let's just consider the symbolic permission notation that's shared with the *chmod* command (as discussed in "Setting Permissions with chmod" on page 67).

In this model, permissions are specified as a sequence of:

    who op perm

where *who* can be any of *a* (all), *u* (user), *g* (group), or *o* (other, that is, everyone who isn't the user or in the user's group). The *op* value for *find* permission strings can only be =, but in the *chmod* command itself there are other *op* possibilities. The possible values for *perm* are shown in Table 5-4.

Table 5-4. Symbolic permission values for perm

Option	Description
r	Read permission
w	Write permission
x	Execute permission
s	Special set-user-ID-on-execution or set-group-ID-on-execution permission

Let's experiment with the *-perm* primary to get a better sense of how these different permission strings can be specified. To find all files in the */usr/bin* directory whose names start with the letter z and that you have write permission for, use the following:

```
$ find /usr/bin -name "z*" -type f -perm +u=w -print
/usr/bin/zcat
/usr/bin/zcmp
/usr/bin/zdiff
/usr/bin/zegrep
/usr/bin/zfgrep
/usr/bin/zforce
/usr/bin/zgrep
/usr/bin/zip
/usr/bin/zipcloak
/usr/bin/zipdetails
```

```
/usr/bin/zipdetails5.16
/usr/bin/zipdetails5.18
/usr/bin/zipgrep
/usr/bin/zipinfo
/usr/bin/zipnote
/usr/bin/zipsplit
/usr/bin/zless
/usr/bin/zmore
/usr/bin/znew
/usr/bin/zprint
```

What's going on here? We don't have write permission on any of these files:

```
$ ls -l /usr/bin/zcat
-rwxr-xr-x  1 root  wheel  52736 Sep 17 01:07 /usr/bin/zcat
```

The problem is that *find* takes the test literally: it looks for files that have write permission *for their owner*. When I said "that you have write permission for," I was misstating the test, in a way that's quite common for Unix folk. To tighten this *find* search to files for which you actually have write permission, you need to add a -*user* predicate. To make this as general as possible, you can use the $USER variable:

```
$ find /usr -type f -user $USER -perm +u=w
```

Try this on your system. If you see any results, you have a problem with the permissions on the files and directories in the */usr* tree and you need to fix it. Since OS X fixes disk permissions automatically in El Capitan, try just restarting your system—that should fix any issues. Making sure your disk permissions are correct keeps applications from telling you that you don't have permission to save a file when you know darn well you do, and keeps security problems and obscure application behavior from cropping up, too.

Using find to Identify Recently Changed Files

One of the most common uses of *find* is to identify files that have been changed within a certain amount of time. This is obviously quite useful for doing system backups, but it can also help ensure that files shared across multiple machines stay in sync, and it's just generally helpful to be able to list which of your files have been updated recently.

Just like the permissions test, the time tests in *find* behave quite differently depending on whether you specify an exact value, a value prefaced with a -, or a value prefaced with a +. Let's have a look:

```
$ find . -cmin 60 -print
$ find . -cmin -60 -print -type f
./Desktop/LearnUnixOSX
./Desktop/LearnUnixOSX/.ch05.asc.swp
./Desktop/LearnUnixOSX/ch05.asc
```

```
./Library/Application Support/AddressBook
./Library/Application Support/AddressBook/.database.lockN
```

These first two tests are for files that were changed *exactly* 60 minutes ago (no surprise, there aren't any) and files that have changed within the last 60 minutes (specified by adding the - to the time), of which there are five. (Depending on how many files you've worked on in the last hour and your current directory, your output from this command will differ.) One of the matches is the directory *./Library/Application Support/AddressBook*. You can easily remove that from the list by using *-type f* as another primary if all you seek in your results is actual files (perhaps for backing up to a DVD).

What do you think will happen if you specify *-cmin +60*? If you're thinking that this command will give your Mac some level of clairvoyance and tell you which files you're going to work on in the next hour, think again. It'll list out all the files that have been changed more than 60 minutes ago, which for me is, well, quite a few files:

```
$ find . -cmin +60 | wc -l
  442435
```

To narrow that down to just plain files that haven't been changed, again I'll just add the *-type f* primary:

```
$ find . -cmin +60 -type f | wc -l
  369990
```

The difference in these two values indicates that there are over 72,000 directories and other nonstandard files on my system that are being matched in the first test. That's quite a few!

This sort of time test can also be cast across the entire filesystem to see what's been changing. The following command identifies all the files owned by *root* that have been changed in the last 10 minutes:

```
$ sudo find / -cmin -10 -type f -user root -print
.fseventsd/00000000005169e5
/.MobileBackups/Computer/2013-05-06-075950/Volume/Users/taylor/Library/
    Containers/com.fiplab.facetabpro/Data/Library/Preferences/
    com.fiplab.facetabpro.plist
/.MobileBackups/Computer/2013-05-06-075950/Volume/Users/taylor/Library/
    Mail/V2/Mailboxes/Deleted Messages (Intuitive.com (IMAP))
    .mbox/965F1F99-FAB0-4EFE-9635-E04F1D6A4D84/Data/3/9/2/Messages/293416.emlx
/.MobileBackups/Computer/2013-05-06-075950/Volume/Users/taylor/Library/
    Preferences/com.zeobit.MacKeeper.Helper.plist
/.MobileBackups/Computer/2013-05-06-085722/Volume/private/
    var/db/.TimeMachine.Results.plist
...
/private/var/log/asl/StoreData
/private/var/log/DiagnosticMessages/2013.05.06.asl
/private/var/log/DiagnosticMessages/StoreData
/private/var/log/system.log
```

```
/private/var/run/.autoBackup
/private/var/run/utmpx
```

If you'd rather work with time units of hours rather than minutes, just use *-ctime* instead of *-cmin*.

find's Faithful Sidekick: xargs

One primary that you might have immediately noticed is missing is a *-grep* or other primary that lets you look *inside* the files to find which contain specific text. It's missing because *find* doesn't know how to actually *open* any files; it can only test attributes.

If *grep* were smart enough to accept a list of filenames from standard input, the solution to searching the contents of a set of files matched by *find* would be ridiculously easy: *find | grep*. Unfortunately, though, that's not one of *grep*'s many skills. So, you're presented with a dilemma: you can generate a list of files to search, but there's no easy way to actually give that list to *grep* in a way that the program can understand.

The solution is to use *xargs*, a partner program to *find*. The *xargs* program turns a stream of filenames into iterative calls to whatever program is specified, with a subset of the filenames listed on the command line itself. This is confusing, so let me step you through a very simple example.

Let's say that the output of *find* is a list of four files: *one, two, three,* and *four*. Using *xargs*, these files could be given to *grep* two at a time by using:

```
find | xargs grep pattern
```

grep sees this as the following two invocations:

```
grep pattern one two
grep pattern three four
```

Make sense? Let's try it out so you can see how this tremendously powerful *find* partner program helps you become a real power command-line user!

```
$ find /var/log -not -name "*.gz" -type f -size +0 -print
/var/log/asl/2015.05.05.G80.asl
/var/log/asl/2015.05.05.U0.asl
/var/log/asl/2015.05.05.U0.G80.asl
/var/log/asl/2015.05.05.U501.asl
/var/log/asl/2015.05.05.U502.asl
/var/log/asl/2015.05.05.U503.asl
...
/var/log/opendirectoryd.log
/var/log/opendirectoryd.log.0
/var/log/performance/StoreData
/var/log/system.log
/var/log/system.log.0.bz2
/var/log/weekly.out
```

```
/var/log/wifi.log
/var/log/wifi.log.0.bz2
/var/log/zzz.log
```

This is a delightfully complex *find* command, but we can step through it together, so I'm sure it'll make sense to you. First off, a sneak preview: you can reverse the logic of any *find* test by prefacing it with the *-not* primary, so the first test is to find all files whose names *do not* match the pattern **.gz*. That ensures we don't search in compressed (*gzip*'d) files.

Next, *-type f* matches just plain files, and *-size +0* matches files that aren't zero bytes in size. The end result can be summed up as "show me a list of all plain files in this directory that don't have a *.gz* file extension and are greater than zero bytes in size."

If you wanted to scan through all these files for any possible security warnings, your first attempt might be:

```
$ find /var/log -not -name "*gz" -type f -size +0 -print |  ↵
  grep -i warning
```

But that won't work, of course, because it's scanning *the filename list itself* for the pattern, and none of the filenames themselves contain the word "warning." To look inside the files, use *xargs* to pass these filenames to *grep* instead, and since you're going to be looking inside these files, add a *sudo* invocation, too:

```
$ find /var/log -not -name "*gz" -type f -size +0 -print |  ↵
  sudo xargs grep -i warning
/var/log/com.apple.launchd/launchd-shutdown.system.log:19014      com.apple.launchd
    1        com.apple.AppleGraphicsWarning 0         Removed
/var/log/install.log:May  5 21:35:24 Macintosh installd[515]:
    kextcache: Warning: Error 12 rebuilding /System/Library/Caches/
    com.apple.corestorage/EFILoginLocalizations
/var/log/install.log:May  5 21:36:31 Macintosh installd[515]:
    PackageKit: Touched bundle System/Library/CoreServices/
    AppleGraphicsWarning.app
/var/log/system.log:May  6 09:10:41 Daves-MBP sudo[1581]:
    taylor : TTY=ttys001 ; PWD=/Users/taylor ; USER=root ;
    COMMAND=/usr/bin/xargs grep -i warning
```

That's the general pattern that you'll use for searching inside lots of files matched by the *find* command, which might include shell scripts, plain-text files, email message archives, and more.

Because Mac OS users often add spaces to filenames, there are times when the *find | xargs grep* command will fail with all sorts of scary "file not found" error messages. Not to worry, just switch from *-print* to *-print0* and then add a *-0* (zero) flag to *xargs*:

```
$ find $HOME -name "html" -print0 | xargs -0 grep -i ↵
intuitive.com
```

This finds all HTML files in my home directory, and searches through them all for references to the *intuitive.com* domain. Better yet, it's smart enough to handle spaces in the filenames, too.

Further Refinements to find

You've already seen the *-not* primary that lets you switch the logic of a *find* primary, but there are a few more refinements that can help you create highly sophisticated filtering patterns. If you don't mind escaping the character, you can use *!* as a substitute for *-not*, but if you don't use it as *\!* the shell inevitably interprets it and generates some screwy error messages.

You can also group one or more tests with parentheses, which is useful given that you can also specify an *-or* to allow logical OR tests, rather than the default AND test between each primary. This is particularly useful with filename matches. For example, you can find all files that end with either *.txt* or *.htm* with this *find* test:

```
$ find . -type f \( -name "*.txt" -or -name ".htm" \) -print
```

Notice that you must escape the elements of the expression so the shell doesn't try to interpret them and end up messing up your command completely. The easy way? Always quote expressions that include the asterisk, and backslash-escape the parens.

Shining a Light on Spotlight

A key feature included in OS X since the release of Mac OS X Tiger is Spotlight, which indexes and stores metadata for all of the files on your system. This means that if you're looking for a file by name, you can use *locate* or *find*, but if you're looking for all images taken with a Nikon camera, or all PDF files that are more than 10 pages long, then Spotlight and its command-line tools are for you.

Spotlight builds what Apple calls a *metadata database* that has a lot of information about the files on the system, in addition to their filenames. Whenever you conduct a Spotlight search—either through the graphical interface or on the command line—this metadata is searched to reveal information about the files on your system and offer up results. The two Spotlight commands that are analogous to the regular Unix commands *ls* and *find* are logically called *mdls* and *mdfind*.

Let's start with the *mdls* command—you're going to be quite impressed!

What's Metadata?

If you've been using computers for even a short time, you're used to certain data being associated with each file you create. The filename, file size, date of creation—that's all file-related data that's familiar to you. But many files have additional, supplemental information.

For example, Microsoft Word records the name and address of the file creator; Adobe Photoshop remembers what version of Photoshop you last used to edit an image file; and even digital cameras write out additional information for each image saved, including the camera name, the date and time the shot was taken, and often the film speed and lens focal length, all in EXIF format. This supplemental information is known as *metadata*, and it's at the heart of Spotlight.

Listing Spotlight Metadata with mdls

Some of the most interesting types of files to explore with *mdls* are the pictures you take with a digital camera. Here's what the *ls* command has to say about the JPEG file *IMG_1912.jpg*: on my system.

```
$ ls -l IMG_1912.JPG
-rwxrwxrwx  1 taylor  staff  2030063 Oct  2 16:33 IMG_1783.JPG
```

Not particularly useful in terms of what's actually *inside* the file. By comparison, here's what the *mdls* command reports:

```
$ mdls IMG_1912.JPG
_kMDItemOwnerUserID              = 501
kMDItemAcquisitionMake           = "Canon"
kMDItemAcquisitionModel          = "Canon PowerShot S95"
kMDItemAperture                  = 2
kMDItemBitsPerSample             = 32
kMDItemColorSpace                = "RGB"
kMDItemContentCreationDate       = 2015-10-02 22:33:56 +0000
kMDItemContentModificationDate = 2015-10-02 22:33:56 +0000
kMDItemContentType               = "public.jpeg"
kMDItemContentTypeTree           = (
    "public.jpeg",
    "public.image",
    "public.data",
    "public.item",
    "public.content"
)
kMDItemDateAdded                 = 2015-10-04 16:02:28 +0000
kMDItemDescription               = "                              "
kMDItemDisplayName               = "IMG_1783.JPG"
kMDItemEXIFVersion               = "2.3"
```

```
kMDItemExposureMode              = 0
kMDItemExposureTimeSeconds       = 0.07692307692307693
kMDItemFlashOnOff                = 0
kMDItemFNumber                   = 2
kMDItemFocalLength               = 6
kMDItemFSContentChangeDate       = 2015-10-02 22:33:56 +0000
kMDItemFSCreationDate            = 2015-10-02 22:33:56 +0000
kMDItemFSCreatorCode             = ""
kMDItemFSFinderFlags             = 0
kMDItemFSHasCustomIcon           = (null)
kMDItemFSInvisible               = 0
kMDItemFSIsExtensionHidden       = 0
kMDItemFSIsStationery            = (null)
kMDItemFSLabel                   = 0
kMDItemFSName                    = "IMG_1783.JPG"
kMDItemFSNodeCount               = (null)
kMDItemFSOwnerGroupID            = 20
kMDItemFSOwnerUserID             = 501
kMDItemFSSize                    = 2030063
kMDItemFSTypeCode                = ""
kMDItemHasAlphaChannel           = 0
kMDItemISOSpeed                  = 1600
kMDItemKind                      = "JPEG image"
kMDItemLogicalSize               = 2030063
kMDItemOrientation               = 0
kMDItemPhysicalSize              = 2031616
kMDItemPixelCount                = 9980928
kMDItemPixelHeight               = 2736
kMDItemPixelWidth                = 3648
kMDItemProfileName               = "sRGB IEC61966-2.1"
kMDItemRedEyeOnOff               = 0
kMDItemResolutionHeightDPI       = 180
kMDItemResolutionWidthDPI        = 180
kMDItemWhiteBalance              = 0
```

Quite a bit more useful information, thanks to Spotlight and its smart file parsing modules! Note that *mdls* offers the following details:

- The camera used (Canon PowerShot S95), as noted by kMDItemAcquisitionMo del
- The dimensions of the image (3648 x 2736), as noted by the kMDItem-PixelWidth and kMDItemPixelHeight items, respectively
- The resolution of the image (180 DPI), as noted by kMDItemResolution HeightDPI and kMDItemResolutionWidthDPI
- Various other digital photo data, including exposure time (kMDItemExposureTime Seconds), focal length of the lens (kMDItemFocalLength), etc.

Here's another example of *mdls* output, this time with a PDF file:

```
$ mdls HXR-MC50U\ Manual.pdf
kMDItemAuthors                 = (
    "Sony Corporation"
)
kMDItemContentCreationDate     = 2015-07-15 15:52:50 +0000
kMDItemContentModificationDate = 2015-07-15 15:52:50 +0000
kMDItemContentType             = "com.adobe.pdf"
kMDItemContentTypeTree         = (
    "com.adobe.pdf",
    "public.data",
    "public.item",
    "public.composite-content",
    "public.content"
)
kMDItemDateAdded               = 2015-07-15 16:10:30 +0000
kMDItemDisplayName             = "HXR-MC50U Manual.pdf"
kMDItemEncodingApplications    = (
    "Mac OS X 10.6.8 Quartz PDFContext"
)
kMDItemFSContentChangeDate      = 2015-07-15 15:52:50 +0000
kMDItemFSCreationDate           = 2015-07-15 15:52:50 +0000
kMDItemFSCreatorCode            = ""
kMDItemFSFinderFlags            = 0
kMDItemFSHasCustomIcon          = (null)
kMDItemFSInvisible              = 0
kMDItemFSIsExtensionHidden      = 0
kMDItemFSIsStationery           = (null)
kMDItemFSLabel                  = 0
kMDItemFSName                   = "HXR-MC50U Manual.pdf"
kMDItemFSNodeCount              = (null)
kMDItemFSOwnerGroupID           = 20
kMDItemFSOwnerUserID            = 501
kMDItemFSSize                   = 9732347
kMDItemFSTypeCode               = ""
kMDItemKind                     = "Portable Document Format (PDF)"
kMDItemLogicalSize              = 9732347
kMDItemNumberOfPages            = 139
kMDItemPageHeight               = 515.906
kMDItemPageWidth                = 362.835
kMDItemPhysicalSize             = 9736192
kMDItemSecurityMethod           = "None"
kMDItemTitle                    = "HXR-MC50U/MC50N"
kMDItemVersion                  = "1.4"
```

For a PDF document, the information includes the number of pages (as noted with kMDItemNumberOfPages; this document has 139), the application used to encode the PDF (Mac OS X 10.6.8 Quartz PDFContext, as noted by kMDItemEncodingApplications), and the date and time that the PDF file was created (2015-07-15 15:52:50, as noted by kMDItemFSCreationDate).

Let's peek at one more file type before we explore what you can actually *do* with the Spotlight data, shall we? This time, it's an MP3 file from my iTunes library:

```
$ mdls "1-12 Can We Still Be Friends.mp3"
_kTimeMachineIsCreationMarker   = 1
kMDItemAlbum                    = "The Very Best Of
Todd Rundgren"
kMDItemAlternateNames           = (
    "/Users/taylor/Music/iTunes/iTunes Media/Music/Todd Rundgren/The Very Best ↵
    Of Todd Rundgren/1-12 Can We Still Be Friends.mp3"
)
kMDItemAudioBitRate             = 227000
kMDItemAudioChannelCount        = 2
kMDItemAudioSampleRate          = 44100
kMDItemAudioTrackNumber         = 12
kMDItemAuthors                  = (
    "Todd Rundgren"
)
kMDItemComment                  = "reference libFLAC 1.2.1 20070917"
kMDItemContentCreationDate      = 2015-06-04 22:26:40 +0000
kMDItemContentModificationDate  = 2015-06-04 22:26:50 +0000
kMDItemContentType              = "public.mp3"
kMDItemContentTypeTree          = (
    "public.mp3",
    "public.audio",
    "public.audiovisual-content",
    "public.data",
    "public.item",
    "public.content"
)
kMDItemDateAdded                = 2015-06-19 13:06:55 +0000
kMDItemDisplayName              = "Can We Still Be Friends"
kMDItemDurationSeconds          = 218.4881632653061
kMDItemFSContentChangeDate      = 2015-06-04 22:26:50 +0000
kMDItemFSCreationDate           = 2015-06-04 22:26:40 +0000
kMDItemFSCreatorCode            = ""
kMDItemFSFinderFlags            = 0
kMDItemFSHasCustomIcon          = (null)
kMDItemFSInvisible              = 0
kMDItemFSIsExtensionHidden      = 0
kMDItemFSIsStationery           = (null)
kMDItemFSLabel                  = 0
kMDItemFSName                   = "1-12 Can We Still Be Friends.mp3"
kMDItemFSNodeCount              = (null)
kMDItemFSOwnerGroupID           = 20
kMDItemFSOwnerUserID            = 501
kMDItemFSSize                   = 6323093
kMDItemFSTypeCode               = ""
kMDItemKind                     = "MP3 audio"
kMDItemLogicalSize              = 6323093
kMDItemMediaTypes               = (
    Sound
```

```
)
kMDItemMusicalGenre            = "(17)"
kMDItemPhysicalSize            = 6324224
kMDItemRecordingYear           = 1997
kMDItemTitle                   = "Can We Still Be Friends"
kMDItemTotalBitRate            = 227000
```

Encoded in each audio file is the artist (kMDItemAuthors), album (kMDItemAlbum), song name (kMDItemTitle), genre (kMDItemMusicalGenre), length of track (kMDItem DurationSeconds), and much more, all accessible thanks to Spotlight and *mdls*.

Finding Files with mdfind

Knowing that there's so much valuable and interesting information available through Spotlight, how do you actually do something useful with it? The answer is by using the *mdfind* command. However, while *find* has weird syntax, *mdfind*'s is even weirder and more unfriendly.

The *mdfind* command matches files in the filesystem that meet a specific criterion or set of criteria, specified as:

```
"metadata_field_name == 'pattern'"
```

For example, to find all photographs taken with a Nikon camera, you'd use the following:

```
$ mdfind "kMDItemAcquisitionModel == 'NIKON*'" | head
/Users/taylor/Library/Mail/V3/IMAP-d1taylor@imap.gmail.com/[Gmail].mbox/
Bin.mbox/0CE78AA8-AE4A-4E62-96D9-D8507B834E99/Data/8/8/Attachments/88376/2
/ValorieCurry.jpg
/Users/taylor/Library/Mail/V3/IMAP-d1taylor@imap.gmail.com/[Gmail].mbox/
Bin.mbox/0CE78AA8-AE4A-4E62-96D9-D8507B834E99/Data/6/8/Attachments/86888/4
/TaraSummers_82873_6.jpg
/Users/taylor/Library/Mail/V3/IMAP-d1taylor@imap.gmail.com/[Gmail].mbox/
Bin.mbox/0CE78AA8-AE4A-4E62-96D9-D8507B834E99/Data/4/8/Attachments/84006/4
/TaraSummers_82873_6 (1).jpg
/Users/taylor/Library/Mail/V3/IMAP-d1taylor@imap.gmail.com/[Gmail].mbox/
All Mail.mbox/0CE78AA8-AE4A-4E62-96D9-D8507B834E99/Data/5/8/Attachments/85629
/1.2/Women of Below Her Mouth.jpg
/Users/taylor/Pictures/Taylor-Web (photos from Peter)/Taylor-Web-6410.jpg
/Users/taylor/Pictures/Taylor-Web (photos from Peter)/Taylor-Web-6406.jpg
/Users/taylor/Pictures/Taylor-Web (photos from Peter)/Taylor-Web-6401.jpg
/Users/taylor/Pictures/Taylor-Web (photos from Peter)/Taylor-Web-6392.jpg
/Users/taylor/Pictures/Taylor-Web (photos from Peter)/Taylor-Web-6391.jpg
/Users/taylor/Pictures/Taylor-Web (photos from Peter)/Taylor-Web-6385.jpg
```

Want to constrain the search to a specific subdirectory? You might be tempted to specify this directly as you would in *find*, but that's not how it's done. Instead, you need to use a flag called *-onlyin*, followed by a directory name. To find all the songs in your Jazz collection, use:

```
$ mdfind -onlyin ~/Music "kMDItemMusicalGenre == 'Jazz'"
```

You can also specify that you want a specific word anywhere in the metadata info by specifying just that word:

```
$ mdfind -onlyin ~ Jazz | head
/Users/taylor/Library/Mail/V3/Mailboxes/Deleted Messages (taylor@intuitive.com)
.mbox/0CE78AA8-AE4A-4E62-96D9-D8507B834E99/Data/1/5/2/Messages/251740.emlx
/Users/taylor/Library/Mail/V3/Mailboxes/Deleted Messages (taylor@intuitive.com)
.mbox/0CE78AA8-AE4A-4E62-96D9-D8507B834E99/Data/1/5/2/Messages/251684.emlx
/Users/taylor/Library/Containers/com.apple.Notes/Data/Library/CoreData/
ExternalRecords/C4B83507-DA59-4500-8793-91E7369D1EFD/ICNote/_records/0
/p10.notesexternalrecord
/Users/taylor/Library/CoreData/ExternalRecords/4AA0727E-5B99-4012-A8DD-
29D8F90E7E80/IMAPNote/_records/0/p29.notesexternalrecord
/Users/taylor/Library/Mail/V3/IMAP-d1taylor@imap.gmail.com/[Gmail].mbox/
All Mail.mbox/0CE78AA8-AE4A-4E62-96D9-D8507B834E99/Data/5/8/Messages/85442.emlx
/Users/taylor/Library/Mail/V3/IMAP-d1taylor@imap.gmail.com/[Gmail].mbox/
All Mail.mbox/0CE78AA8-AE4A-4E62-96D9-D8507B834E99/Data/5/8/Messages/85444.emlx
/Users/taylor/Library/Mail/V3/IMAP-d1taylor@imap.gmail.com/[Gmail].mbox/
All Mail.mbox/0CE78AA8-AE4A-4E62-96D9-D8507B834E99/Data/5/8/Messages/85682.emlx
/Users/taylor/Library/Mail/V3/IMAP-d1taylor@imap.gmail.com/[Gmail].mbox/
Spam.mbox/0CE78AA8-AE4A-4E62-96D9-D8507B834E99/Data/4/8/Messages/84599.emlx
/Users/taylor/Library/Mail/V3/IMAP-d1taylor@imap.gmail.com/[Gmail].mbox/
Spam.mbox/0CE78AA8-AE4A-4E62-96D9-D8507B834E99/Data/4/8/Messages/84742.emlx
/Users/taylor/Library/Mail/V3/IMAP-d1taylor@imap.gmail.com/[Gmail].mbox/
Bin.mbox/0CE78AA8-AE4A-4E62-96D9-D8507B834E99/Data/8/8/Messages/88241.emlx
```

This output is quite interesting because it matches not only files where the word "Jazz" is part of the Spotlight metadata (as in the iTunes files), but also files that have "Jazz" in their name (the BlogWorld Expo document *jazz-performances.doc*), and even a plain-text file where the word "Jazz" appears in the text itself (*art_dolls.txt*). Pretty nifty, eh?

Making Spotlight Useful

Before leaving Spotlight, and certainly before we give up and assume that it's only useful on the command line, let's have a look at a couple of simple Unix commands that can extract useful information from the *mdls* information stream.

Curious about the size in pixels of your JPEG files? You can quickly ascertain their height and width by using *grep*:

```
$ mdls IMG_1912.JPG | grep -E '(PixelHeight|PixelWidth)'
kMDItemPixelHeight      = 4752
kMDItemPixelWidth       = 3168
```

You can identify the duration of an audio file without loading it into iTunes or any other audio player by using:

```
$ mdls "06 Elise affair.mp3" | grep Duration
kMDItemDurationSeconds          = 280.9774
```

You can also use *find* and *xargs* to identify files by name and then extract specific characteristics:

```
$ find . -name "*jpg" -print0 | xargs -0 mdls | grep FocalLength
```

Or, you can actually use *mdfind* in the same manner (it does have a *-0* option that makes it possible to match filenames that have spaces without things breaking):

```
$ mdfind -0 "kMDItemFocalLength == '35'" | xargs -0 mdls | ↵
  grep -E '(PixelHeight|PixelWidth|DisplayName)'
kMDItemDisplayName          = "Little-Hand.jpg"
kMDItemPixelHeight          = 532
kMDItemPixelWidth           = 800
kMDItemDisplayName          = "Peanut.jpg"
kMDItemPixelHeight          = 531
kMDItemPixelWidth           = 800
```

This last search matches all pictures on the entire system with a focal length of 35 (meaning, they were taken with a 35 mm lens), and then displays the name, height, and width of each of the images it finds.

These commands really beg for a simple shell script or two, where you could actually parse the output and reformat it as desired. We'll talk about writing shell scripts a bit later in the book, but here's a sneak preview of what such a script could do:

```
$ photosize Peanut.jpg
800x531 at 300DPI
```

The Spotlight commands accessible from the command line still haven't been refined quite yet. You can get started with the information shown here, but don't be surprised if future revisions turn the Spotlight commands into really powerful tools you can use for all sorts of tasks.

## CHAPTER 6

Redirecting I/O

Many Unix programs read input (such as from a file) and write output in a standard way that lets them work with one another. This exchange of information is commonly known in Unix circles as *I/O* (pronounced "eye-oh," which is short for input/output). In this chapter, we discuss some of these tools and learn how to connect programs and files in new and powerful ways.

This chapter generally *doesn't* apply to programs, such as the *vi* editor, that take control of your entire Terminal window. (*less* does work in this way, however.) It also doesn't apply to graphical programs that open their own windows on your screen, such as iTunes or Safari. On the other hand, the vast majority of Unix commands that you use on the command line are line-oriented, and they're exactly why I/O redirection is included in OS X's Unix.

The difference between "screen-oriented" and "line-oriented" is a bit tricky to figure out when you're just starting. Think of it this way: if you can use arrow keys to move up and down, it's a screen-oriented program. The *vi* editor is the classic example of a screen-oriented program. If the input or output is all shown line by line, as in the *ls* command's output, then it's a line-oriented command. Almost all Unix commands are line-oriented, as you'll see in this chapter.

Standard Input and Standard Output

What happens if you don't give a filename argument in a command line? Most programs take their input from your keyboard instead (after you press Return to start the program running, that is). The keyboard you use to type commands into the Terminal is what's called the program's *standard input*. As soon as you hit that Return key, you're providing the shell with input.

As a program runs, the results are usually displayed on your Terminal screen. What you see displayed in the Terminal is the program's *standard output*. So, by default, each of these programs takes its information from the standard input and sends the results to the standard output. It turns out that where programs read their information from and where their output goes to can both be changed, depending on what you type on the command line. In Unix terminology, this is called *I/O redirection*.

If a program writes to its standard output (normally the screen), you can make it write to a file instead by using the greater-than symbol (>) operator, followed by the name of the file to which the output should be saved. If you'd prefer connecting the output of one program to the input of another—as you saw in "Pipes and Filters" on page 141 when the output of *find* was given to the *wc* (word count) program to count the total number of output lines rather than just listing them all—you can build a pipe. Command pipes are specified by using a pipe operator (|), which connects the standard output of one program to the standard input of the next program in the pipeline. We'll look at this in more detail shortly.

If a program doesn't normally read from files, but reads from its standard input, you can direct it to read from a file instead by using the less-than symbol (<) operator, followed by the name of the file.

Input/output redirection is one of the most powerful and flexible features of the Unix system and a big reason why power users still prefer its command-line interface to a graphical interface.

The *tr* (character translator) program allows us to demonstrate input redirection, because it reads from standard input, normally the keyboard. Here's how to use the input redirection operator to convert all vowels to x's in the *todo* file:

```
$ cat todo
1. Wake up
2. Look in mirror
3. Sigh
4. Go back to bed.
$ tr '[aeiou]' '[xxxxx]' < todo
1. Wxkx xp
2. Lxxk xn mxrrxr
3. Sxgh
4. Gx bxck tx bxd.
```

Can you see what's happened here? The *cat* command shows what's in the file, a simple four-step to-do list. The second command, *tr*, replaces every vowel in the input file (*todo*, which replaced standard input because of the < notation) with the corresponding character in the second set (all x's), displaying the output on the standard output (the Terminal window).

Putting Text in a File

Instead of always letting a program's output come to the screen, you can redirect output to a file. This is useful when you'd like to save program output or when you put files together to make a bigger file.

cat

cat, which is short for "concatenate," reads files and outputs their contents one after another, without stopping. To display files on the standard output (your screen), use:

```
cat file(s)
```

For example, let's display the contents of the file */etc/bashrc*. This system file is the global login file for the *bash* shell:

```
$ cat /etc/bashrc
# System-wide .bashrc file for interactive bash(1) shells.
if [ -z "$PS1" ]; then
   return
fi

PS1='\h:\W \u\$ '
# Make bash check its window size after a process completes
shopt -s checkwinsize

[ -r "/etc/bashrc_$TERM_PROGRAM" ] && . "/etc/bashrc_$TERM_PROGRAM"
```

With *cat*, you cannot go back to view the previous screens, as you can when you use a pager program such as *less* (unless you're using a Terminal window with a sufficiently large scrollback buffer, that is). Because of this, *cat* is mainly used with redirection, as we'll see in a moment.

If you enter *cat* without a filename, it just sits there without a system prompt, leaving you to wonder what's happening. Nothing's broken, however; *cat* simply reads from the keyboard (as we mentioned earlier) until the end-of-file character is sent, and echoes each line of what you type to standard output (normally your screen). You can exit by pressing Control-D, which ends the input file for the program.

When you add > *filename* to the end of a command line, the program's output is diverted from the standard output to a file. The > symbol is called the *output redirection operator*.

For example, let's use *cat* with the output redirection operator. The file contents that you'd normally see on the screen (from the standard output) are diverted into another file, which we'll then read by using *cat* again, this time without any redirection:

```
$ cat /etc/bashrc > mybashrc
$ cat mybashrc
# System-wide .bashrc file for interactive bash(1) shells.
```

```
if [ -z "$PS1" ]; then
    return
fi

PS1='\h:\W \u\$ '
# Make bash check its window size after a process completes
shopt -s checkwinsize

[ -r "/etc/bashrc_$TERM_PROGRAM" ] && . "/etc/bashrc_$TERM_PROGRAM"
```

Don't Step on Your Files!

When you use the > operator, be careful not to accidentally overwrite a file's contents. Your system may let you redirect output to an existing file. If so, the old file's contents will be lost forever (or, in Unix lingo, "clobbered"). Be careful not to overwrite a much-needed file!

Many shells can protect you from this risk. In *bash* (the default shell for OS X), use the command *set noclobber*. Enter the command at a shell prompt to have it take effect for the current session, or put it in your shell's *~/.profile* file for it to take effect for each new session you start. After that, the shell won't allow you to redirect onto an existing file and overwrite its contents.

Note that this doesn't protect against overwriting by Unix programs such as *cp*; it works only with the > redirection operator. For more protection, you can set Unix file access permissions (see "Setting Permissions with chmod" on page 67).

An earlier example showed how *cat /etc/bashrc* displays the file */etc/bashrc* on-screen. The example here adds the > operator, so the output of *cat* goes to a file called *mybashrc* in the working directory. Displaying the *mybashrc* file shows that its contents are the same as the file */etc/bashrc* (in this simple case, the effect is the same as using the copy command *cp /etc/bashrc mybashrc*).

You can use the > redirection operator with any program that sends text to its standard output—not just with *cat*. For example:

```
$ who > users
$ date > today
$ ls
mylogin    today    users    ...
```

Here, we've sent the output of *who* to a file called *users*, and the output of *date* to the file named *today*. Listing the directory shows the two new files. Let's look at the output from the *who* and *date* programs by reading these two files with *cat*:

```
$ cat users
taylor    console  Oct  1 10:03
taylor    ttys000  Oct  5 12:26
```

```
$ cat today
Mon Oct  5 12:29:37 MDT 2015
```

You can also use the *cat* program and the > operator to make a small text file. I told you earlier to type Control-D if you accidentally enter *cat* without a filename, because in this case, the *cat* program takes whatever you type on the keyboard as input.

That means the following command takes input from the keyboard and redirects it to a file:

```
cat > filename
```

Try the following example:

```
$ cat > new-todo
Finish report by noon
Lunch with Ashley at WF
Swim at 5:30
^D
$
```

cat takes the text that you typed as input (in this example, the three lines that begin with Finish, Lunch, and Swim), and the > operator redirects it to a file called *new-todo*. Type Control-D *once*, on a new line by itself, to signal the end of the text. You should get a shell prompt.

You can also create a bigger file from smaller files with the *cat* command and the > operator. This form creates a file *newfile*, consisting of *file1* followed by *file2*:

```
cat file1 file2 > newfile
```

This highlights that the name *cat* comes from *concatenate*, meaning, "put a bunch of things together." Here's what I mean:

```
$ cat today todo > diary
$ cat diary
Mon Oct  5 12:29:37 MDT 2015
1. Wake up
2. Look in mirror
3. Sigh
4. Go back to bed.
```

You shouldn't use redirection to add a file to itself. For example, you might hope that the following command would merge today's to-do list with tomorrow's, but this example isn't going to give you what you expect:

```
$ cat todo todo.tomorrow > todo.tomorrow
```

It works, but it will run for all eternity because it keeps copying the file over itself. If you cancel it with Control-C and use *ls* to examine the file, you'll see that it's gotten quite large:

```
^C
$ ls -sk todo*
    4 todo
61436 todo.tomorrow
```

ls -sk shows the size in kilobytes, so it's grown to about 61 megabytes! The right way to do this is to either use a temporary file (as you'll see in a later example) or simply use a text editor program.

You can add more text to the *end* of an existing file, instead of replacing its contents, by using the >> (append redirection) operator. Use it as you would the > (output redirection) operator. So, the following appends the contents of *file2* to the end of *file1*:

```
cat file2 >> file1
```

This doesn't affect the contents of *file2* since it is being read from, not written to.

For example, let's append the contents of the file *users* and the current date and time to the file *diary*. Here's what it looks like:

```
$ cat users >> diary
$ date >> diary
$ cat diary
Mon Oct  5 12:29:37 MDT 2015
1. Wake up
2. Look in mirror
3. Sigh
4. Go back to bed.
taylor   console  Oct  1 10:03
taylor   ttys000  Oct  5 12:26
Mon Oct  5 12:29:37 MDT 2015
```

Unix doesn't have a redirection operator that adds text to the beginning of a file, but you can accomplish the same thing by renaming the old file, then rebuilding the contents of the file as needed. For example, maybe you'd like each day's entry to go at the beginning of your *diary* file. To achieve this, simply rename *diary* to something like *older.diary*, make a new *diary* file with today's entries, then append *older.diary* (with its old contents) to the new *diary*. For example:

```
$ mv diary older.diary
$ date > diary
$ cat users >> diary
```

```
$ cat older.diary >> diary
$ rm older.diary
```

This example could be shortened by combining the two *cat* commands into one, giving both filenames as arguments to a single *cat* command. That wouldn't work, though, if you were making a real diary with a command other than *cat users*.

Pipes and Filters

We've seen how to redirect input from a file and output to a file. You can also connect two programs *together* so the output from one program becomes the input of the next, without ever being written to disk. Two or more programs connected in this way form a *pipe*. To make a pipe, place a vertical bar (|) on the command line between the two commands.

When a pipe is set up between two commands, the standard output of the command to the left of the pipe symbol becomes the standard input of the command to the right of the pipe symbol. Any two commands can form a pipe, as long as the first program writes to standard output and the second program reads from standard input. For example:

```
$ ls -l $HOME | colrm 1 30
 170 Sep 27 19:24 Applications/
 510 Oct  5 12:05 Desktop/
2788 Sep 24 11:07 Documents/
 612 Oct  5 11:43 Downloads/
 612 Oct  2 18:27 Dropbox/
2074 Oct  5 12:19 Library/
 646 Jun 19 12:30 Movies/
 238 Sep 20 10:54 Music/
1530 Oct  4 20:40 Pictures/
2516 Sep 22 20:15 Presentations/
 170 Jun 19 01:06 Public/
 136 Jun 20 16:35 VirtualBox VMs/
 578 Oct 13  2014 bin/
  29 Oct  5 12:31 diary
  68 Oct  3 16:45 images/
 265 Oct  5 12:28 mybashrc
  59 Oct  5 12:30 new-todo
 760 Oct  3 23:40 sample
 179 Oct  3 23:46 shells
  29 Oct  5 12:29 today
  64 Oct  5 12:29 users
```

This example combines *ls -l* with the *colrm* (column remove) command to give you a listing that just includes file size, modification date, and name.

You could take this example one step further and redirect its output to a file, as in:

```
$ ls -l $HOME | colrm 1 30 > homedirlist.txt
```

That command line starts by listing the files, uses *colrm* to strip out the extraneous information that *ls -l* returns, and then redirects the remaining information into a new file, named *homedirlist.txt*.

You just can't do that in the Finder!

When a program takes its input from another program, performs some operation on that input, and writes the result to the standard output (or pipes it to yet another program), it is referred to as a *filter*. A common use of filters is to modify output. Just as a common filter culls unwanted items, Unix filters can restructure output so you get just what you need.

Most Unix programs can be used to form pipes. Some programs that are commonly used as filters are described in the next sections. (Note that these programs aren't used only as filters or parts of pipes, though; they're also useful in their own right.)

wc

The *wc* program is one of the most useful pipe programs, believe it or not. By default, the program counts characters, words, and lines in the input file or standard input, but you can constrain the output to report just characters (*-c*), words (*-w*), or lines (*-l*). Counting lines turns out to be wonderfully useful.

A classic example is identifying how many "core" files are in the filesystem.

Core files are identified with the suffix *.core;* they're crashed program debugging datafiles and can be deleted to free up disk space as needed.

This is done with a call to *find* with the output piped to *wc*:

```
$ sudo find / -name "*.core" -print | wc -l
13
```

sudo helps sidestep any permissions problems here and will probably prompt you for the administrative password when used.

A more common use of *find* and *wc* together is to count larger output streams. For example, are you wondering how many directories you have within your *Documents* directory? You might be surprised:

```
$ find ~/Documents -type d -print | wc -l
    1002
```

You can see how having a single number displayed is far superior to having all 1,002 directory names stream past!

tr

Another simple and helpful program for command pipes is *tr*, the translator utility. The most common use for this command is to replace all occurrences of one character with another character. Here's how you would replace all occurrences of *x* with *y*:

```
tr "x" "y"
```

More usefully, *tr* can also work with sets of characters (you can either list them all in a range or specify a named range like *lower* or *alpha*), so it's an easy way to turn all lowercase text into uppercase:

```
tr "[:lower:]" "[:upper:]" < file1
```

For example:

```
$ tr "[:lower:]" "[:upper:]" < todo
1. WAKE UP
2. LOOK IN MIRROR
3. SIGH
4. GO BACK TO BED.
```

The *tr* command has a number of different options for power users, including *-c* to invert the specified pattern (that is, if you specify *tr -c "abc"*, the program outputs anything other than a, b, or c) and *-d* to delete any characters from the first pattern specified.

To remove all vowels from the input, you could use:

```
$ tr -d "[aeiou]" < todo
1. Wk p
2. Lk n mrrr
3. Sgh
4. G bck t bd.
```

The *tr* command can be quite useful in other situations, too. Wondering how many words appear in a large text file? *tr* can figure this out with a little help from the *-s* flag, which tells it to output only one occurrence of a character if more than one is found:

```
$ tr -cs "[:alpha:]" "\n" < alice.txt | wc -l
29061
```

Here, we can see that Lewis Carroll's *Alice's Adventures in Wonderland* contains just over 29,000 words.

You can download this text for yourself at *http://intuitive.com/ wicked/scripts/alice.txt.gz.*

Like the *wc* command, *tr* may not seem too useful by itself, but when you start building up more complex pipes, you'll be surprised by how frequently it's useful to translate case and fix similar problems.

grep

As you learned in the previous chapter, *grep* searches the contents of files for lines that contain a certain pattern. The syntax is:

```
grep "pattern" file(s)
```

Most of the earlier discussion, however, focused on how *grep* can help you search through files to find lines that match a specified pattern. In fact, *grep* is a tremendously useful command for pipes, too, because it can help you easily weed out the few lines you care about from hundreds or thousands of lines of information.

As an example, let's use the *mdfind* command to identify files on the system that reference the word "ipod" (*mdfind*, a part of Spotlight, is discussed in "Shining a Light on Spotlight" on page 126). The default command with *wc* reveals that there are 1,310 matches:

```
$ mdfind ipod | wc -l
    1310
```

It turns out that many of these are actually related to the scripting Automator utility and other library files. They're easily identified by their *Library* directory location, however, so *grep*, with its useful -v option (which returns everything but lines that match this pattern), helps us identify how many files *aren't* in the *Library* subdirectory:

```
$ mdfind ipod | grep -v "Library" | wc -l
    204
```

Of those 204, how many are within my home directory?

```
$ mdfind ipod | grep -v "Library" | grep "/taylor/" | wc -l
    191
```

Notice here that you can build pipes that are 2, 3, 4, or even 10 or 20 commands long. Unix has no limit on how complex your pipes can be, and I commonly work with pipes that are six or seven commands long.

head and tail

When you have output of hundreds or thousands of lines, being able to peek in and see the first few or last few lines is critically important. Those two tasks are enabled by the helpful *head* and *tail* commands. With both commands, the default action is to show 10 lines (the first 10 for *head*, and the last 10 for *tail*). You can change this by specifying *n*, where *n* is the desired number of lines. To see just the first three lines, use *head -3*, and to see the last 15, use *tail -15*.

For example, we can see that the last 15 words of *Alice's Adventures in Wonderland* are:

```
$ tr -cs "[:alpha:]" "\n" < alice.txt | tail -15
in
all
their
simple
joys
remembering
her
own
child
life
and
the
happy
summer
days
```

In addition to using *head* and *tail* to view the beginning or end of files, with a little bit of fancy footwork, you can use them to view any range of lines in a file. Want to see lines 250–255? You could use:

```
$ head -255 alice.txt | tail -5
it so very much out of the way to hear the Rabbit say to itself,
'Oh dear! Oh dear! I shall be late!' (when she thought it over
afterwards, it occurred to her that she ought to have wondered at
this, but at the time it all seemed quite natural); but when the
Rabbit actually took a watch out of its waistcoat-pocket, and looked
```

This could also be accomplished by using other Unix commands, and that's part of the power of Unix: there's usually more than one way to solve a problem at the command line.

sort

The *sort* program arranges lines of text alphabetically or numerically. The following example sorts the lines in the *food* file alphabetically. *sort* doesn't modify the file itself; it just reads the file and displays the result on standard output (in this case, the Terminal):

```
$ sort food
Afghani Cuisine
Bangkok Wok
Big Apple Deli
Isle of Java
Mandalay
Sushi and Sashimi
Sweet Tooth
Tio Pepe's Peppers
```

By default, *sort* arranges lines of text alphabetically. Many options control the sorting, and Table 6-1 lists some of them.

Table 6-1. Some sort options

Option	Description
-n	Sort numerically (for example, 10 sorts after 2); ignore blanks and tabs.
-r	Reverse the sorting order.
-f	Sort upper- and lowercase together.
-k x	Sort by the key at position *x*.

Don't forget that more than two commands may be linked together with a pipe. Taking a previous pipe example using *grep*, you can further sort the files modified in January by order of size. The following pipe uses the commands *ls*, *grep*, and *sort*:

```
$ ls -l | grep "Jan" | sort -n -k 5
drwx------   2 taylor taylor  264 Jan 13 10:02 Music/
drwx------   4 taylor taylor  264 Jan 29 22:33 Movies/
drwxr-xr-x   3 taylor taylor  264 Jan 24 21:24 Public/
drwx------  95 taylor taylor 3186 Jan 29 22:44 Pictures/
```

Both *grep* and *sort* are used here as filters to modify the output of the *ls -l* command. This pipe sorts all files in your working directory modified in January by order of size, and prints them to the Terminal screen. The *sort* option *-n* forces a numeric (rather than alphabetic) sort, and *-k 5* uses the fifth field as the sort key. So, the output of *ls*, filtered by *grep*, is sorted by the file size (this is the fifth column, starting with 264).

sort is also a powerful tool for identifying the extremes of a list. A common use is to identify the largest files on the system, which can be done by using *find* and *xargs* to generate a list of all files, one per line, including their size in 512-byte blocks, then feeding that to *sort -rn* (reverse, numeric) and looking at the top few:

```
$ find . -type f -print0 | xargs -0 ls -s1 | sort -rn | head
29015568 ./Movies/iMovie Events.localized/Nest Thermo Upgrade (raw)/
clip-2015-09-28 10;49;07.mov
```

```
14435072 ./VirtualBox VMs/Solaris 11/sol-11_2-vbox-disk1.vmdk
12043048 ./Movies/iMovie Events.localized/New Event 9-4-15 - Day 3/
clip-2015-09-04 10;15;15.mov
11295976 ./Movies/Untitled.fcpbundle/galileo/Transcoded Media/High Quality
Media/2014-02-06 10_32_44 (id).mov
8673216 ./Movies/DVD Images/MOMO and the Thieves of Time DVD.img
8305664 ./Documents/Virtual Machines.localized/Windows 10 x64.vmwarevm/Virtual
Disk-s020.vmdk
8305664 ./Documents/Virtual Machines.localized/Windows 10 x64.vmwarevm/Virtual
Disk-s018.vmdk
8305664 ./Documents/Virtual Machines.localized/Windows 10 x64.vmwarevm/Virtual
Disk-s017.vmdk
8305536 ./Documents/Virtual Machines.localized/Windows 10 x64.vmwarevm/Virtual
Disk-s021.vmdk
6340608 ./Documents/Virtual Machines.localized/Windows 10 x64.vmwarevm/Windows
8 x64-25a2bb34.vmem
```

Coupled with the power of *find*, you should be able to see how you can identify not only the largest files, but also the largest files owned by a particular user (hint: use *find -user username* to match all files owned by that user).

uniq

Another command that's quite useful in pipes is the oddly named *uniq* (which would be easier to remember if it were spelled correctly: *unique*). Give *uniq* a stream of input, and it silently eliminates consecutive duplicate lines. Add the *-c* flag, and *uniq* not only removes duplicate lines, but also lists a count of how frequently each line occurs.

If you're thinking that *sort* and *uniq* are a good pair, you're absolutely correct! For example, figuring out how many unique words occur in the book *Alice's Adventures in Wonderland* is a simple task:

```
$ tr -cs "[:alpha:]" "\n" < alice.txt | uniq | wc -l
    29033
```

Or is it? That's not correct, because in this situation, *uniq* needs to have the input sorted. Add that step and the number changes dramatically:

```
$ tr -cs "[:alpha:]" "\n" < alice.txt | sort | uniq | wc -l
    3285
```

Further, we should also ensure that all the letters are lowercase, so that "Hello" and "hello," for example, are counted as one word, not two. This can be done by using our friend *tr* to translate everything to lowercase:

```
$ tr -cs "[:alpha:]" "\n" < alice.txt | tr "[A-Z]" "[a-z]" | sort | uniq | wc -l
    2900
```

So now you know—the entire novel is written using only 2,900 different words.

Piping Output to a Pager

The *less* program, which we met in Chapter 4, can also be used as a filter. A long output normally zips by you on the screen, but if you run text through *less*, the display stops after each page or screen of text (that's why such programs are called *pagers*: they let you see the output page by page).

Let's assume that you have a long directory listing. (If you want to try this example and need a directory with lots of files, use *cd* first to change to a system directory such as */bin* or */usr/bin*.) To make it easier to read the sorted listing, pipe the output through *less*:

```
$ cd /bin
$ ls -l | sort -nk 5 | less
total 5168
-rwxr-xr-x  1 root   wheel     17984 Sep 17 01:07 sleep
-rwxr-xr-x  1 root   wheel     18032 Sep 17 01:07 echo
-rwxr-xr-x  1 root   wheel     18064 Sep 17 01:07 rmdir
-rwxr-xr-x  1 root   wheel     18080 Sep 17 01:07 wait4path
-r-xr-xr-x  1 root   wheel     18144 Sep 17 01:07 domainname
-rwxr-xr-x  1 root   wheel     18176 Sep 17 01:07 pwd
...
-rwxr-xr-x  1 root   wheel    378624 Sep 17 01:07 tcsh
-rwxr-xr-x  1 root   wheel    573600 Sep 17 01:07 zsh
-r-xr-xr-x  1 root   wheel    628496 Sep 17 01:07 bash
-r-xr-xr-x  1 root   wheel    632672 Sep 17 01:07 sh
-r-xr-xr-x  1 root   wheel   1394432 Sep 17 01:07 ksh
:
```

less reads a screen of text from the pipe (consisting of lines sorted by order of file size), then prints a colon (:) prompt. At the prompt, you can type a *less* command to move through the sorted text. *less* reads more text from the pipe, shows it to you, and even enables you to go backward to reread previous text if you want. When you're done viewing the sorted text, type the **q** command at the colon prompt to quit *less*. Table 6-2 contains a list of useful commands to use along with *less*.

Table 6-2. Useful less commands to remember

Command	Meaning
d	Scroll down (forward) one half of the screen size.
u	Scroll up (backward) one half the screen size.
b	Scroll back one screen.
f	Scroll forward one screen.
g	Jump to the beginning of the file.

Command	Meaning
G	Jump to the end of the file.
/pat	Scroll forward until a line containing the specified pattern is found.
?pat	Scroll back until a line containing the specified pattern is found.
n	Repeat previous search.
:n	Move to the next file in the file list (if more than one file was specified).
v	Open up the file in the *vi* editor.
q	Quit.

Printing

Sometimes there's no substitute for hard copy for information that's sent to your printer and printed on a piece of paper. You can generate printouts from within the Terminal, of course, though it prints *everything* in the buffer, not just the text that's visible in the Terminal window itself. You can also select a portion of text, choose Shell→Export Selected Text As, then open that file in TextEdit and print it, but that's rather a hassle.

Instead, it turns out that you can print files directly from the Unix command line in OS X, and there are two ways to do this. If you want the pure Unix solution, use the *lp* command series; but if you have a Bonjour network and one or more printers accessible through Bonjour, you can queue up printouts from the command line, too.

The Unix Way

The command used for sending information to the printer is *lp*, and there are a set of *lp*-related commands that you'll need to become familiar with if you want to actually print something. To start, you need to ensure that you have at least one printer configured in OS X. If you haven't done so yet, set up your printer by going to Apple Menu→System Preferences→Printers & Scanners, then clicking on the "+" button to add a printer to your system. Once you have at least one printer configured, you can identify it by name with the *lpstat* command.

lpstat

With the *-a* flag, *lpstat* shows everything about the known printers:

```
$ lpstat -a
EPSON_Artisan_837 accepting requests since Thu Jul 23 07:36:53 2015
```

```
Samsung_ML_191x_252x_Series___MiniMe accepting requests since Mon Oct  5
00:01:15 2015
```

In this case, you can see that I have two printers, both online and accepting print jobs. To see which of your possible printers is the default, use the *-d* option:

```
$ lpstat -d
system default destination: Samsung_ML_191x_252x_Series___MiniMe
```

 If you have printers hooked up through Bonjour, *lpstat* will see them too, which is particularly helpful!

If you really want to learn a lot about your printers, print queues, and more, use the *-t* option:

```
$ lpstat -t
scheduler is running
system default destination: Samsung_ML_191x_252x_Series___MiniMe
device for EPSON_Artisan_837: dnssd://EPSON%20Artisan%20837._ipp._tcp.local./
?uuid=cfe92100-67c4-11d4-a45f-a4ee573ee596
device for Samsung_ML_191x_252x_Series___MiniMe: dnssd:
//Samsung%20ML-191x%20252x%20Series%20%40%20MiniMe._ipps._tcp.local./printers/
Samsung_ML_191x_252x_Series?uuid=0acc075d-b11a-3b36-4b7c-f5317fefa479
EPSON_Artisan_837 accepting requests since Thu Jul 23 07:36:53 2015
Samsung_ML_191x_252x_Series___MiniMe accepting requests since Mon Oct  5
00:01:15 2015
printer EPSON_Artisan_837 is idle.  enabled since Thu Jul 23 07:36:53 2015
printer Samsung_ML_191x_252x_Series___MiniMe is idle.  enabled since Mon Oct  5
00:01:15 2015
```

Everything looks good!

lp

You actually add a job to the printer queue by using the *lp* command. Printing the output of an *ls -l* command is easy:

```
$ ls -l | lp
request id is Samsung_ML_191x_252x_Series___MiniMe-93 (0 file(s))
```

The request ID is rather ugly, but unless you need to remove a job because you've changed your mind, you shouldn't need to pay attention to anything more than that the print job has been accepted.

A few seconds later, your printout should emerge from the printer.

The first time you print out more than a single page of content, you'll realize that *lp* is a crude printing tool without any capability to paginate, add any sort of header or footer, and so on.

pr

The *pr* program does minor formatting of files on the Terminal or for a printer. For example, if you have a long list of names in a file, you can format it on-screen into two or more columns.

The syntax is:

```
pr option(s) filename(s)
```

pr changes the format of the file only on the screen or on the printed copy; it doesn't modify the original file. Table 6-3 lists some *pr* options.

Table 6-3. Some pr options

Option	Description
-n	Produces *n* columns of output.
-d	Double-spaces the output.
-h header	Prints *header* at the top of each page.
-t	Eliminates printing of header and top/bottom margins.

Other options allow you to specify the width of columns, set the page length, and so on. For a complete list of options, see the manpage (*man pr*).

Before we get into using *pr*, here are the contents of a sample file named *food*:

```
$ cat food
Sweet Tooth
Bangkok Wok
Mandalay
Afghani Cuisine
Isle of Java
Big Apple Deli
Sushi and Sashimi
Tio Pepe's Peppers
```

Let's use some *pr* options to make a two-column report with the header "Restaurants":

```
$ pr -2 -h "Restaurants" food

Oct  5 12:30 2015 Restaurants Page 1

Sweet Tooth                     Isle of Java
Bangkok Wok                     Big Apple Deli
Mandalay                        Sushi and Sashimi
Afghani Cuisine                 Tio Pepe's Peppers
```

The text is output in two-column pages. The top of each page has the date and time, the header (if none is specified, the name of the file is used as the header), and the page number. To send this output to the default OS X printer instead of to the Terminal screen, create a pipe to the *lpr* printer program:

```
$ pr -2 -h "Restaurants" food | lpr
```

## CHAPTER 7

Multitasking

OS X can do many jobs at once, dividing the processor's time between running applications and system processes so quickly that it looks as if everything is running at the same time. This is called *multitasking*. As new applications are launched, processes are started, and others go idle or shut down entirely, the system monitors each of these tasks and doles out memory and CPU resources on the fly to make sure everything runs smoothly.

Most users think of multitasking in terms of the way OS X handles applications like Adobe Photoshop, Microsoft Word, Mail, Messages, Safari, and so on—allowing you to have multiple applications open, each with its own windows. But on the Unix side, OS X allows you to run multiple Unix programs and/or processes at the same time as well. These processes can all be run and managed through a single Terminal window, with a little help from something called *job control*. Even if you're using a window system, you may want to use job control to do several things inside the same Terminal window. For instance, you may prefer to do most of your work from one Terminal window, instead of having multiple Terminal windows open when you really don't need to.

Why else would you want job control? Suppose you're launching a Unix program that takes a long time to run. On an old-school, single-task operating system, you would enter the command and wait for the job to finish, returning you to the command prompt (which is your indication that you're free to enter a new command). In OS X and other modern operating systems, however, you can enter new commands in the "foreground" while one or more programs are running in the "background."

When you enter a command as a background process, the shell prompt reappears immediately so that you can enter a new command. The original program runs in the background, but you can use the same Terminal window to do other things during that time. Depending on your system and your shell, you may be able to close the

Terminal window or even completely log off from OS X while the background process completes.

Running a Command in the Background

Running a program as a background process is most often done to free a Terminal when you know the program is going to take a long time to complete. It's also done whenever you want to launch a new application from an existing Terminal window, so you can keep working in the existing Terminal window, as well as within the new application.

To run a program in the background, all you need to do is add the & character at the end of the command line before pressing the Return key. The shell then assigns and displays a process ID (PID) number for the program:

```
$ sort bigfile > bigfile.sort &
[1] 372
```

Sorting is a good example, because it can take a while to sort huge files.

The PID for this program is 372. The PID is useful when you want to check the status of a background process or if you need to cancel it. To check on the status of the process, use the *ps* command with the following two options: *-f* to have expanded output, and *-p* because you're specifying a process ID. The full command for this example is:

```
$ ps -fp 372
  UID   PID PPID  C STIME   TTY          TIME CMD
  501   372 16901  0 10:12AM ttys001   0:00.00 sort
```

To cancel a process, use the *kill* command, followed by the PID of the process you want to cancel. In this instance, the command would look like:

```
$ kill 372
```

Fortunately, you don't need to remember the PID every time, because there are Unix commands (explained in the next section) to check on the processes you have running. Also, *bash* writes a status line to your screen when a background process finishes.

In *bash*, you can put an entire sequence of commands separated by semicolons (;) into the background by putting an ampersand (&) at the end of the command line. In other shells, enclose the command sequence in parentheses before adding the ampersand:

```
(command1; command2) &
```

OS X's Unix shells also have a feature (mentioned earlier) called *job control* that allows you to use the *suspend character* (usually Control-Z) to suspend a program running in the foreground. The program pauses, and you get a new shell prompt. You can then do anything else you like, including putting the suspended program into the background using the *bg* command. The *fg* command brings a suspended or background process to the foreground.

For example, you might start *sort* running on a big file, then decide you want to edit another file. You can stop *sort* with Control-Z, and then put it in the background with the *bg* command. The shell then gives you another shell prompt, at which you can start using *vi* while *sort* runs merrily in the background:

```
$ sort hugefile1 hugefile2 > sorted
...time goes by...
^Z
Stopped
$ bg
[1]    sort hugefile1 hugefile2 > sorted &
$ vi test.txt
```

Checking on a Process

If a background process seems to be taking forever to run, or if you change your mind and want to stop a process, you can check the status of the process and even cancel it.

ps

When you enter the *ps* (process status) command, you get a variety of useful information about the processes that are running, including how long a process has been active and the Terminal from which it was launched. Not sure you're the person who launched a process? The *tty* program shows the name of the Terminal where you're logged in. This is especially helpful when you're logged in to multiple machines, as the following code shows:

```
$ ps
  PID TTY            TIME CMD
  409 ttys000    0:00.04 -bash
  813 ttys001    0:00.02 -bash
$ tty
/dev/ttys000
```

In the preceding output, s000 corresponds to the Terminal window for ttys000 (which is the current window, as the *tty* command shows), and s001 denotes a second Terminal window. In its basic form, *ps* lists the following:

Process ID (PID)
    A unique number assigned by Unix to the process

Terminal name (TTY)
    The Unix name for the terminal from which the process was started

Runtime (TIME)

The amount of CPU time (in minutes and seconds) that the process has used

Command CMD

The name of the process

In Unix, each Terminal window has its own name. The previous example shows processes running in two windows: s000 and s001. If you want to see the processes that a certain user is running, use the following construct:

```
ps -U username
```

where *username* is the username of someone logged in to the system.

To see all processes running on the system, use *ps -ax*. The *-a* option shows processes from all users, and the *-x* option shows processes that are not connected with a Terminal session. Many of these processes are a core part of OS X, while others may be graphical programs you are running, such as Safari. The *head -20* in the following command line limits the output to the first 20 lines:

```
$ ps -ax | head -20
  PID TTY           TIME CMD
    1 ??         9:41.93 /sbin/launchd
   42 ??         2:05.18 /usr/libexec/UserEventAgent (System)
   43 ??         3:46.72 /usr/sbin/syslogd
   45 ??         0:07.54 /usr/libexec/kextd
   46 ??         1:55.25 /System/Library/Frameworks/CoreServices.framework/
Versions/A/Frameworks/FSEvents.framework/
Versions/A/Support/fseventsd
   50 ??         0:02.28 /System/Library/CoreServices/appleeventsd --server
   51 ??         2:18.30 /usr/libexec/configd
   52 ??         0:19.18 /System/Library/CoreServices/powerd.bundle/powerd
   57 ??         2:04.30 /usr/libexec/airportd
   59 ??         0:01.35 /usr/libexec/warmd
   60 ??         8:53.56 /System/Library/Frameworks/CoreServices.framework/
Frameworks/Metadata.framework/Support/mds
   64 ??         0:00.72 /System/Library/CoreServices/iconservicesd
   65 ??         0:00.05 /System/Library/CoreServices/iconservicesagent
   66 ??         0:40.39 /usr/libexec/diskarbitrationd
   68 ??         1:34.73 /usr/libexec/coreduetd
   69 ??         0:00.04 /usr/libexec/wdhelper
   71 ??        13:52.00 /System/Library/CoreServices/backupd.bundle/Contents/
Resources/mtmfs --tcp --resvport --listen localhost --oneshot --noportmap
--nobrowse
   72 ??         1:53.06 /usr/libexec/opendirectoryd
   73 ??         0:00.28 /usr/sbin/wirelessproxd
```

The output of *ps -ax* can be baffling, since almost all the processes listed are the low-level system tasks required for OS X to run happily on your system.

In the preceding list, notice the OS kernel extensions module *kextd*, the configuration management daemon *configd*, the audio utility *coreaudiod*, the low-level disk management program *diskarbitrationd*, the *CoreServices*, etc. These are processes that a regular user shouldn't have to worry about. Just beware before you try killing one of these processes; doing so could cause your system to crash.

You can find out what processes are being run as *root* by using *-U root*:

```
$ ps -ax -U root | head
  PID TTY           TIME CMD
    1 ??         9:42.22 /sbin/launchd
   42 ??         2:05.19 /usr/libexec/UserEventAgent (System)
   43 ??         3:46.73 /usr/sbin/syslogd
   45 ??         0:07.54 /usr/libexec/kextd
   46 ??         1:55.26 /System/Library/Frameworks/CoreServices.framework/
Versions/A/Frameworks/FSEvents.framework/Versions/A/Support/fseventsd
   50 ??         0:02.28 /System/Library/CoreServices/appleeventsd --server
   51 ??         2:18.30 /usr/libexec/configd
   52 ??         0:19.18 /System/Library/CoreServices/powerd.bundle/powerd
   57 ??         2:04.30 /usr/libexec/airportd
```

You can also change the output, of course, by specifying yourself as the account with the $LOGNAME environment variable (*ps -ax -U $LOGNAME | head*), though the results will probably look identical until you get to the last few processes on the list. And if you want to see more information about the process names, try using the *-w* flag. You can even use it more than once to get even more, like *-ww* or *-www*.

When you're just learning how to interpret the oft-confusing output of the *ps* command, you might find it quite helpful to simultaneously run the Activity Monitor (*/Applications/Utilities*), shown in Figure 7-1.

It's useful to change the filter at the top of the Activity Monitor from the default of "My Processes" to "All Processes" using the View menu in the program. This gives you a much better sense of what's happening on your computer, and if you do have a runaway application or one that's locked, it often doesn't show up in the My Processes view anyway.

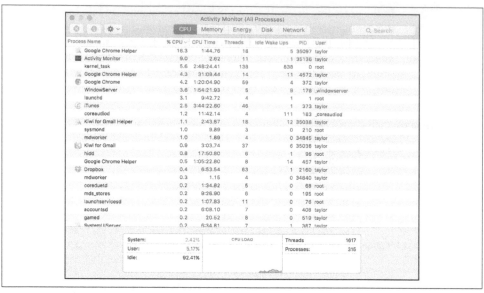

Figure 7-1. The Activity Monitor also shows running processes

top

A better way to see what applications are running and which are taking up the most resources is to use the helpful *top* command. Figure 7-2 shows *top* in action.

```
●●●                      taylor — top — 90×26
Processes: 315 total, 2 running, 12 stuck, 301 sleeping, 1448 threads      13:13:44
Load Avg: 0.70, 0.64, 0.75  CPU usage: 0.72% user, 1.57% sys, 97.69% idle
SharedLibs: 204M resident, 21M data, 28M linkedit.
MemRegions: 81695 total, 5616M resident, 125M private, 2333M shared.
PhysMem: 15G used (2409M wired), 576M unused.
VM: 887G vsize, 467M framework vsize, 1408(0) swapins, 7488(0) swapouts.
Networks: packets: 41488102/34G in, 89294962/86G out.
Disks: 3367348/140G read, 2365108/89G written.

PID    COMMAND     %CPU TIME     #TH  #WQ #PORT MEM   PURG  CMPRS PGRP  PPID
35148  top         2.7  00:00.40 1/1  0   21    3216K 0B    0B    35148 34062
35142  mdworker    0.0  00:00.03 3    0   49    1928K 0B    0B    35142 1
35141  mdworker    0.0  00:00.03 3    0   49    1948K 0B    0B    35141 1
35140  mdworker    0.0  00:00.03 3    0   50    1880K 0B    0B    35140 1
35139  mdworker    0.0  00:00.04 3    0   59    2128K 0B    0B    35139 1
35138  mdworker    0.0  00:00.07 3    0   60    2444K 0B    0B    35138 1
35137  systemstats 0.0  00:01.87 2    1   27    23M   0B    0B    35137 1
35136  Activity Mon 0.0 00:04.25 10   7   222+  46M-  33M+  0B    35136 1
35120  mdworker    0.0  00:00.04 3    0   49    1892K 0B    0B    35120 1
35119  mdworker    0.0  00:01.76 3    0   53    2996K 0B    0B    35119 1
35118  mdworker    0.0  00:01.69 3    0   53    3004K 0B    0B    35118 1
35113  mdworker    0.0  00:01.73 3    0   53    3180K 0B    0B    35113 1
35110  Calendar    0.0  00:15.82 3    0   229   80M   236K  0B    35110 1
35107  apple.Device 0.0 00:00.03 2    1   33    1516K 0B    0B    35107 1
35105  ath         0.0  00:00.15 4    0   42    1924K 0B    0B    373   373
35104  PTPCamera   0.0  00:00.23 5    0   143   4688K 0B    0B    35104 1
```

Figure 7-2. The top command shows processes running, sorted by CPU usage

If you're curious what commands consume the most system resources, leave *top* running in a Terminal window while you work. However, do be aware that *top* itself consumes some system resources, so if you're not paying attention to its output, you can quit *top* by typing **q**. You can always start it up again if things seem to be oddly slow on your computer.

top packs a lot of information into its display—considerably more than we have space to explain here. However, look at the first few lines and you'll get some quick insight into how well your system configuration matches the needs of the processes you're running. You can grab a snapshot of the first seven lines of output with this command (the flag used is a lowercase "L" followed by the digit one):

```
$ top -l 1 | head -8
Processes: 316 total, 3 running, 12 stuck, 301 sleeping, 1615 threads
2015/10/06 13:16:09
Load Avg: 0.44, 0.59, 0.71
CPU usage: 4.31% user, 12.94% sys, 82.73% idle
SharedLibs: 204M resident, 21M data, 28M linkedit.
MemRegions: 82102 total, 5634M resident, 125M private, 2340M shared.
PhysMem: 15G used (2442M wired), 570M unused.
VM: 889G vsize, 467M framework vsize, 1408(0) swapins, 7488(0) swapouts.
```

What you should look for here is high CPU usage (anything over about 25 percent is usually considered high, unless you're running something like Photoshop or some other CPU-intensive task) or too little free memory (I have 570M free—as shown at the end of the second-to-last line—out of a 16 GB RAM configuration, not a ton of space).

 Swapping is based on the idea that the memory needed for an application can be broken into *pages*, as many as needed for the app at that particular moment. As multiple processes compete for the system memory, memory pages that haven't been accessed for a while are temporarily copied to a special place on the hard disk, and those pages are given to applications that need them now. The process of swapping an older page for a newer one is called a *pageout* or *swapout*.

To display processes sorted by CPU usage (rather than process ID), use:

```
$ top -o cpu
```

If you find this view to be more useful than *top*'s traditional view, you can add this as an alias to your *.profile* file:

```
alias top='/usr/bin/top -s 5 -o cpu'
```

This updates *top*'s display every five seconds rather than the default of every second, and sorts the results by highest CPU usage to lowest. For more information on *top*, visit its manpage (*man top*).

If you see a process in *top* that seems to be a resource hog, you can give its PID value to *ps* to find out more about that specific job. If you know that Apple Mail is running as process 317, for example, *ps -p 317* will give you more process-related information.

Watching System Processes

The *ps -ax* command tells you which system processes are running, but if you want to see what they are up to, you'll need to look in the *system log*. To view the system log, use the command *tail*. If you use the *-f* option, *tail* follows the file as it grows. So, if you open up a new Terminal window and issue the following command, you can monitor the informational messages that come out of system utilities:

```
$ tail -f /var/log/system.log
Oct  6 13:15:45 Daves-MacBook-Pro Kiwi for Gmail[35036]: [d1taylor@gmail.com]
GOT MESSAGE. RESTARTING IDLE
Oct  6 13:15:45 Daves-MacBook-Pro Kiwi for Gmail[35036]: [d1taylor@gmail.com]
STARTING IDLE
Oct  6 13:15:45 Daves-MacBook-Pro Kiwi for Gmail[35036]: [d1taylor@gmail.com]
GMFeed updateUnreadCountImportantUsingImap
Oct  6 13:15:45 Daves-MacBook-Pro Kiwi for Gmail[35036]: [d1taylor@gmail.com]
GMFeed updateUnreadCountImportantUsingImap: searchResult != nil
Oct  6 13:15:55 Daves-MacBook-Pro Kiwi for Gmail[35036]: [d1taylor@gmail.com]
GMFeed getMessagesUsingImap - BEFORE
Oct  6 13:15:55 Daves-MacBook-Pro Kiwi for Gmail[35036]: [d1taylor@gmail.com]
GMFeed getMessagesUsingImap - ON START with info count 10
Oct  6 13:15:55 Daves-MacBook-Pro Kiwi for Gmail[35036]: [d1taylor@gmail.com]
getMessages starting from uid: 238151
Oct  6 13:15:55 Daves-MacBook-Pro Kiwi for Gmail[35036]: [d1taylor@gmail.com]
getMessagesUsingImap[fetchOperation] - BEFORE
Oct  6 13:15:55 Daves-MacBook-Pro Kiwi for Gmail[35036]: [d1taylor@gmail.com]
getMessagesUsingImap[fetchOperation] msg count: 1
Oct  6 13:16:35 Daves-MacBook-Pro syslogd[43]: ASL Sender Statistics
```

When you're done, use Control-C to quit *tail*'s monitoring and get a new command prompt. You can also see some system messages by running the Console application (*/Applications/Utilities*). Launch the Console, then click on the Show Logs List icon in the toolbar. You'll see that there's a nice list of all the logfiles on your Mac, and if you click on one, you can read through it for critical errors or just monitor what's been written to the logfile, exactly as you can with the *tail -f* command.

Canceling a Process

You may decide that you shouldn't have put a process in the background, or that the process is taking too long to execute. You can cancel a background process if you know its PID.

---

kill

The *kill* command terminates a process. This has the same basic result as using the Finder's Force Quit option, though it can be more graceful, as you'll see. To *kill* a process, use the following format:

kill *PID(s)*

 OS X includes a very helpful utility called Force Quit, accessible from the Apple menu (Apple Menu→Force Quit, or Option-⌘-Esc), which can be quite useful when applications are stuck or non-responsive. However, commands entered into the Terminal window can only be canceled from the command line—they don't show up in the Force Quit window. Additionally, Force Quit doesn't show you administrative processes. To stop Unix programs and administrative processes, you must use either the command line or the Activity Monitor (*/Applications/Utilities*).

kill terminates the designated PIDs (shown under the PID heading in the *ps* listing). If you do not know the PID of the process you want to kill, you should first run *ps* to display the status of your processes.

The following example illustrates how to enter two commands—*sleep* and *who*—on the same line, and designate those to run as a background process. The *sleep n* command simply causes a process to "go to sleep" for *n* seconds:

```
$ (sleep 60;who) &
[1] 981
$ ps
  PID TTY           TIME CMD
  409 ttys000    0:00.09 -bash
  981 ttys000    0:00.00 -bash
  982 ttys000    0:00.00 sleep 60
  813 ttys001    0:00.02 -bash
  912 ttys001    0:00.58 vi ch07.asc
$ kill 981
[1]+  Terminated: 15                    ( sleep 60; who )
```

Here, I decided that 60 seconds was too long to wait for the output of *who*. The *ps* listing showed that *sleep* had the PID number 982, so I used this PID to *kill* the *sleep* process. You should see a message like "Terminated" or "Killed"; if you don't, use another *ps* command to make sure the process has been killed (or that you killed the right process).

Now *who* executes immediately—as it's no longer waiting on *sleep*—and displays a list of users logged in to the system.

killall

If you'd rather not worry about finding the PID for a particular process, you can always use the *killall* command, which lets you kill processes by name instead. Since it's possible to inadvertently kill a different process with the same name (like your Terminal application or your shell), I strongly recommend that you always start by using the *-s* option so *killall* shows you what it'll do without actually killing anything:

```
$ (sleep 60;who) &
[2] 990
$ killall -s make
No matching processes belonging to you were found
$ killall -s who
No matching processes belonging to you were found
$ killall -s sleep
kill -TERM 991
kill -TERM 986
```

Did it surprise you that there's no match to *killall -s who* even though *sleep;who* is running in the background? The reason it didn't match is because the *who* command itself isn't yet running, but the *sleep* command is; you can see that it's matched by the third instance of *killall*.

If you have eagle eyes, you'll notice that the *sleep* command's PID isn't the same as the PID given by the shell when the *sleep;who* command was dropped into the background. That's because when a job is put into the background, the shell copies itself, and then the *copy shell* (Unix folk call that the *subshell*) manages the commands. It's the subshell that has PID 990, and *sleep* is a subprocess of that shell, so it gets a different PID: 991. When *sleep* finishes and the *who* command runs, that'll have yet another PID (most likely 992).

To kill the *sleep* process, simply remove the *-s* flag from the *killall* command, or, if you're curious, replace it with *-v* so you can see what the program does:

```
$ killall sleep
-bash: line 52:    995 Terminated: 15          sleep 60
taylor    console  May 14 10:50
taylor    ttys000  May 14 11:39
taylor    ttys001  May 14 11:56
$ killall -v sleep
No matching processes belonging to you were found
[1]+  Done                    ( sleep 60; who )
```

Notice that the first *killall* killed the *sleep* process, which immediately caused *who* to be run. When I tried to use *killall* again with the *-v* flag, it was too late and there was no longer a *sleep* command running.

The Process Didn't Die When I Told It To

Some processes can be hard to kill. If a normal *kill* is not working, try entering:

```
kill -9 PID
```

Or, if you're using *killall*, try:

```
killall -9 name
```

This is a sure kill, and can destroy almost anything, including the shell itself. Most Unix folk refer to the *-9* option as "terminate with extreme prejudice," a nod to the popular James Bond movie series.

Also, if you've run an interpreted program (such as a shell script), you may not be able to kill all dependent processes by killing the interpreter process that got it all started. You may need to kill them individually; however, killing a process that is feeding data into a pipe generally kills any processes receiving that data.

Launching GUI Applications

One great feature of OS X's Unix command line is that you can interact with the graphical applications in Aqua. For example:

- Drag a file or folder from the Finder onto a Terminal window and watch as its full pathname gets dropped in after the command prompt.

- Want to use *vi* to edit a text file that's on your Desktop? Just type *vi* on the command line, followed by a space, and then drag the file onto the Terminal window.

- When viewing a file in the Finder, you'll see what's known as a *proxy icon* in the Finder's title bar that shows you what directory you're in. Type *cd* followed by a space, then drag the proxy icon into the Terminal window and press Return; you'll be taken to that same exact location, just in the Terminal.

If you can have the Finder interact with the Terminal, it should be no surprise to you that you can also have the Terminal interact with other graphical applications on the Mac. For this, OS X offers the *open* command.

open

By default, the *open* command works identically to double-clicking an icon in the Finder. To open up a picture file called *peanut.jpg* in your default picture editor, use:

```
$ open peanut.jpg
```

If you don't have a graphics-editing application like Photoshop installed, the image opens in Preview (*/Applications*). If Preview is already running, the *peanut.jpg* image file opens in a new window.

The *open* command also lets you work at the command line with file matching, since it accepts more than one filename at a time. For example, if you need to open up a bunch of Microsoft Word files in a directory, just use:

```
$ open *.doc
```

You can, however, get things a bit confused, because sometimes the system doesn't know what to do with certain files. For example, try issuing the following command:

```
$ open .profile
```

The default application that's used when there's no specific binding is TextEdit, which works in this instance, but look what happens when you try to open something it can't recognize:

```
$ open .sample.swp
No application knows how to open /Users/taylor/Desktop/.sample.swp.
```

In this case, *open* just couldn't figure out what to do with this temporary scratch file from the *vi* editor. That's because *open* uses a file's creator and/or type code to determine which application should be used to open a particular file. Since *vi*'s scratch files don't have a creator or type code, the command gets confused and ends up doing nothing.

What Are Creator and Type Codes?

Unlike other operating systems, whenever you create and save a file with an application on the Mac, the application you use assigns its creator and type codes to the file. These codes are four characters in length and can contain upper- and lowercase letters, numbers, and even spaces. OS X uses these codes to figure out which icon gets assigned to certain files and, more importantly, to determine the default application for opening that file.

For example, in the Terminal, you can create a blank file on your Desktop with the following command:

```
$ touch ~/Desktop/myFile.txt
```

As you can see from the file extension (*.txt*), this is a plain-text file. If you were to double-click on this file, and if you didn't have another graphical text editor on your system, the file would open in TextEdit.

However, if you rename that file and give it a *.doc* extension:

```
$ mv myFile.txt myFile.doc
```

---

you can trick the system into thinking that it's a Word file. Don't believe me? Just try double-clicking the file and see which application opens it!

If you've installed the Xcode Tools (*https://developer.apple.com/technologies/tools/*) on your Mac, you can use a couple of special command-line utilities to peek inside a file to see its creator and type codes. For example, the following displays the output of the *GetFileInfo* command (located in */usr/bin*) when used on a Word file:

```
$ GetFileInfo Column.42.docx
file: "/Users/taylor/Documents/Linux Journal/Column.42.docx"
type: "W8BN"
creator: "MSWD"
attributes: avbstclinmedz
created: 09/02/2015 20:45:22
modified: 09/07/2015 20:45:22
```

Here you can see that the creator code is MSWD, short for Microsoft Word. Note that some of this information is also available with *mdls*, as explored in "Listing Spotlight Metadata with mdls" on page 127.

Useful Starting Options for Use with open

The *open* command has a lot of power accessible through command options. For example, if you want to stream a bunch of input into a text file then open it in an Aqua file, you can do so by using the *-f* option:

```
$ mdfind NIKON | open -f
```

This quick call to Spotlight generates a list of all filenames that reference or include NIKON. It would be easy to generate a printout with TextEdit, too.

The most useful option for use with *open* is *-a*, which is used to specify an application to open. For example, you can launch Messages with the generic *open* command, but you need to know where it's located on your system:

```
$ open messages
The file /Users/taylor/Desktop/messages does not exist.
```

Add the *-a* option, though, and *open* knows that you're talking about an application, so it'll search in the */Applications* directory to find and launch it:

```
$ open -a messages
```

Notice that *open* is smart enough to ignore case: the actual application is called Messages. You can also use the *open -a* command to open applications that are in a subdirectory of */Applications*. Want to launch the Console (located in */Applications/Utilities*)? Use *open -a console*. Ready to compare the output of Activity Monitor to the *ps* command, as discussed earlier in this chapter? Launch Activity Monitor with *open -a "activity monitor"*.

If you want to open a file with TextEdit, there's another option to *open* that's worth knowing: use *open -e*, and whatever you specify will be opened with the TextEdit program, regardless of its type. For example, if you wanted to open an HTML file in TextEdit instead of with BBEdit, you could use the following:

```
$ open -e ~/Sites/someFile.html
```

The *open* command will then look in your *Sites* folder for the file *someFile.html* and open it in TextEdit.

Making open More Useful

open makes it a breeze to launch your favorite applications, but because it requires that you type in the full application name, a few aliases are in order:

```
alias word="open -a Microsoft\ Word"
alias excel="open -a Microsoft\ Excel"
alias gc="open -a GraphicConverter\ 9"
```

With these added to your *.profile* file, you can easily launch Graphic Converter by just entering *gc*, and launch Microsoft Excel with *excel* and Microsoft Word with *word*.

A more sophisticated approach would be to use a shell script wrapper that would give its arguments to *open* and, if they failed, try to figure out what application you were talking about. It's an advanced topic, but here's how that script might look:

```
#!/bin/sh

# open2 - a smart wrapper for the cool OS X 'open' command
#    to make it even more useful. By default, open launches the
#    appropriate application for a specified file or directory
#    based on the Aqua bindings, and has a limited ability to
#    launch applications if they're in the /Applications dir.

# first off, whatever argument we're given, try it directly:

open=/usr/bin/open

if ! $open "$@" >/dev/null 2>&1 ; then
  if ! $open -a "$@" >/dev/null 2>&1 ; then

    # More than one arg?  Don't know how to deal with it: quit
    if [ $# -gt 1 ] ; then
      echo "open: Can't figure out how to open or launch $@" >&2
      exit 1
    else
      case $(echo $1 | tr '[:upper:]' '[:lower:]') in
        acrobat     ) app="Acrobat Reader"         ;;
        address*    ) app="Contacts"               ;;
        chat        ) app="Messages"               ;;
        cpu         ) app="Activity Monitor"       ;;
        dvd         ) app="DVD Player"             ;;
```

```
        word        ) app="Microsoft Word"              ;;
        excel       ) app="Microsoft Excel"             ;;
        prefs       ) app="System Preferences"          ;;
        qt|quicktime ) app="QuickTime Player"           ;;
        * ) echo "open: Don't know what to do with $1" >&2
            exit 1
      esac
      echo "You asked for $1 but I think you mean $app." >&2
      $open -a "$app"
    fi
  fi
fi

exit 0
```

This script has a simple table of nicknames for common applications, allowing you to use *open2 qt* to launch QuickTime Player, for example.

 This script is based on one in my book, *Wicked Cool Shell Scripts* (No Starch Press), which explains 101 powerful and interesting shell scripts. You can learn about the book, and download this script for yourself, at *http://intuitive.com/wicked/*.

## CHAPTER 8

Taking Unix Online

A network lets computers communicate with each other, share files, send email, and much more. Unix systems have been networked for more than 30 years, and OS X has had networking as an integral part of the system design from day one. In fact, Apple-Talk was the first computer network that let computers connect directly together without needing a server in the middle.

This chapter introduces Unix networking: remotely accessing your Mac from other computers and copying files between computers. It also shows you how the Terminal's "New Remote Connection" feature can make common connections a breeze once you've set them up initially.

Remote Logins

There may be times when you need to access your Mac, but you can't get to the desk it's sitting on. If you're working on a different computer, you may not have the time or inclination to stop what you're doing, walk to your Mac, and log in (laziness may not be the only reason for this: perhaps someone else is using your Mac when you need to get on it, or perhaps your Mac is miles away). OS X's File Sharing (System Preferences→Sharing→File Sharing) lets you access your files, but there may also be times you want to use the computer interactively, perhaps to move files around, search for a particular file, or perform a system maintenance task.

If you enable Remote Login (System Preferences→Sharing→Remote Login), as shown in Figure 8-1, you can access your Mac's Unix shell from any networked computer that can run the Secure Shell (*ssh*) client.

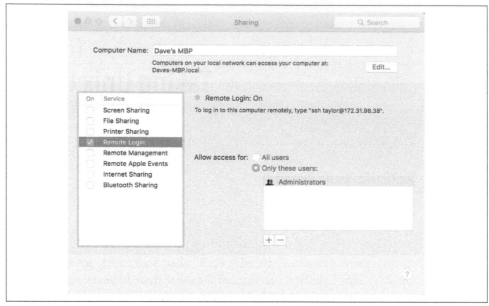

Figure 8-1. Enabling Remote Login in the Sharing preferences panel

The *ssh* client program is included with OS X (access it from within the Terminal) and all Unix and Linux systems. And just in case you need to access your Mac from a Windows system, there are a number of different *ssh* applications available, the two best of which are:

- SSH (*http://www.ssh.com*)
- OpenSSH (*http://www.openssh.com/*)

Figure 8-2 shows how remote login programs such as *ssh* work. In a local login, you interact directly with the shell with the Terminal application. In a remote login, you run a remote-access program (such as SSH) on your local system, and that program lets you interact with a shell program on the remote system. When you enable Remote Login, the Sharing panel displays instructions for logging in to your Mac from another computer. This message is shown in Figure 8-1, roughly in the middle of the window:

```
To log in to this computer remotely, type "ssh taylor@172.31.98.38".
```

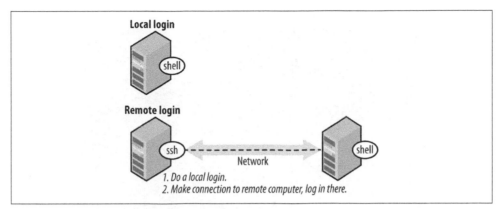

Figure 8-2. Local login, remote login

To log in to your Mac from a remote Unix system, use the command displayed in the Sharing panel, as shown in the following sample session. Here, a user on a Red Hat Linux system is connecting to an OS X computer (the first time you connect, you'll be asked to vouch for your Mac's authenticity):

```
$ ssh taylor@172.31.98.38
The authenticity of host '172.31.98.38 (172.31.98.38)' can't be established.
ECDSA key fingerprint is SHA256:KtU5bcJtQFn8ZBsPqZaUs0xkhTi9gVlXi5xZX/kgrL8.
Are you sure you want to continue connecting (yes/no)? yes
Warning: Permanently added '172.31.98.38' (ECDSA) to the list of known hosts.
Password:
Last login: Tue Oct  6 23:43:07 2015
```

 If you have a firewall running, you need to open up a network port to allow remote connections into your computer from outside your network if you want it to work bidirectionally. If you're just using *ssh* to connect outwards, you should be fine regardless of firewall settings. You can learn more about how to do this by starting with Apple's Help system. In the Finder, use Command-? to launch Help Viewer, then search for "firewall."

To log in to your Mac from a Windows machine using PuTTY, launch the PuTTY application, specify SSH (the default on the latest version, but not older versions of PuTTY), and type in your OS X system's IP address, as shown in the Mac's Sharing panel. PuTTY prompts you for your OS X username and password. Figure 8-3 shows a sample PuTTY session.

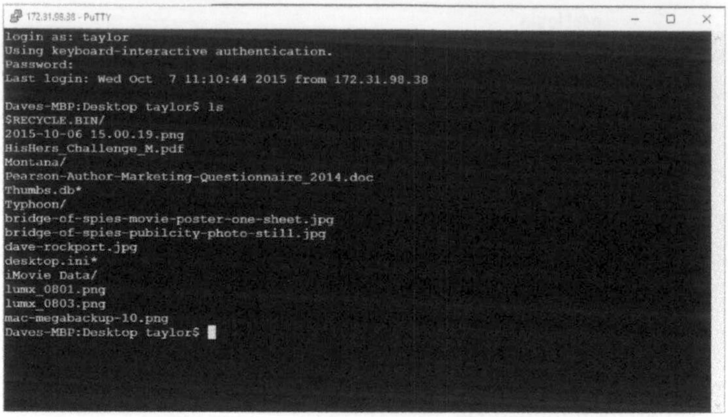

Figure 8-3. Connecting to OS X with PuTTY

For the most part, being connected via *ssh* is identical to using the Terminal application itself. You can even use the *open* command (discussed in Chapter 7) to launch applications on the Macintosh system, which can surprise the heck out of anyone who might be watching the screen! Of course, you won't be able to use the applications if you're remote.

> To run OS X applications remotely from another Mac, enable Screen Sharing in System Preferences→Sharing. In the Screen Sharing description, you can also click Computer Settings to enable access from non-Mac computers using Virtual Network Computing (VNC) software. Once you've enabled Screen Sharing, open the Finder on another Mac on the same network, and find your Mac in the list. You'll see an option to connect to the screen. If you've got "Back to My Mac" enabled under iCloud, you don't even need to be on the same network to connect from one Mac to another!

One of the very few differences is that the system records the Internet address of the system from which you're connected remotely, as shown in this *who* output:

```
$ who
taylor    console   Oct 13 16:56
taylor    ttys000   Oct 13 17:00
taylor    ttys001   Oct 13 17:10 (1)72.31.98.38
```

The third entry is a remote connection by a user on a different computer.

Web Access

Unlike previous editions of OS X, El Capitan does not include an option for starting the web server automatically. You can either install OS X Server from the Mac App

Store, or you can start the web server manually from the Terminal, with this command:

```
$ sudo apachectl start
```

Use this command to make sure that the web server starts each time you boot the computer:

```
$ sudo defaults write /System/Library/LaunchDaemons/org.apache.httpd \ ↵
  Disabled -bool false
```

Remote Access and the Outside World

If your Macintosh has an IP address that was assigned by an AirPort Base Station or other type of network router running the Dynamic Host Control Protocol (DHCP), then it's probable that your machine is inaccessible to the outside world. Because of this, you will be able to connect to your Mac only from machines on your local network. You can allow remote users to connect by using the AirPort Utility (if you have an AirPort Base Station) and following these steps:

1. Select your Base Station and click Edit.
2. Click the Network button in the toolbar.
3. Under Port Settings, click the Add (+) button to add a public TCP port that you want to map to a private IP address and TCP port on your local network.

In older versions of the AirPort Utility, or in configuration utilities for other network routers or access points, the configuration steps will be similar. Just look for Port Forwarding.

For Remote Login via *ssh*, you must map port 22 to your Macintosh; use port 80 for Personal Web Sharing. Other gateways may support this feature as well.

If you use this technique, the IP address shown in the Sharing preferences panel will be incorrect. You should use your AirPort Base Station's WAN address when you connect from a computer outside your local network.

Remote Access to Other Unix Systems

You can also connect to other systems from OS X. To do so, launch the Terminal application, and then start a program that connects to the remote computer. In addition to *ssh*, some typical programs for connecting over a computer network include *telnet*, *rsh* (remote shell), and *rlogin* (remote login). All of these are supported by and included with OS X. In any case, when you log off of the remote computer, the remote login program quits and you get another shell prompt from your Mac in the Terminal window.

My websites are running on a remote NetBSD system, and I use *ssh* from the Terminal window on my Mac so often that I have an alias to make it easy to pop on and tweak things:

```
alias vps="ssh dtaylor@intuitive.com"
```

 While you can use *ssh*, *telnet*, *rsh*, or *rlogin* to connect to a remote system, security experts highly discourage the use of anything other than *ssh*, because none of the others are as secure. This means that when you type in your username and password, the information could be sent "in the clear" to the remote system, exposing you to possible "sniffers," who will then be able to log in as if they were you. Better safe than sorry: insist that the remote system support *ssh*, and use it exclusively!

The syntax for *ssh* is:

```
ssh remote-user@remote-hostname
```

For example, when Dr. Nelson wants to connect to the remote computer named *biolab.medu.edu*, her first step is to launch the Terminal. Next, she'll need to use the *ssh* program to reach the remote computer. Her session will look something like this:

```
Welcome to Darwin!

$ ssh nelson@biolab.medu.edu
nelson@biolab.medu.edu's password:

biolab$
.
.
.
biolab$ exit
Connection to biolab.medu.edu closed.
$
```

As you can see, the shell prompt from her account on the *biolab* server includes the hostname. This is helpful, because it reminds her when she's logged in remotely, and after exiting the remote system, she'll also know when she's back in her own territory. If you use more than one system but don't have the hostname in your prompt, see "Changing the Command Prompt" on page 33 in Chapter 2 to find out how to add it.

When you're logged on to a remote system, keep in mind that the commands you type take effect on the remote system, not on your local one! For instance, if you use *lpr* to print a file (see "Printing" on page 149), the printer it comes out from won't be the one sitting under your desk, but one that might be hundreds or thousands of miles away.

The programs *rsh*, *rlogin*, and *ssh* generally don't give you a login: prompt. These programs assume that your remote username is the same as your local username. If they're different, you'll need to provide your remote username on the command line of the remote login program, as shown earlier for *ssh*.

You may be able to log in without typing your remote password or passphrase. In *ssh*, you can run an *agent* program, such as *ssh-agent*, that asks for your passphrase once, then handles authentication every time you run *ssh* or *scp* (secure copy) afterward. Otherwise, you'll be prompted after entering the remote login command line.

The following are four sample *ssh* and *rsh* command lines. The first pair shows how to log in to the remote system *biolab.medu.edu* when your username is the same on both the local and remote systems. The second pair shows how to log in if your remote username is different (in this case, *jdnelson*). Note that the OS X versions of *ssh* and *rsh* may support both syntaxes shown, depending on how the remote host is configured:

```
$ ssh biolab.medu.edu
$ rsh biolab.medu.edu
$ ssh jdnelson@biolab.medu.edu
$ rsh -l jdnelson biolab.medu.edu
```

About Security

Today's Internet and other public networks have users who try to break into computers and snoop on other network users. While the popular media calls these people *hackers*, the correct term to use is *crackers*. (Most hackers are self-respecting programmers who enjoy pushing the envelope of technology, but never cause trouble on remote systems.)

Keep in mind that with *ssh*, *telnet*, and related programs, the "shell" you're in, the programs you run, and the CPU you utilize are all on the remote system. What you see on your local Terminal screen is essentially just a bunch of text characters being transmitted back and forth across the network to show you what's going on remotely.

Most remote login programs (and file transfer programs, which we cover in the next section) were designed 25 or more years ago, when networks were friendly places with cooperative users. Those programs (many versions of *telnet* and *rsh*, for instance) make a cracker's job easy. They transmit your data, including your password, across the network in a way that allows even the most inexperienced cracker to read it. Worse, some of these utilities can be configured to allow access without passwords, opening up a huge security hole.

SSH is different; it was designed with security in mind. It sends your password (and everything else transmitted or received during your SSH session) in a secure way. For more details on SSH, start with the *ssh* manpage; then, if you want to know (lots) more, I recommend the book *SSH, The Secure Shell: The Definitive Guide*, by Daniel J. Barrett, Richard Silverman, and Robert G. Byrnes (O'Reilly).

Transferring Files

You may need to copy files between computers. For instance, you can put a backup copy of an important file you're editing onto a computer in another building or another city, or copy a file from your local computer onto a central computer, where your colleagues can access it. Or you might want to download 20 files from an FTP server, but don't want to go through the tedious process of clicking on them one by one in a web browser.

If you need to do this sort of thing often, you may be able to set up a networked file-system connection; then you'll be able to use the Finder or local programs such as *cp* and *mv* to help you move files around on your own network. But Unix systems also have command-line tools such as *scp* and *rcp* for transferring files between computers. These often work more quickly than most graphical applications, and believe it or not, they're pretty easy to use, as we'll explore in this section.

scp and rcp

OS X includes both *scp* (secure copy) and *rcp* (remote copy) programs for copying files between two computers. In general, you must have accounts on both computers to use these commands. The syntax of both *scp* and *rcp* is similar to that of *cp*, but they also let you add the remote hostname to the start of a file or directory pathname. The syntax of each argument is:

```
hostname:pathname
```

hostname is needed only for remote files. You can copy from a remote computer to the local computer, from the local computer to a remote computer, or between two remote computers (aka "third-party copy").

The *scp* program is much more secure than *rcp*, so I suggest using *scp* to transfer private files over insecure networks such as the Internet. For privacy, *scp* encrypts the file and your passphrase during the transfer of the data.

The general syntax for scp is:

```
scp [[user@]host1:]FromFile [[user@]host2:]ToFile
```

For both the *From* and *To* files, if either is on a remote host, you need to specify the hostname. And if any remote host involves a different username than what you are currently using locally, you must specify that as well.

For example, suppose you want to copy the files *report.may* and *report.june* from your home directory on the computer named *w2.intuitive.com* and put the copies into your working directory (.) on the machine you're presently logged into. If you haven't set up an SSH agent that lets you use *scp* without typing your passphrase (password), *scp* asks you for it:

```
$ scp w2.intuitive.com:report.may w2.intuitive.com:report.june .
Enter passphrase for RSA key 'taylor@mac':
```

To use wildcards in the remote filenames, put quotation marks ("*name*") around each remote name. Quotes tell the local shell not to interpret special characters, such as wildcards, in the filename. The wildcards are passed, unquoted, to the remote shell, which interprets them *there*.

You can use absolute or relative pathnames; if you use relative pathnames, they start from your home directory on the remote system. For example, to copy all files from your remote *w2* account's *food/lunch* subdirectory into your local working directory (.), enter:

```
$ scp "w2.intuitive.com:food/lunch/*" .
```

Unlike *cp*, the OS X versions of *scp* and *rcp* don't have an *-i* safety option. If the files you're copying already exist on the destination system (in the previous example, that's your local machine), those files are overwritten. To be safe, always use *ls* to check what's in the destination directory before you copy files.

Two useful command options for use with *scp* are *-p*, which preserves the creation and modification dates of the original file in the copy, and *-r*, which lets you recursively copy folders and their contents to the remote system. For example, to copy everything in my *Pictures* directory to the *w2* server, I would use:

```
$ scp -r ~/Pictures w2.intuitive.com:.
```

If your system has *rcp*, your system administrator may not want you to use it for system security reasons. Another program, *ftp*, is more flexible than *rcp* (but much less secure than *scp*, which is itself less secure than *sftp*).

FTP

The File Transfer Protocol, or FTP, is a standard way to transfer files between two computers. Many users of earlier Mac OS versions are familiar with Fetch (*http://www.fetchsoftworks.com*), a shareware graphical FTP client that runs on all versions of OS X. There are also a number of graphical FTP programs available from the Mac App Store (search for "ssh" or "ftp"). While Fetch offers an easy-to-use interface, it also comes with a price tag, which begs the question: why spend your hard-earned cash on Fetch when you get FTP services for free with Unix?

The Unix *ftp* program does FTP transfers from the command line. Since it's fast, easy, and portable, I'll cover the standard *ftp* program here.

To start *ftp*, identify yourself to the remote computer by giving the username and password for your account on that remote system.

 Sending your username and password over a public network with *ftp* means that snoopers might see them, and then use them to log in to your account on that system. Instead, you should use *sftp*, because it uses SSH for an encrypted, secure FTP connection.

A special kind of FTP, *anonymous FTP*, happens if you log in to the remote server with the username *anonymous*. The password is your email address, such as *taylor@intuitive.com*. (The password isn't usually required; it's a courtesy to the remote server.) Anonymous FTP lets anyone log in to a remote system and download publicly accessible files to their local systems.

Command-line ftp

To start the standard Unix *ftp* program, provide the remote computer's hostname:

```
ftp hostname
```

ftp prompts for your username and password on the remote computer. This is something like a remote login (see "Remote Logins" on page 169, earlier in this chapter), but *ftp* doesn't start your usual shell. Instead, *ftp* has its own prompt and uses a special set of commands for transferring files. Table 8-1 lists the most important *ftp* commands.

Table 8-1. Some ftp commands

Command	Description
put *filename*	Copies the file *filename* from your local computer to the remote computer. If you give a second argument, the remote copy will have that name.
mput *filenames*	Copies the named files (you can use wildcards) from the local computer to the remote computer.
get *filename*	Copies the file *filename* from the remote computer to your local computer. If you give a second argument, the local copy will have that name.
mget *filenames*	Copies the named files (you can use wildcards) from the remote computer to the local computer.

Command	Description
prompt	A "toggle" command that turns prompting on or off during transfers with the *mget* and *mput* commands. By default, *mget* and *mput* will prompt you with *mget filename ?* or *mput filename ?* before transferring each file; you answer **y** or **n** each time. Typing **prompt** once, from an ftp> prompt, stops the prompting; all files will be transferred without question until the end of the *ftp* session. Or, if prompting is off, typing **prompt** at an ftp> prompt resumes prompting.
hash	Displays progress marks on file uploads and downloads so you can gauge progress. Particularly helpful with large transfers.
cd pathname	Changes the working directory on the remote machine to *pathname* (*ftp* typically starts at your home directory on the remote machine).
lcd pathname	Changes *ftp*'s working directory on the local machine to *pathname*. (*ftp*'s first local working directory is the working directory from which you started the program.) Note that *ftp*'s *lcd* command changes only *ftp*'s working directory. After you quit *ftp*, your shell's working directory will not have changed.
dir	Lists the remote directory (like *ls -l*).
pwd	Displays the present working directory.
binary	Tells *ftp* to copy the file(s) that follow it without translation. This preserves pictures, sound, or other data.
ascii	Transfers plain-text files, translating data if needed. For instance, during transfers between a Microsoft Windows system (which adds Control-M to the end of each line of text) and a Unix system (which doesn't), an ASCII-mode transfer removes or adds those characters as needed.
passive	Toggles the setting of passive mode. This may help *ftp* to run correctly if you are behind a firewall. If you put the command export FTPMODE=passive in your *.profile* file, all your *ftp* sessions will use passive mode.
quit or *bye*	Ends the *ftp* session and takes you back to a shell prompt.
!cmd	Gives the specified command to a shell, displays its output, then returns to the *ftp* program.

Here's an example. Kiana moves into the local directory she wants to use as a starting point (a good idea whether you're uploading or downloading). She then lists the files in her current directory to see what's there, and uses *ftp* to connect to an FTP server located at *rhino.zoo.edu*. After using her username and password to log on, Kiana changes remote directories to the *work* subdirectory, then gets the *todo* file and downloads that to her local machine. After receiving the "Transfer complete" message, Kiana uses the *!ls* command to make sure that the file she transferred is on her local machine. Then, with the knowledge that the file is there, she quits the FTP session:

```
$ cd downloads
$ ls
afile    ch2      somefile
$ ftp rhino.zoo.edu
Connected to rhino.zoo.edu.
Name (rhino:kiana): ktaylor
Password:
ftp> cd work
ftp> dir
total 3
-rw-r--r--  1 csmith   mgmt     47 Feb  5  2001 for.ed
-rw-r--r--  1 csmith   mgmt    264 Oct 11 12:18 message
-rw-r--r--  1 csmith   mgmt    724 Nov 20 14:53 todo
ftp> get todo
local: todo remote: todo
227 Entering Passive Mode (17,254,16,11,224,18).
150 Opening BINARY mode data connection for todo (724 bytes)
226 Transfer complete.
724 bytes received in 00:00 (94.06 KB/s)
ftp> !ls
afile    ch2      somefile    todo
ftp> quit
$ ls
afile    ch2      somefile    todo
```

We've explored the most basic *ftp* commands here. Entering **help** at an ftp> prompt gives a list of all available commands; entering **help** followed by an *ftp* command name gives a one-line summary of that command.

sftp: ftp to secure sites

If you can only use *ssh* to connect to a remote site, chances are it won't support regular *ftp* transactions either, due to higher security restrictions. That's a good thing, though, and I encourage you to always defer to using *sftp* if it's an option, particularly if you're on a public WiFi or other public network.

The good news is that OS X also includes *sftp*, a version of *ftp* that's part of the *ssh* package and works similarly to regular *ftp*. To run the program, type **sftp** at the command line. Here's an example:

```
$ cd Downloads
$ sftp taylor@intuitive.com
taylor@intuitive.com's password:
Connected to intuitive.com.
sftp> cd mybin
sftp> dir -l
drwxr-xr-x    0 24810    100         1024 Jun 26 20:18 .
drwxr-xr-x    0 24810    100         1536 Sep 16 18:59 ..
-rw-r--r--    0 24810    100          140 Jan 17  2014 .library.account.info
-rwxr-xr-x    0 24810    100         3312 Jan 27  2014 addvirtual
-rw-r--r--    0 24810    100          406 Jan 24  2014 trimmailbox.sh
```

```
-rwxr-xr-x    0 24810    100       1841 Jan 24  2014 unpacker
-rwxr-xr-x    0 24810    100        946 Jan 22  2014 webspell
sftp> get webspell
webspell                               100%  946      4.7KB/s   00:00
sftp> quit
$ ls -l webspell
-rwxr-xr-x  1 taylor   taylor   946 25 Sep 11:28 webspell
```

The *sftp* program also has a very useful option that you can specify when you're copying files. The -P option causes the program to preserve the original file's creation and modification date and time information:

```
sftp> get -P webspell
```

Additional helpful commands include *lcd*, *lls*, and *lmkdir*, to change your location in the local filesystem, list the files in the current local working directory, and make a new local directory, respectively. You can also use the *!* escape to access any Unix command from within *sftp*. Like the *ftp* program, *sftp* also has built-in help, which you can access by typing **help** at the prompt.

FTP with a web browser

If you need a file from a remote site, and you don't need all the control that you get with the *ftp* program, you can use a web browser to download files using anonymous FTP. To do that, enter a URL (location) with this syntax:

```
ftp://hostname/pathname
```

For instance, *ftp://somecorp.za/pub/reports/2001.pdf* downloads the file *2001.pdf* from the directory */pub/reports* on the host *somecorp.za*. In most cases, you can start with just the first part of the URL—such as *ftp://somecorp.za*—and browse your way through the FTP directory tree to find what you want. If your web browser doesn't prompt you to save a file, use its Save menu command.

If you are using the Safari browser, it will open *ftp:* directories by mounting them in the Finder as if you specified the *ftp* URL in the Finder itself, as explained later in this chapter.

FTP with curl

A faster way to download a file is with the *curl* (copy from URL) command. For example, to save a copy of the *2001.pdf* report in the current directory, enter:

```
$ curl -O ftp://somecorp.za/pub/reports/2001.pdf
```

Without the -O option (that's a capital letter O, not a zero), *curl* dumps the file to the standard output (your screen). If you want to read a text file from an Internet server, you can combine *curl* and *less*:

```
$ curl ftp://ftp.oreilly.com/pub/README.ftp | less
```

You can also use *curl* with web pages, but this brings the page up in HTML source view:

```
$ curl http://www.oreilly.com | less
```

One strategy you could use, though it isn't necessarily optimal, is to save HTML pages locally, then open them in Safari:

```
$ curl http://www.oreilly.com > oreilly.html
$ open oreilly.html
```

or in Google Chrome:

```
$ curl http://www.oreilly.com > oreilly.html
$ open -a "Google Chrome" oreilly.html
```

Keep in mind that any graphics referenced by that page won't have been retrieved by *curl*, so it's likely to be a bit messy. Indeed, there are better ways to work with HTML pages on the command line, but they're beyond the scope of this book.

FTP from the Finder

You can also mount remote FTP directories using the Finder, and then continue accessing them with Finder actions, or access them with standard Unix commands in the Terminal. In the Finder, choose Go→Connect to Server, then type *ftp://* followed by the name of the server that you want to access (such as *ftp.oreilly.com*). Figure 8-4 shows how this appears in the Finder.

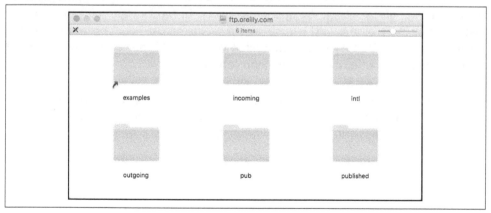

Figure 8-4. Connecting to an FTP server in the Finder

If a password is required, another window pops up, asking you to authenticate with a valid username and password. Enter those correctly—or, depending on the remote settings, select "Guest"—and the new FTP disk appears on your Desktop. It is now accessible in the */Volumes* directory, as shown here:

```
$ ls -l /Volumes/
total 16
lrwxr-xr-x  1 root    admin     1 Oct  1 10:02 BigHD@ -> /
drwxrwxrwx  0 root    wheel     0 Oct  7 14:35 MobileBackups/
dr-xr-xr-x  1 taylor  staff   512 Oct  7 14:39 ftp.oreilly.com/
drwxrwxr-x@ 38 taylor staff  1360 Sep  5 20:08 red/
```

When you're done with the FTP server, you can use the *umount* command to disconnect:

```
$ umount /Volumes/ftp.oreilly.com
```

It's considerably easier than using the *ftp* program!

Other FTP solutions

One of the pleasures of working with Unix within the OS X environment is that there is a wealth of great graphical Mac applications. In the world of FTP-based file transfer, the choices are uniformly excellent, starting with Fetch, FlashFTP, Transmit, Cyberduck, YummyFTP, and Viper FTP, and encompassing many other possibilities. To see what options you have, just open the App Store and search for "ftp."

Easy Shortcuts with New Remote Connection

The Terminal application has a very helpful feature that can make connecting to remote systems via *telnet*, *ssh*, *ftp*, or *sftp* a breeze, once it's set up. New Remote Connection is available via the Shell menu and is shown in Figure 8-5.

To add a service, click on the + icon on the left side of the window. More commonly, you'll add servers, which you can do by clicking on the + icon on the right side of the window. This produces a window that asks for the hostname or host IP address, which is easily entered, as shown in Figure 8-6.

Once added in one area, the new server is available for all services, so to connect to my web server using SSH, I can simply choose *ssh* then the new server name, as shown in Figure 8-7. Finally, the connection to my server is a breeze: specify the username, and click Connect. Easy enough!

Figure 8-5. New Remote Connection offers simple shortcuts

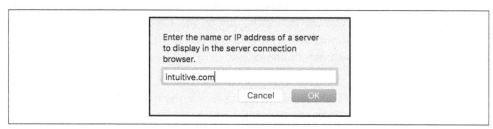

Figure 8-6. Adding a new server to New Remote Connection

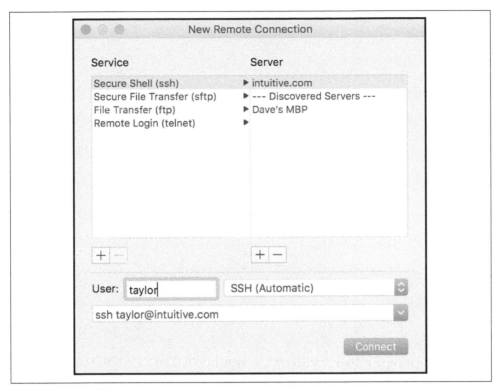

Figure 8-7. intuitive.com

## CHAPTER 9

Of Windows and X11

OS X comes with great applications, and a trip to Apple's App Store can bag you quite a few more, but there's also a flood of applications available to you solely because of OS X's Unix core. Many of these are applications that have been around for a long time, and many are flowing in from other members of the Unix family, including Linux and FreeBSD.

What's different about these applications is that they're not commercial apps like Microsoft Office or Adobe Photoshop, they're not shareware like Graphic Converter and Fetch, and they're not free, public domain applications. Most of the programs available to the Mac community from Unix are a part of the active open source movement. They're free to download—including source code, if you want it—but there are constraints on what you can do with the programs. If you're a programmer and make any modifications, you are obligated to share those changes with the rest of the open source community. It's certainly a very different distribution model for software, but don't let the lack of a price tag fool you: open source applications are often as good as, or even better than their commercial counterparts. Added bonus: having large teams of programmers building open source apps means that if you do report a bug, the fix can appear quickly, even sometimes the same day—a level of responsiveness that Apple and Microsoft certainly can't match.

Much open source software comes from university research. This chapter talks about one of these wonderful open source applications: the X Window System, Version 11. X11, as it's called, is a graphical interface for Unix that's been around a long, long time. Although OS X's shiny interface is fantastic, there are many powerful Unix programs that require X11.

In earlier versions of OS X, Apple included X11, but the latest release marks the company redirecting you to an open source X11 project called XQuartz (*http://*

xquartz.macosforge.org/). You can go there directly, or you can simply double-click on the "X11" icon in */Applications/Utilities*.

In the latter instance, you'll be shown a message like the one in Figure 9-1.

Figure 9-1. Time to install X11 from XQuartz

 One warning before we start: while typical Mac applications—freeware, shareware, or commercial—are a breeze to install thanks to OS X's Installer, Unix applications don't have the same easy interface. This means that different programs have different installation methods (sometimes requiring you to type in a sequence of commands in the Terminal, for example). The latest X11 installer is easy, but once you get to individual X11 applications like GIMP, it can get tricky fast. To address this problem, a team of dedicated programmers have created a powerful software distribution and installation system called Homebrew (*http://brew.sh/*). There are a couple of alternatives, too: MacPorts (*http://www.macports.org*) and Fink (*http://www.finkproject.org*).

X11

The X Window System (commonly called X11) is the standard graphical user interface for almost all Unix and Linux systems. While OS X is built upon a Unix core, it turns out to be an exception to this rule because its default graphical interface is Aqua, and it's not directly X11-compatible. On OS X, a combination of components called the Quartz Compositor (sometimes just referred to as Quartz), OpenGL, and the CoreGraphics library are responsible for drawing what appears on your screen.

In an X11-based system, an application called an *X server* creates what you see on the screen. The programs that run under X11, such as office applications, web browsers, and terminal windows, are known as *X clients*. X servers and clients talk to each other using standard Unix networking protocols: if an X11 word processor needs to pop up

---

a dialog asking whether you want to save a document, it makes a network connection to the X server and asks it to draw that window. Because X11 is networked in this way, you can run an X client on a Unix system in another office or across the planet, and have it displayed by your computer's X server.

X servers are typically full-screen applications, which means they completely take over your display. Figure 9-2 shows a full-screen X server running on a Linux computer. Three applications are running: an xterm (which is similar to OS X's Terminal), a clock app, and a web browser showing the OS X El Capitan landing page at Apple.com. In addition, a taskbar is visible along the side of the screen. This belongs to the *window manager*, an X11 program that takes care of putting frames and window controls (such as close, resize, and zoom) around application windows. The window manager provides the overall look and feel, and also lets you launch applications and log out of X11. X11 users have many window managers to choose from; the one shown in Figure 9-2 is *lxde*.

Figure 9-2. An X server running on Linux

When X11 was included with OS X, Apple shipped what's called a *rootless* X server. Now the path to X11 is through XQuartz, the open source version of X11 that's compatible with Quartz and, of course, OS X El Capitan and previous versions of the operating system. It, too, is rootless. What's that mean? Simple: it's an X server that won't take over your entire screen. XQuartz's X11 implementation, which includes the X server, many common X clients, and a software development kit for writing X11 applications, is derived from an implementation of X11 called X.Org (*http:// www.x.org*). This is the X11 release used on Linux, FreeBSD, NetBSD, OpenBSD, and many other Unix operating systems.

Apple also created an X11 window manager, *quartz-wm*, which draws X11 windows that look and behave much like Quartz windows.

Using X11

You can most easily launch X11 by double-clicking on the X11 icon, located in */Applications/Utilities*. Most likely, once it launches, nothing will appear to happen. Look closely at the menu bar on the top of your Mac's screen, however, and you'll see X11 appear with its minimal menu options.

You can launch a new xterm window by selecting the Terminal item from its Applications menu (or using ⌘-N). Don't confuse this with OS X's Terminal application! Under X11, the program you use to type in Unix commands is also a terminal, except it's an X11-based terminal window, thus the name *xterm*. When you select the Applications menu, you'll see a list of shortcuts to other X11-based applications. By default, there are options for:

- *Terminal*, which starts a new xterm
- *xman*, which lets you browse Unix manpages
- *xlogo*, which pops up a window displaying the X logo

Figure 9-3 shows X11 running along with these three applications and a manpage browser information window from *xman*.

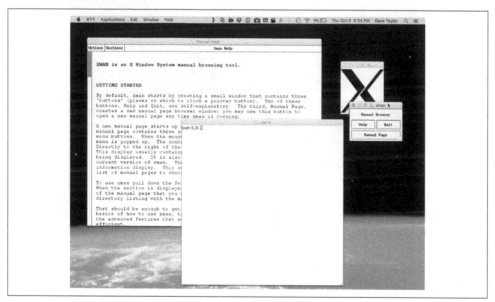

Figure 9-3. X11 running on the Mac

X11 includes many other applications as well. To see a list, examine the X11 application directory with the following command:

```
$ ls /opt/X11/bin/
```

If you're going to be working with X11 applications, you'll want to put */usr/X11/bin* or */opt/X11/bin* in your PATH by editing your *.profile* file (if you're using *bash*) or your *.login* file (if you're using *tcsh*). For *bash* users, add this line:

```
PATH=${PATH}:/usr/X11/bin ; export PATH
```

tcsh users should add this line:

```
setenv PATH ${PATH}:/usr/X11/bin
```

The next time you launch a Terminal or xterm window, you'll be able to type in all the X11 application names at the command line without specifying where they're located.

Before you add this to your PATH, however, open a Terminal and type **echo $PATH**. The XQuartz installer may have already done this for you.

Here are a few of the utilities included with OS X's X11:

bitmap
An X11 bitmap (*.xbm*) editor.

glxgears
An OpenGL 3D graphics demonstration. OpenGL applications running under Apple's X11 implementation have the benefit of full 3D hardware acceleration.

glxinfo
Displays information about OpenGL capabilities.

oclock
An X11-based clock application.

xcalc
A calculator program that runs under X11.

xeyes
A pair of eyeballs that follow the mouse cursor around the screen.

xhost
Gives another computer permission to open windows on your display.

xkill
Changes your cursor to the "cursor of doom." Any X11 window you click in will be shut down. If you change your mind and don't want to kill an app, press Control-C. This won't kill any Aqua applications; it works only on X11 applications.

xload
Displays the CPU load.

xwud

An image display program for X11.

None of these X11 applications included with OS X's X11 package are very interesting, and their interfaces are retro 1980s in complexity and use of color, as you'll quickly realize, but bear with me; there are a wealth of great X applications available online.

Differences Between OS X and X11

There are some significant differences between X11 and the OS X interface that you need to watch out for. Although Apple's X11 does a great job of minimizing these differences, there are still some quirks that may throw you off:

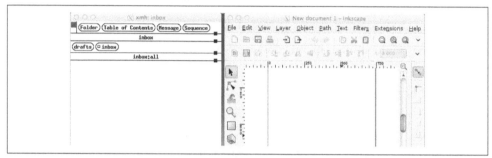

Figure 9-4. Comparing X11 menu styles

Mouse focus

OS X's Aqua interface doesn't care where your mouse is located: the application in front of the other apps is the one that sees your keystrokes. X11 doesn't work that way (depending on your X11 settings), and you might find that it uses something called *mouse focus* to decide where your keyboard input should be sent. Even having your mouse on the scrollbar or just slightly off the edge of the application window leaves you in limbo. Don't be surprised if this happens: just move your cursor into the middle of the target application window and you'll be fine.

Cutting and pasting

If you press ⌘-C (copy) while you have something selected in an X11 window, you can paste it into another OS X application. But that's where the similarity ends: to paste something into an X11 window, you can't use ⌘-V. Instead, use Option-click (you must enable three-button emulation in X11's preferences first). If you have a three-button mouse, press the middle button to paste into an X11 window.

X11 application menus

The menu at the top of the screen always belongs to X11 itself. Individual X11 applications may have their own menus near the top of their main windows.

Figure 9-4 shows two different types of X11 application menus: a classic X11 menu from *xmh* (an X11 mail reader) and a more modern X11 menu from *Ink-Scape* (a vector drawing application).

Be careful with ⌘-Q

If you press ⌘-Q (quit) while running an X11 application, this shuts down all of X11 and any X applications you're running. Because of this, you'll get a warning if you try to do this when there are X11 clients running. Look for a quit option on the X11 application's own menu, or click the close button on its window.

Scrolling in the xterm

By default, the xterm doesn't have scrollbars. However, as in the Terminal, you can use a keystroke to scroll up and down. Unfortunately, it's not the same keystroke: the Terminal uses ⌘-Page Up and ⌘-Page Down (or, if you're using a MacBook or MacBook Pro, Shift-Fn up arrow or Shift-Fn down arrow), while the xterm expects Shift-Page Up and Shift-Page Down.

Launching applications from the xterm

When you type the name of an X11 program in the xterm, it launches, but the xterm window appears to hang because it is waiting for the program to exit. To avoid this problem, you can append the *&* character after the program name to put it in the background. Another option is to press Control-Z after the program starts, and type **bg** to put the program in the background. (See Chapter 7 for a refresher on how to place Unix processes in the foreground or background.)

X11, .bashrc, and .profile

If you've customized your Unix shell by editing *~/.profile*, applications that run under X11, including the xterm, won't respect the settings in that file. To correct this problem, put any essential settings in your *~/.bashrc* file, which X11 *does* read.

Customizing X11

One of the big differences between X11 and OS X is that X applications expect that you have a three-button mouse. Meanwhile, Apple still assumes that you have a single-button mouse and you don't mind occasionally holding down the Control key to emulate right-mouse-button actions. X11 is built on a three-button mouse, so as an X user, you need to know how to get to all of those buttons. That's one of the key preferences accessible from the X11→Preferences menu, as shown in Figure 9-5.

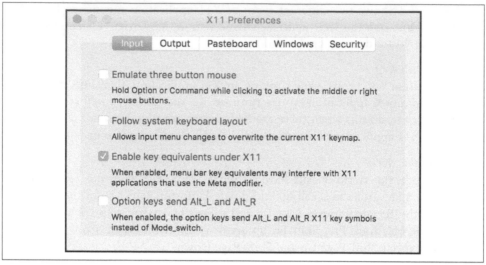

Figure 9-5. Configuring X11 Input preferences

You should leave the other configuration options set to their default values, unless you're an absolute wizard at working with X and know how to tweak it to match the Apple hardware configuration. Set these wrong and you can throw the proverbial spanner in the works, causing X11 to not work or to display everything unreadably.

The Output tab offers additional preferences: most notably, you can switch out of so-called *rootless* mode, which allows X11 to take over your entire screen. If you do this, make sure that you write down that Option-⌘-A lets you leave full-screen mode, or you might end up having to reboot to figure out how to get back to the familiar world of Aqua and OS X!

Customizing X11's Applications menu

You can customize X11's Applications menu by selecting Applications→Customize. Click the Add Item button to add an X11 application to the menu. Specify the menu title in the Menu Name column, and use the Command column for the command to execute. You can also add any necessary parameters or switches here. For example, to change the Terminal/xterm menu item so it uses white text on a dark blue background, rather than the boring default of black text on a white background, add the switches *-bg darkblue -fg white* (see Figure 9-6).

 Although the Application menu item for xterm is named Terminal, it's not the same as OS X's Terminal application. To avoid confusion, many people rename it "xterm" in the menu.

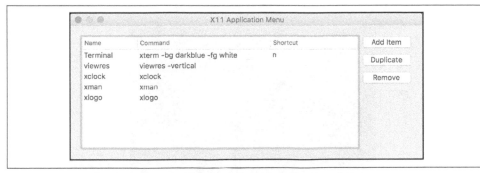

Figure 9-6. Configuring the xterm to launch with different colors

You can also specify a shortcut in the Shortcut column. The shortcut key must be used with the Command (⌘) key, so the n in the Terminal/xterm entry specifies the ⌘-N keystroke.

X11 and the Internet

Since the X Window System is built on a network model, it should be no surprise that you can launch X applications on your computer and have them actually display on an X11 system somewhere else on the network. What's cool is that you can also do the opposite and have remote computer systems run applications that actually display and work on your own computer. It's a bit tricky to set things up properly, however, so I'll recommend you check out some of the many Internet resources on the subject, starting with Lucy Lim's guide to forwarding an X11 session through SSH (*http://www.mit.edu/people/lucylim/MacX11.html*).

GIMP, the X11 Graphics Editor

Before we leave the topic of X11, I'd like to showcase one of the very slick apps that are available. The freeware application GIMP is a graphics and photo editor that competes with expensive commercial programs like Photoshop. Yes, it's an awkward name, but look beyond that, as it's surprisingly powerful and user-friendly.

You can learn more about GIMP on OS X at *http://www.gimp.org*, or you can go straight to the SourceForge download page (*http://sourceforge.net/projects/gimponosx/*).

Once you've downloaded GIMP, you can launch it with a simple double-click, as with any other Mac application. It works within the X11 world, though it doesn't look too different from an Aqua application. In Figure 9-7, I've loaded in a wonderful shot of Earth from NASA's archive (taken from Apollo 8 as it orbited the moon, if you're curious).

Figure 9-7. GIMP has a zillion graphics and photo editing options, making it comparable to Adobe Photoshop

As you can also see in Figure 9-7, there are a lot of different options, filters, tools, and utilities for photo creation and editing built into the GIMP framework. If you can do it in Photoshop, odds are pretty good you can figure out a way to do it in GIMP too, just without the huge price tag.

To learn more about how to work with GIMP, take a look at the documentation (*http://docs.gimp.org/2.8/en/*).

 As of GIMP 2.8.2, you don't even need X11 installed; it'll run native within the Aqua OS X environment.

## CHAPTER 10

Where to Go from Here

Now that you're almost at the end of this guide, let's look at some ways to continue learning about the Unix side of OS X. Documentation is an obvious choice, but it isn't always in obvious places, so I'll give you a few pointers on where to look. You can also learn how to save time by taking advantage of other shell features—aliases, functions, and scripts—that let you shorten a repetitive job and "let the computer do the dirty work."

Oh, and there's the fun factor, too. Have I mentioned yet that it's really fun to master the command line and learn how to create sophisticated command pipes and, down the road, shell scripts, even if you don't consider yourself a programmer? Give yourself some time to become comfortable, and you too might find *ls* and *vi* fun alternatives to the sameness of working within the Mac's Aqua interface day in and day out.

Documentation

You might want to know more about the options to the programs I've introduced here, and get more information about them and the many other Unix programs out there. You're now ready to consult your system's documentation and other resources.

The man Command

Different versions of Unix have adapted Unix documentation in different ways. Almost all Unix systems have documentation derived from a manual, originally called the *Unix Programmer's Manual*. The manual has numbered sections; each section is a collection of manual pages, often called *manpages*, and each program has its own manpage. Section 1 has manpages for general Unix programs such as *who* and *ls*.

OS X ships with a selection of individual manpages, and you can also read them online. If you want to know the correct syntax for entering a command or the particular features of a program, enter the command *man*, followed by the name of the command about which you need information.

For example, if you want to find information about the program *vim*, the fancy version of *vi* included with OS X, enter:

```
$ man vi
VIM(1)                                                              VIM(1)

NAME
       vim - Vi IMproved, a programmers text editor

SYNOPSIS
       vim [options] [file ..]
       vim [options] -
       vim [options] -t tag
       vim [options] -q [errorfile]

       ex
       view
       gvim gview evim eview
       rvim rview rgvim rgview

DESCRIPTION
       Vim  is a text editor that is upwards compatible to Vi.  It can be used
       to edit all kinds of plain text.  It is especially useful  for  editing
       programs.
   ...
```

The output of *man* is filtered through the *less* pager in OS X, as mentioned in Chapter 4.

 Manpages are displayed using a program that doesn't write the displayed text to the Terminal's scroll buffer. This can be quite annoying, because if you need to scroll back, you can't. Fortunately, there's an easy fix: just specify *TERM="ansi"* on the command line, or add the line export TERM="ansi" to your ~/.*profile* file, and the manpages will remain in the Terminal's scroll buffer.

After you enter the command, the screen fills with text. Press the space bar or Return to read more, and press **q** to quit.

OS X also includes a command called *apropos* (actually an alias for *man -k*) to help you locate a command if you have an idea of what it does but aren't quite sure of its correct name. Enter *apropos* followed by a descriptive word, and you'll get a list of commands that might help. To get this working, however, you need to first build the *apropos* database. This is done when OS X runs its weekly maintenance job, which you can also run manually with the following command:

```
$ sudo periodic weekly
Password:
```

Don't be surprised if it takes a few minutes for the *periodic* command to complete once you've entered your admin password; it's doing quite a lot of work building the index.

 If you don't want to wait for *periodic* to finish up, don't forget that you can append an *&* and have the job run in the background (as discussed in Chapter 7)—but don't expect the *apropos* command to work properly until you've finished building the database.

Once you've rebuilt your *apropos* database, you can use *apropos* (or its easier-to-remember cousin, *man -k*) to find all commands related to *zip*, for example, with:

```
$ man -k zip | grep '(1)'
bzcmp(1), bzdiff(1)        - compare bzip2 compressed files
bzip2(1), bunzip2(1)       - a block-sorting file compressor, v1.0.6
bzcat                      - decompresses files to stdout
bzip2recover               - recovers data from damaged bzip2 files
bzmore(1), bzless(1)       - file perusal filter for crt viewing of bzip2
                             compressed text
funzip(1)                  - filter for extracting from a ZIP archive in a pipe
gzip(1)                    - compression/decompression tool using Lempel-Ziv
                             coding (LZ77)
unzip(1)                   - list, test and extract compressed files in a ZIP
                             archive
unzipsfx(1)                - self-extracting stub for prepending to ZIP archives
zforce(1)                  - force gzip files to have a.gz suffix
zip(1)                     - package and compress (archive) files
zipcloak(1)                - encrypt entries in a zipfile
zipdetails(1)              - display the internal structure of zip files
zipgrep(1)                 - search files in a ZIP archive for lines matching a
                             pattern
zipinfo(1)                 - list detailed information about a ZIP archive
zipnote(1)                 - write the comments in zipfile to stdout, edit
                             comments and rename files in zipfile
zipsplit(1)                - split a zipfile into smaller zipfiles
znew(1)                    - convert compressed files to gzipped files
```

If you use *man -k* and get tons of output, don't forget that you can use a standard Unix pipe to trim the results. Only interested in regular user commands, for example? Add *grep '(1)'* as I've done above and it'll eliminate all the uninteresting matches by constraining the results to just those that are from section 1 of the manpage database (similarly, *'(2)'* would limit it to section 2, and so on). Here's another example:

```
$ man -k postscript | grep '(1)'
cupstestdsc(1)             - test conformance of postscript files (deprecated)
```

```
grops(1)                      - PostScript driver for groff
pfbtops(1)                    - translate a PostScript font in .pfb format to ASCII
```

Problem Checklist: man Says There's No Manual Entry for the Command

Some commands aren't separate Unix programs; they're part of the shell. On OS X, you'll find the documentation for those commands in the manual page for *bash* or in the busy manpage for *builtin*.

If the program isn't a standard part of your Unix system—that is, if you or your system staff added the program to your system—there may not be a manual page, or you may have to configure the *man* program to find the local manpage files.

The third possibility is that you don't have all the manpage directories in your MAN PATH variable. If so, add the following to your *.profile* file, then open a new Terminal window for the settings to take effect:

```
export MANPATH=${MANPATH}:/opt/X11/share/man:/opt/local/share/man
```

Documentation on the Internet

The Internet changes so quickly that any list of online Unix documentation I gave you would soon be out of date. Still, the Internet is a great place to find out about Unix systems. Remember that there are many different versions of Unix, so some documentation you find may not be completely right for you. Also, some information you'll find may be far too technical for your needs (many computer professionals use and discuss Unix). But don't be discouraged! Once you've found a site with the general kind of information you want, you can come back later for more.

The premier place to start your exploration of online documentation for OS X Unix is the Apple website. But don't start on the home page—start either on the OS X page (*http://www.apple.com/osx*) or the open source projects page (*http://developer.apple.com/opensource*).

Many Unix command names are plain English words, which can make searching hard. If you're looking for collections of Unix information, try searching for the Unix program named *grep*. My favorite search engine works just fine for this. You've probably heard of it: Google (*http://www.google.com*).

Here are some other places to try:

Magazines
> Some print and online magazines have Unix tutorials and links to more information. Macintosh magazines include *MacTech* (*http://www.mactech.com*) and *MacWorld* (*http://www.macworld.com*). I also write a monthly shell scripting and

---

Unix command-line column for *Linux Journal* (*http://www.linuxjournal.com*) that you may find enjoyable.

Publishers

Publishers such as O'Reilly (*http://www.oreilly.com*) have areas of their websites that feature Unix and host articles written by their books' authors. They may also have books online (such as O'Reilly's Safari (*http://www.safaribooksonline.com*) service) with subscriptions available for a small monthly fee. Subscribing to such a service is a good way to learn a lot quickly without needing to buy a paper copy of a huge book, most of which you might not need.

Universities

Many schools use Unix-like systems and will have online documentation. You'll probably have better luck at the computer services division (which services the whole campus) than at the computer science department (which may be more technical).

OS X–related websites

Many OS X websites are worthy of note, though they're run by third parties and may change by the time you read this. Information on Darwin can be found at Pure Darwin (*http://www.puredarwin.org*), and Mac OS X Hints (*http://www.macosxhints.com*) offers valuable information and hints. I also have a popular Q&A site (Figure 10-1) that addresses many Unix and OS X questions, and I invite you to visit with your questions (*http://www.AskDaveTaylor.com*).

One more site well worth a bookmark is O'Reilly's MacDevCenter (*http://www.macdevcenter.com*). Oh, and two more, if you like Mac rumors and discussion about the world of Apple products: MacRumors (*http://www.macrumors.com*) and MacInTouch (*http://www.macintouch.com*).

Figure 10-1. AskDaveTaylor.com has tons of Mac and Unix tutorial content

Books

Bookstores, both traditional and online, are full of computer books. The books are written for a wide variety of needs and backgrounds. Unfortunately, many books are rushed to press, written by authors with minimal Unix experience, and are full of errors. Before you buy a book, read through parts of it. Does the style (brief or lots of detail; chatty and friendly or organized as a reference) fit your needs? Search the Internet for reviews; online bookstores may have readers' comments on file.

Customizing Your Unix Experience

One of the great values of Unix is that it's flexible, and what's the point of all this flexibility if you can't bend it to meet your own needs? Let's finish up this book with a brief tour of the different ways you can reshape your OS X Unix world.

Shell Aliases and Functions

If you find yourself typing command names that are hard for you to remember, or command lines that seem too long, you'll want to learn about *shell aliases* and *shell functions*. These shell features let you abbreviate commands, command lines, and long series of commands. In most cases, you can replace them with a single word or a word and a few arguments. For example, a long pipeline (see "Pipes and Filters" on page 141) could be replaced by an alias or function. I also use aliases to ensure that certain commands always have the options I prefer, without my needing to type them. As an example:

```
alias grep='grep --color=always'
```

Making an alias or function is almost as simple as typing in the command line or lines that you want to run. References earlier in this chapter have more information; for more on aliases in this text, see "Creating Aliases" on page 38.

Programming

Shell aliases and functions are actually a simple case of shell programming. There are a number of different ways that you can delve into the world of programming, ranging from the lightweight interpreted shell script to full C++, PHP, or Ruby development. They're all supported within the OS X environment.

Shell scripts

I mentioned earlier that the shell is the system's command interpreter. It reads each command line you enter in your terminal and performs the operation that you call for. Your shell is chosen when your account is set up.

The shell is just an ordinary program that can be called by a Unix command. However, it contains some features (such as variables, control structures, and so on) that make it similar to a programming language. You can save a series of shell commands in a file, called a *shell script*, to accomplish specialized functions.

Programming the shell should be attempted only when you are reasonably confident in your ability to use Unix commands. Unix is quite a powerful tool, and its capabilities become more apparent when you try your hand at shell programming.

Take time to learn the basics. Then, when you're faced with a new task, take time to browse through sites like Stack Overflow (*http://stackoverflow.com/*) and other references to find programs or options that will help you get the job done more easily. Once you've done that, learn how to build shell scripts so that you never have to type a complicated command sequence more than once.

Let's take a closer look at a shell script to give you some flavor of what can be done. The following script reads lines out of a file called *tweets.txt* and prints those that are too long to be sent to Twitter (more than 130 characters—Twitter works on 140-character messages, and this leaves room for your name):

```
#!/bin/sh

while read tweet
do
```

```
    length="$(echo $tweet | wc -c)"
    if [ $length -ge 130 ] ; then
      echo $length -- $(echo $tweet | cut -c1-30)...
    fi
done < tweets.txt

exit 0
```

You can try this script by entering these few lines into *vi, pico,* or another Unix text editor of your choice. (See Chapter 4 for additional information on editing files.)

After typing in this script, save the file and name it something like *tweetcheck,* since that's what the program does. (Giving a script a descriptive name helps you quickly identify it later, when you need to use it.) The first line indicates what program should run the script; like most scripts, this is written for the Bourne shell, */bin/sh.* The *while* loop reads lines from the file (specified at the end of the loop), and the *$( )* notation sends whatever's inside to a subshell for separate execution, replacing it all with the output of the command (in this case, the number of characters in the line). An *if* test checks to see if it's over 130 characters, and *echo* is used to output those lines that match.

To make a shell script act as if it's a new program rather than just a text file, you use *chmod +x* to make it executable. Then you can run it by typing in its name if it's in your current PATH (see Chapter 2 for more information on setting and customizing your PATH), or with the *./* prefix to indicate that; otherwise specify its full pathname.

This is really the tip of the iceberg with shell scripts. For more information, see my book *Wicked Cool Shell Scripts* (No Starch Press), or take a look at *Unix in a Nutshell* (O'Reilly) by Arnold Robbins or *Unix Power Tools* (O'Reilly) by Jerry Peek, Shelley Powers, Tim O'Reilly, and Mike Loukides.

Turning shell scripts into AppleScript droplets

A very cool trick with OS X is to turn a shell script into a *droplet,* an application that can have files dropped onto it from the Finder. To accomplish this feat, you'll need to download and launch a copy of Fred Sanchez's DropScript utility (*http://www.mit.edu/people/wsanchez/software/darwin/DropScript-0.5.dmg*).

At its simplest, a droplet script accepts one or more files, given as command-line arguments, which are then processed in some manner. As a simple example, here's a droplet script that prints whatever files you give it:

```
#!/bin/sh
pr "$@" | lpr
```

This can be turned into a droplet by dragging the shell script icon over the Drop-Script application in the Finder. It creates a new version called *dropfilename* that's fully drag-and-drop-enabled. For example, if this script were called *print-text*, the droplet would be called *dropprint-text*.

Perl, Python, and Ruby

If shell script programming seems too limiting, you might want to try learning Perl, Ruby, or Python. These languages are also interpreted from source files full of commands and have a steeper learning curve than the shell. Also, because you've already learned a fair amount about the shell and Unix commands by reading this book, you're almost ready to start writing shell scripts now; on the other hand, a programming language takes longer to learn. But if you have sophisticated needs, learning one of these languages is another way to use even more of the power of your OS X system.

Don't underestimate what you can do with shell scripting, though. It's very powerful, and we've only touched on its features here!

C and C++

In addition to Perl, Python, and Ruby, OS X also ships with compiled programming languages, for where there's an intermediate step between writing a program and having it ready to run on your system. This is how Mac applications themselves are written, including both Unix commands and the graphical Aqua utilities that make the Mac such a great environment. A few variants that you might have heard of are Objective-C (a variant of the C programming language that's popular with Mac developers) and Cocoa (an OS X–only development environment). These are also quite complex and can take years to fully master, but if you want to begin learning, you'll be glad to know that a full development environment is included with your OS X system once you've installed Xcode (*http://bit.ly/dl-xcode*) from the App Store.

Index

Symbols

! character, 126, 181
(hash), xvi, 27, 34
$ (dollar sign), xvi, 33, 34, 90, 114
$LOGNAME environment variable, 157
& character, 154, 193, 199
() (parentheses), 126
* (asterisk), 5, 52, 78, 114
+ operator, 114
- (dash), 15, 57
. (dot), 35, 51, 55
.. (dot dot), 46, 51, 99
.. shortcut, 12, 51
/ (forward slash), 7, 42, 62, 75
; (semicolon), 154
< operator, 136
= operator, 69
> operator, 24, 136-140
>> operator, 140
? (question mark), 78, 114
@ (ampersand), 52
[] (brackets), 78
\ (backslash), 24, 45
^ character, 114
^M sequences, 86
{} (braces), 78
| (pipe) operator, 110, 115, 136
~ (tilde), 5, 7, 27, 34, 99-100

A

absolute pathnames, 44-45
access modes (see permissions)
Activity Monitor, 157
admin users, 72

Adobe Photoshop, 127
AirPort Utility, 173
aliases, 36, 48, 103-103
   and shell functions, 202
   in .profile file, 38
ampersand (@), 52
anonymous FTP (File Transfer Protocol), 178
ANSI escape sequences, 23
Apple Developer's Site, 9
AppleScript
   manipulating Terminal with, 24
   running from shell, 17, 24
   turning shell scripts into droplets, 204
Applications folder, 11
applications, free, 7-8
apropos command, 198
Aqua interface, xi, 1, 192
archiving files, 105-107
   with gzip program, 105-106
   with tar program, 106-107
arguments, 14
asterisk (*), 5, 52, 78, 114
attributions, xvi
audio files, metadata in, 131

B

background processes, 154-155
backslash (\), 24, 45
Barrett, Daniel, 175
bash shell, xvi, 14, 19, 138, 154, 191, 200
.bashrc file, 35, 39, 193
BBEdit, 86
BEL character, 23
bg command, 155

bin directory, 43
blocks, 56
BLOCKSIZE environment variable, 53
bold text, xiv
braces ({}), 78
brackets ([]), 78
bzip2, 105

C

C language, 205
C++ language, 205
Cameron, Debra, 96
carriage returns, removing, 86
case sensitivity, 15
cat command, 31, 79
    adding text to file, 137-141
    looking inside files with, 80-81
cd command, 10, 11, 30, 48-49, 163, 179
character classes
    in regular expressions, 113
    with tr command, 143
chgrp command, 70
chmod command, 67-70, 121
chown command, 70
chsh command, 32
CMD header, 4
Cocoa, 205
colons in filenames, 75
colors
    in Terminal, 19
    matches in, 112
colrm command, 141
Command mode, vi editor, 87
command prompt, 33-35
commands
    displaying all, 9
    recalling previous, 28-29
    syntax for, 14-16
    types of, 17-18
    why use, 1
compressing files, 105-107
    with bzip2, 105
    with gzip program, 105-106
    with tar program, 106-107
concatenate, 139
configd process, 157
constant-width text, xiv
context matches, 111
control characters, 30

Control symbol, xv
copy shell, 162
.core files, 142
coreaudiod process, 157
CoreGraphics library, 188
coreservices process, 157
correcting commands, 30-31
cp command, 5, 10, 38, 52, 71, 98-100, 138,
    176-177
CPU usage, determining, 159
crackers, 175
creator codes, 164
csh shell, 19, 32, 35
curl command, 181
cutting and pasting in X11, 192
Cyberduck, 183

D

daemon, 3
DARPA (Defense Advanced Research Projects
    Agency), xi
Darwin, xi, 7
dash (-), 15, 57
databases, for metadata, 126
date command, 14, 16, 27, 29, 36, 91, 138
date command (mistyped), 30
dev directory, 50, 62
devfs partition, 63
df command, 63
directories
    access permissions, 65
    completing names of, 29
    defined, 6
    directory tree, 43, 96
    files in, 49-50
        and wildcards, 78-80
        names of, 75-78
        removing, 101-103
    home directory, 42
    listing files in, 11, 51-59
        ls command, 51-55
        permissions for, 57-59
    mkdir command, 97-98
    overview, 41
    relative pathnames for, 46-47
    shared, 65
    structure of, 43-44
    vs. folders, 6-7
    working directory, 42-43, 47-49

W

wc command, 112, 115, 118, 142-144

websites for OS X-related information, 201

while loop, 204

who command, 16, 28, 138, 161, 172, 197

Wicked Cool Shell Scripts (Taylor), 19, 116, 167, 204

wildcards, 5, 78-80
    * (asterisk) as, 78
    ? (question mark) as, 78
    deleting files with, 102
    in remote filenames, 177
    [] (brackets) as, 78
    {} (braces) as, 78

window manager, 189

windows group, saving, 25

word processors, 85-96
    and shell configuration files, 37
    defined, 85
    Emacs, 95-96
    Pico, 95-95
    vi editor, 87-94

Word, Microsoft, 37, 127

working directory, 42-43
    and cd command, 48-49
    and pwd command, 47

WYSIWYG (What You See Is What You Get), 85

X

X11 (X Window System, Version 11), 188-195
    and .bashrc file, 193
    and .profile file, 193
    customizing, 193-195
    cutting and pasting in, 192
    GIMP graphics editor, 195-196
    mouse focus in, 192
    utilities for, 191-192
    vs. OS X, 192-193

xargs command, 124-126, 146

Xcode Tools, 9, 165

.xls extension, 76

xmh application, 193

XQuartz, 187, 189

xterm application, 190
    launching applications from, 193
    scrolling in, 193

Z

.zip files, 105

zsh shell, 19, 32

About the Author

Dave Taylor has a master's degree in education and an MBA, and has written 20 business and technical books, including *Learning Unix for Mac OS X* (O'Reilly), *Wicked Cool Shell Scripts* (NoStarch Press), and *Teach Yourself UNIX in 24 Hours* (SAMS). He was a contributor to BSD 4.4 Unix and his software is included in many major Unix distributions. He is a columnist for *Linux Journal*, runs a popular tech Q&A site called *AskDaveTaylor.com*, and lives in Boulder, Colorado with his three wonderful children. You can find Dave on all the major social networks by starting at *DaveTaylorOnline.com*.

Colophon

The animal on the cover of *Learning Unix for OS X* is the mountain lion (*Felis concolor*), also known as a cougar, puma, mountain cat, catamount, or panther, depending on the region. This large, solitary cat has the greatest range of any large wild terrestrial mammal in the Western Hemisphere, extending from the Yukon in Canada to the southern Andes of South America. Although large, the mountain lion is more genetically similar to the domestic cat than to true lions. Like smaller felines, the mountain lion is nocturnal.

Adult mountain lions generally are a solid red or brown color. This permits them great camouflage while stalking their prey in the desert, mountainous regions, and forests. Full-grown male mountain lions can weigh upwards of 150 pounds and be 8 feet long, including the tail. Females are smaller and weigh around 80 pounds. They live for approximately 8–10 years in the wild and up to 20 years in captivity, although only 1 in every 6 kittens survives to reach adulthood. They are extremely agile creatures, as their long hind limbs allow them to cover a distance of 40 feet in a single leap.

There is a difference in the structure of their voice box from other large cats. Due to this, mountain lions cannot roar; instead, they produce a high-pitched scream. This shrill scream has earned them a place in American folklore. To the Apache and Walapai of Arizona, the wail of the mountain lion was a harbinger of death. The Algonquins and Ojibwas believed that the mountain lion lived in the underworld and was wicked, whereas it was a sacred animal to the Cherokee.

The mountain lion holds the Guinness record as the animal with the most names, presumably due to its wide distribution across North and South America. It has over 40 names in English alone. The first recorded English use of "puma" was in 1777—it had come from the Spanish, who in turn borrowed it from the Peruvian Quechua language in the 16th century, where it means "powerful."

The cover image is from Shaw's *Zoology*. The cover font is Adobe ITC Garamond. The text font is Minion Pro by Robert Slimbach; the heading font is Myriad Pro by Robert Slimbach and Carol Twombly; and the code font is UbuntuMono by Dalton Maag.

Get even more for your money.

Join the O'Reilly Community, and register the O'Reilly books you own. It's free, and you'll get:

- $4.99 ebook upgrade offer
- 40% upgrade offer on O'Reilly print books
- Membership discounts on books and events
- Free lifetime updates to ebooks and videos
- Multiple ebook formats, DRM FREE
- Participation in the O'Reilly community
- Newsletters
- Account management
- 100% Satisfaction Guarantee

Signing up is easy:

1. Go to: oreilly.com/go/register
2. Create an O'Reilly login.
3. Provide your address.
4. Register your books.

Note: English-language books only

To order books online:
oreilly.com/store

For questions about products or an order:
orders@oreilly.com

To sign up to get topic-specific email announcements and/or news about upcoming books, conferences, special offers, and new technologies:
elists@oreilly.com

For technical questions about book content:
booktech@oreilly.com

To submit new book proposals to our editors:
proposals@oreilly.com

O'Reilly books are available in multiple DRM-free ebook formats. For more information:
oreilly.com/ebooks

O'REILLY®